D1433891

Explorations in Sociology

British Sociological Association conference volume series

Social Conceptions of Time

Structure and Process in Work and Everyday Life

Edited by

Graham Crow and Sue Heath

First published 2002 by
PALGRAVE MACMILLAN
Houndmills, Basingstoke, Hampshire RG21 6XS and
175 Fifth Avenue, New York, N.Y. 10010
Companies and representatives throughout the world.

PALGRAVE MACMILLAN is the global academic imprint of the Palgrave
Macmillan division of St Martin's Press, LLC and of Palgrave Macmillan Ltd.
Macmillan® is a registered trademark in the United States, United Kingdom
and other countries. Palgrave is a registered trademark in the European
Union and other countries.

ISBN 0–333–98499–4

This book is printed on paper suitable for recycling and
made from fully managed and sustained forest sources.

A catalogue record for this book is available
from the British Library.

Library of Congress Cataloging-in-Publication Data

Social conceptions of time : structure and process in work and everyday
life / edited by Graham Crow & Sue Heath.
    p. cm. – (Explorations in sociology)
Includes bibliographical references and index.
ISBN 0-333-98499-4
1. Time – social aspects. 2. Time – Psychological aspects. I. Crow, Graham.
II. Heath, Sue. III. Series.

HM656 .S63 2002
304.2′3–dc21

2002024878

10 9 8 7 6 5 4 3 2 1
11 10 09 08 07 06 05 04 03 02

Printed and bound in Great Britain by
Antony Rowe Ltd, Chippenham and Eastbourne

Contents

List of Figures

List of Tables

Acknowledgements

Many people have helped in the production of this volume, which arises out of the British Sociological Association conference that was organized around the theme of 'Making time/marking time' held at the University of York in April 2000. Thanks are due in particular to the staff of the BSA's Durham offices, notably Judith Mudd, Nicky Gibson and Debbie Brown, without whose efficiency and good humour the conference would have been an unrecognizably different experience. Thanks should go too to our conference co-organizers, Graham Allan and Gill Jones of Keele University. Colleagues of ours in the Department of Sociology and Social Policy at the University of Southampton have helped in many other ways as we have prepared the current volume, not least by providing a supportive and lively environment within which to work. Particular thanks are due to Susan Halford for her helpful comments on Chapter 1. A special mention should be made of the contribution of Alan Warde, who kindly offered to work on preparing the chapter by Davina Chaplin following her death; we are especially grateful to him for this. And finally, thanks are due to the team at Palgrave for all their work in getting the volume to publication.

Other books by the editors

Graham Allan and Graham Crow (eds) *Home and Family* (Macmillan, 1989)

Graham Allan and Graham Crow *Families, Households and Society* (Palgrave, 2001)

Graham Crow *Comparative Sociology and Social Theory* (Macmillan, 1997)

Graham Crow *Social Solidarities* (Open University Press, 2002)

Graham Crow (ed.) *The Sociology of Rural Communities* (Edward Elgar, 1996)

Graham Crow and Graham Allan *Community Life* (Harvester Wheatsheaf, 1994)

Michael Hardey and Graham Crow (eds) *Lone Parenthood* (Harvester Wheatsheaf, 1991)

Rosemary Deem, Kevin Brehony and Sue Heath *Active Citizenship and the Governing of Schools* (Open University Press, 1995)
Fiona Devine and Sue Heath *Sociological Research Methods in Context* (Macmillan, 1999)
Sue Heath *Preparation for Life?* (Ashgate, 1997)

Notes on Contributors

Koen Breedveld is a Research Fellow in the Time, Media and Culture research unit at the Social and Cultural Planning Office (SCP) in the Netherlands. He has particular interests in the use and ordering of time.

Marilyn Carroll is a Research Associate at the European Work and Employment Research Centre (EWERC), Manchester School of Management, UMIST. Her research interests include employment in small firms, working time and the 'work-life' balance. She has worked on projects on 'The Management of Employment Change' and 'The Future of Work' and has co-written published work on recruitment in small firms and women's pay in the banking sector.

Davina Chaplin was a Lecturer at the University of Central Lancashire. She had research interests in consumption, tourism and leisure and published papers in a number of places including *Leisure Studies* and the *Journal of Consumer Studies and Home Economics*. Her PhD thesis on second homes in rural France was awarded in 2000.

Graham Crow is Reader in Sociology at the University of Southampton. His research interests include the sociology of family, household and community relationships, comparative sociology, and sociological theory. He is currently co-editor of *Sociological Research Online* and his most recent book is *Social Solidarities: Theories, Identities and Social Change* (Open University Press, 2002).

Rosemary Deem is Professor of Education at the University of Bristol and Director of the Learning and Teaching Support Network Education Subject Centre ESCalate. Her research interests include higher education, organizational cultures, gender and education, women's leisure, and educational governance and management.

Colette Fagan is a Senior Lecturer in the Department of Sociology at the University of Manchester. Her research focuses on work and gender relations, with particular interests in international comparisons and working-time. Recent publications include *Part-time Prospects: an international comparison* (1998, co-edited with Jackie O'Reilly, Routledge), *Women's Employment in Europe: trends and prospects* (1999, with Jill Rubery and Mark Smith, Routledge), and a paper in the journal *The American Behavioural Scientist*.

Jonathan Gershuny is the Director of the Institute for Social and Economic Research at the University of Essex, and has been responsible, for a number of years, for both the British Household Panel Study and the Multinational Time Use Study. His most recent book is *Changing Times: Work and Leisure in Post-industrial Societies* (Oxford University Press, 2000).

Jackie Goode's research interests include the sociology of food, the intra-household distribution of income, changes in higher education, and parliamentary selection procedures for Westminster. She is currently at the Management Centre, King's College London, undertaking research within the ESRC 'Innovative Health Technologies' programme. Her ongoing involvement in research on collecting emerged from an academic interest in patterns of consumption, the operation of markets, and issues of identity.

Sue Heath is a Senior Lecturer in Sociology at the University of Southampton. Her research interests include the sociology of youth, young adults and household formation, and the sociology of education. Recent publications include *Sociological Research Methods in Context* (with Fiona Devine, Macmillan–now Palgrave Macmillan, 1999) and papers in the *British Journal of Sociology of Education*, the *Journal of Youth Studies* and *Housing Studies*.

Sam Hillyard is a Lecturer in Sociology attached to the Institute for the Study of Genetics, Biorisk and Society at the University of Nottingham. She recently completed doctoral research at the University of Warwick and worked as the researcher on an ESRC-funded project entitled 'New Managerialism and the Management of UK Universities' at Lancaster University.

Mary Holmes is a Lecturer in the Sociology department at the University of Aberdeen. Her recent publications include articles in *Time and Society* and in *Women's Studies International Forum*, and she is presently editing a book on anger and politics.

David Knights is Professor of Organisational Analysis and Head of the School of Management at Keele University. He is the editor of the journal *Gender, Work and Organisation*. Recent publications include *Management Lives: Power and identity in Work Organisation* (Sage, 1999, with Hugh Willmott) and *The Re-engineering Revolution: Critical Studies of Corporate Change* (Sage, 2000, co-edited with Hugh Willmott). His recent research has focused on ICT and virtuality, call centres, and financial services education and social exclusion.

Wim Knulst is Professor in the Leisure Studies department at Tilburg University in the Netherlands, having worked for many years at the Social and Cultural Planning Office (SCP).

Michael Neary is a Lecturer in Sociology at the University of Warwick, and was previously a youth and community worker. He has published on a wide range of subjects including youth training, child labour, money and the human condition, and globalization. His most recent research has been in East Asia, exploring labour relations in Korea.

Pamela Odih is a Lecturer in Sociology at Goldsmiths College, University of London. Her specialist areas include, gender, consumption, time and social theory, and she has published chapters and articles on these subjects in several places including the journal *Time and Society*.

Glenn Rikowski teaches at University College, Northampton. His research interests include education and education policy, the labour process, and the UK horological industry. He is currently working on projects concerned with unemployment, the 'businessification' of schools, and lifelong learning among horologists and jewellery workers.

Ken Roberts is Professor of Sociology at the University of Liverpool. His books include *Leisure* (Longman, 1970), *Contemporary Society and the Growth of Leisure* (Longman,1978) and *Leisure in Contemporary Society* (CAB International, 1999).

Elizabeth Bortolaia Silva is a Senior Research Fellow in Sociology, and Research Director of the National Everyday Cultures Programme at the Open University. Her recent publications include *Good Enough Mothering? Feminist Perspectives on Lone Motherhood* (1996, Routledge),

The 'New' Family (1999, co-edited with Carol Smart, Sage) and a paper in *The Sociological Review*.

Mark Smith is a Lecturer in Employment Studies at the Manchester School of Management, UMIST, where he is also a member of the European Work and Employment Research Centre (EWERC). He has research interests in atypical work, women's employment, working time and new working patterns. His publications include *Women's Employment in Europe: Trends and Prospects* (with Jill Rubery and Colette Fagan, Routledge, 1999).

John Urry is Professor of Sociology at Lancaster University. His recent books include *Sociology Beyond Societies* (Routledge, 2000), *Global Complexity* (Blackwell, 2002), and *The Tourist Gaze* (Sage, 2002, second edition).

Andries van den Broek is Head of the Time, Media and Culture research unit at the Social and Cultural Planning Office (SCP) in the Netherlands.

Tracey Warren is a Lecturer in Sociology in the School of Sociology and Social Policy at the University of Nottingham. She has researched various aspects of work, gender and inequality. Her recent publications include articles in *Sociological Review*, *Work, Employment and Society*, *Journal of European Social Policy*, *Sociological Research Online*, and *Gender, Work and Organisation*.

1
Introduction

Graham Crow and Sue Heath

Time is an essential but elusive dimension of social inquiry. It is essential because any understanding of social relationships needs to get to grips with how they endure or change over time. It is elusive because the time dimension of social relationships is rarely (if ever) straightforward, and always connected to wider debates and disagreements about the nature and causes of continuity and change. The early sociologists all confronted the problems of studying time. The rise of industrial societies was taken by several observers to indicate the presence of a process of social evolution, among whom Durkheim stands out due to his concern about the adverse effects on social solidarity of change that he considered to be overly rapid (Lockwood, 1992). Durkheim's comment that 'The past predetermines the future' (1984, p. 302) was made in the context of his discussion of the importance of habit in social and economic life, his argument being that new patterns of behaviour necessarily take time to become established and that abrupt change is inevitably disruptive. Marx identified the opposite problem of change taking place too slowly or not at all, as in the Asiatic societies that he described as being characterized by 'millennial stagnation' (in Sayer, 1989, p. 148), and (with specific reference to China) 'vegetating in the teeth of time' (in Avineri, 1969, p. 343). Weber rejected the idea of social change unfolding in an orderly, evolutionary fashion, but his analysis of the rationalization process still led him to explore the preconditions that allowed Benjamin Franklin's admonition 'Remember, that *time* is money' (cited in Weber, 1930, p. 48, emphasis in original) to gain widespread currency. Simmel's question 'What is the relationship between time and the other components of history?' (1980, p. 127) dates from the same period in which the classical sociologists in their different ways attempted to understand the world as it

1

changed around them and were thereby led to try to make sense of time sociologically.

The sense that time is crucial to the understanding of social relationships is at least as strong today as it was a century ago. Recent contributions to the literature suggest that we live in *Changing Times* (Gershuny, 2000), an age of *Time Pioneers* (Hörning *et al.*, 1995), and that we have entered *The 24 Hour Society* (Kreitzman, 1999), or have become locked into *The Time Bind* (Hochschild, 1997), to take but four titles from a rejuvenated field of research. This rediscovery by contemporary writers of the full importance of the temporal dimension of social relationships followed a long period during which it had been relatively neglected by social theorists, but there is much about current debates that is familiar to historians of social theory, as several commentators have noted (Adam, 1990; Hassard, 1990; Urry, 1996). Young's (1988) analysis of the rhythmic and habitual character of much of our social life has explicitly Durkheimian foundations, to take one example. A very different illustration of the same point would be the intellectual debt to Goffman and several other predecessors that Giddens (1984) acknowledges as influences on the development of his account of the structuration of social systems. It can also be noted that there are numerous antecedents of the often-voiced proposition that the pace of life is speeding up and of the related suggestion that the rate of social change is accelerating (Eriksen, 2001; Shaw, 1998). Ours is by no means the first generation to grapple with the problem of studying time in social life, and the insights (as well as the limitations) of earlier contributions to the sociology of time provide a valuable starting-point for much of the best current research.

There are several broad themes running through the contemporary sociology of time, of which three are particularly important to note in introducing the contributions to this volume. The first of these themes is that there are many different ways of thinking about time. Sociologists, like physicists, have been led 'to recognise a "plurality of times"' (Wallerstein, 1991, p. 33), and consideration of this point has gone well beyond the influential but problematic distinction between natural time and social time. Among the many types of time discussed by Nowotny (1994) are public time and private time, work time and free time, women's time and men's time, individual time and global time, and cyclical and linear time. Literally dozens of other types of time have been distinguished (Bender and Wellbery, 1991; Lash *et al.*, 1998). Many of these distinctions are subversive of the taken-for-granted world of time understood as a linear process captured by clocks and calendars. The way in which contemporary sociologists of time approach their subject has been transformed so that, as Adam puts it, 'It needs to be conceived as a multivariate with each variant implicating all the others. At the very least, therefore, we would be concerned with time, temporality, tempo, timing, duration, sequence, and rhythmicity as the mutually implicating structural aspects of time' (1998, p. 202). McNeill's (1995) wide-ranging study of the practical obstacles to 'keeping together in time' provides a vivid illustration of why we should be surprised not by how little synchronization there is in social relationships but by how much there is, given the enormous scope that exists for people to be out of step with those around them. Zerubavel's point that 'Temporal symmetry, which involves synchronizing the activities of different individuals, is actually one of the fundamental principles of social organization' (1981, p. 65) is all too easily overlooked; because they are so familiar to us, the rhythms of social life are in a very real sense 'hidden'.

The second theme relating to recent work in the sociology of time to which it is important to draw attention is the significance of the methodological strategies adopted by researchers. Increasingly sophisticated tools have become available to researchers who are concerned to explore various dimensions of time in social life, for example in relation to the longitudinal study of time use, the value attached to time, and sequence alignment (Merz and Ehling, 1999). Sociologists have been able to draw upon developments in other disciplines, as they have when, like economists, they are confronted with the need to smooth out time series data in order to reveal the general trend and not to be misled by minor fluctuations (Marsh 1988). The ongoing debate about the relationship between sociology and history has also helped to sharpen awareness of what is needed in order to capture the complexity of the connection between time and social change (Engelstadt and Kalleberg, 1999). The diversity of methodological tools available is a reflection of the presence of a range of problems to be researched. As Young and Schuller have observed about the study of social rhythms, some 'require a very wide-angle lens to bring them into focus, and would be completely invisible to the social scientist peering at a more limited segment of historical time. Conversely, the broad sweep of history at the macro level cannot capture the infinity of pulses that sustain particular households, housegods, workplaces or individuals in their daily lives' (1988, p. 14). The existence of an impressive array of findings about the place of time in contemporary social life demonstrates that researchers have risen to the challenge of developing imaginative techniques of investigation. Chattoe and Gilbert's (1999) analysis of time and uncertainty in household budgeting provides a good illustration of this point. Methodological innovation is currently being given a further spur by the need to capture the nature of the flows which cross national frontiers with increasing regularity in an age of globalization and which have, according to Urry (2000), made study in terms of 'society', the conventional unit of sociological analysis, increasingly problematic.

The third broad theme connecting research in the field of the sociology of time relates to the unavoidable engagement with issues of causality. The quest to discover what forces lie behind the social changes that are manifest in the various aspects of our lives has prompted Giddens to observe that 'We need not accept all aspects of Marx's account to see the significance of what might be called the "commodification of time" in modern society' (1987, p. 150). Others have taken up this idea and identified the development of global capitalism as the driving force behind 'time–space compression' (Harvey, 1989), although Giddens's (1999) own account of globalization treats it as the product of a combination of forces of which economic ones are only a part, albeit a very important part. Hochschild's account of what she refers to as 'the current speed-up in work and family life in the United States' (1996, p. 14) provides a good illustration of the value of paying attention to non-economic causes of changes in time use. Her argument that the increase in the number of hours women spend at work is rooted less in financial considerations than in a desire to escape from the pressures of home life goes against the conventional wisdom concerning the causal connection between work and family life, that family is the dependent variable. Mulgan and Wilkinson's observation that 'large majorities would continue to work even if there was no financial need' (1997, p. 79) also goes against conventional wisdom by questioning the presumption that people in post-industrial societies will have a preference for leisure over work. Nor should it be presumed that the escape from work will even be an option. Recent developments in this and in other areas of life have had the effect of shattering 'the modernist illusion that historical time was moving ahead toward some indefinite but well-advertised improvement upon present circumstances' (Lemert, 1997, p. 162). Divorced from the assumption of social progress, sociologists are free to consider alternative scenarios, including the view that social relationships are characterized to an important degree by repetition and the reworking of tradition (Giddens, 1996).

The contributions to this volume add to these debates in a number of ways. In relation to the theme of the many faces of time, several contributors seek to explore the distinction between work time and other types of time. The conventional distinction between work time and leisure time is problematic for a number of reasons. Gershuny's chapter reveals the importance of recognizing the significance of trends in relation to unpaid work as well as paid work, a distinction that links to the contrast between women's time and men's time that Holmes draws upon to investigate the unequal opportunities that exist to participate in the public sphere. The political economy of time is concerned with time as an unevenly distributed resource, and this issue is particularly prominent in the consideration given by the contributors to the second section of the volume to how people allocate time to paid work and to domestic responsibilities. The importance of gender is emphasized by Fagan, and by Smith and Carroll, and it is also treated as a vital factor by Warren, and by Deem and Hillyard, albeit that the latter pair of chapters direct more attention to the complex interplay of class and gender inequalities. Hareven's (1982) notion of 'family time' offers another point of departure for thinking about different types of time, and the influence of family practices on people's experience of time is central to the accounts of everyday life in the chapters by Silva, Goode and Chaplin. The contributions to this volume frequently return to the theme elaborated upon by Nippert-Eng (1996), that the boundary between home and work is problematic in a temporal sense as well as a spatial one. The activities that make up people's lives do not fall neatly into work time and home time, any more than they fall into public time and private time, or any of the other analytical dualisms that have been developed.

The methodological challenges that the study of time in social life presents have been responded to in a variety of ways. The majority of the contributions to this volume report on empirical research, evenly divided into chapters that draw upon quantitative data and chapters that are reliant on qualitative data. Comparison of national data sets on time use drawing on diary and survey material allows Gershuny and Fagan to discuss emergent trends in different types of societies. Within individual societies it is also possible to chart the process of change, as van den Broek, Breedveld and Knulst do in relation to patterning of daily life in the Netherlands in recent decades. The chapter by Roberts, which explores the relationship between hours of work and leisure among a nationally representative sample of English respondents, demonstrates the potential of quantitative data to confound popular conceptions, as does the analysis of data from the British Household Panel Survey by Warren. Quantitative data also have the potential to illuminate differences in the forces that operate at a more local level to influence people's time allocation decisions, as Smith and Carroll show in their analysis of two local authority policies. The arguments that these chapters advance are in many ways complementary to those of contributors who adopt more qualitative approaches. The theme of rhythms and routines highlighted by van den Broek, Breedveld and Knulst, for example, is also prominent in the analysis of the ethnographic and interview data on time in everyday life collected by Chaplin and Silva. The longer-term collecting habits described by Goode's interviewees might also be mentioned in this context. The interview data collected by Deem and Hillyard nicely illustrate how people often have to juggle several different activities as part of the management of their time, and their point about the difficulties of maintaining boundaries around different types of time is also a key conclusion of the documentary analysis carried out by Holmes. The ethnographic methods employed by Knights and Odih in their chapter on work in call centres are equally revealing about the processes whereby time is made, and their qualitative data about what it is like to work under surveillance help to explain why it is that the statistics for staff turnover are so high.

The explanations of the patterns and trends identified in the various chapters are no less diverse than the subject matter that the contributors discuss, although some common points of reference can be identified. Several of the contributors cast doubt on the efficacy of analyses framed in terms of the concept of globalization. Urry does so on the grounds that the processes involved are more complex than globalization analyses allow, arguing that complexity theory offers a more fruitful starting-point for the attempt to capture movement in time and space more adequately than conventional causal analysis is able to. Roberts also casts doubt on the extent to which globalization explains changes in work time, while the chapters by Gershuny and Fagan suggest that welfare state regimes can have some modifying influence on the impact of global economic forces. The move away from the 'male breadwinner' model of welfare provision has been taken in contrasting directions in different countries, as several of the contributors note, with the result that there is no uniformity in the impact of welfare state regimes on time budgets. The doubts voiced by Gershuny about the utility of Marx's labour theory of value are contested by Neary and Rikowski, whose chapter develops the argument that Marx's political economy approach still has an important role to play in the explanation of the speeding up of the pace of life that is widely

experienced. Technological developments would necessarily figure promi-
nently in any account of the processes that have made possible the type
of work regulation described by Knights and Odih, although they are
careful to avoid adopting a technologically determinist perspective, pre-
ferring instead to explore the negotiated character of time in the workplace. The account of change in Dutch society advanced by van den
Broek, Breedveld and Knulst refers to the effects of that country's secularization, a process that has unfolded alongside the feminization of the
labour force and the spread of a more informal and individualized culture.
Individualization is also discussed by Silva, who arrives at similar conclusions about the greater difficulty in achieving the synchronization of
social relationships that such a development entails. All of these trends
have helped to create an increasingly diverse pattern of social relationships, which require continued monitoring of the methods and analytical
frameworks employed by researchers. The variety of household types in
Silva's sample demonstrates the importance for the analysis of time use of
capturing the diversity of lifestyles that exists beyond the much-
researched married couple. In similar fashion, the recognition of household diversity is increasingly a feature of analysis based on large data sets,
made possible by their being redesigned in order to capture living arrangements beyond the married couple, for example cohabitation. The
welcome recognition of gay and lesbian couple households in the 2001
Census of Population is a further indication of how times are changing in
this respect.

The chapters in this volume serve to confirm that time is necessarily
central to the understanding of social life. They are sufficiently diverse in
their focus on different aspects of time, in their employment of different
methodologies, and in their underlying theoretical assumptions to
convey at least some sense of the range of ideas, practices and debates
that make up the sociology of time. They are united by the shared convic-
tion of their authors that the social dimensions of time and the temporal
dimensions of social relationships are still imperfectly understood, and
that a better understanding of these issues is a matter of very real consequence. By illuminating the structures and processes that are to be found
in work and everyday life, they show that there are many faces of time,
all of them made in different ways. As Landes (2000) has shown, we have
been 'making time' for a very long time indeed, and time is central to the
ways in which social relationships are (more or less) organized. The contributions to this volume suggest that there are good reasons to believe
that the sociological study of these phenomena will continue to repay
those who undertake it.

Part I
The Political Economy of Time

2
Time, Complexity and the Global

John Urry

> Time is the substance I am made of. Time is a river which sweeps me along, but I am the river. (Borges, 1970, p. 269)

> ... man is nothing; he is, at most, the carcass of time. (Karl Marx, in Marx and Engels, 1976, p. 127)

Introduction

This chapter presumes that a new kind of social science 'paradigm', that of globalization, is currently being developed and reproduced. I examine some connections between this emergent globalization paradigm and another paradigm, that of complexity. The latter is also emerging as a contending new paradigm for the social sciences, having already been established in physics, cosmology, chemistry, biology, ecology, management, economics and so on. Through the prism of time/time-space I counterpose these two emergent paradigms for the social sciences, of globalization and complexity (I use 'paradigm' here loosely).

I begin by outlining how complexity transforms the scientific understanding of time and provides notions pertinent to the social sciences. Time will be shown to be irreducible, irreversible, asymmetrical and multiple. Second, I consider how some components of complexity have entered social science through the globalization paradigm. This paradigm in effect authorizes certain complexity-innovations, especially those of non-linear interdependencies between peoples, places, organizations and technological systems across the world. Third, however, I try to show that much work done on globalization is insufficiently 'complex' in its analyses. Instead I develop the concept of 'global hybrids', of networks and fluids roaming the globe in strikingly diverse temporal frames. In conclusion, I consider how we should conceive of the emergent and apparently self-organizing level of the global, of how to capture the emerging character of 'global complexity'.

Times

Pre-twentieth-century science operated with Newtonian time (see Urry, 2000, ch. 5). It is time as absolute; according to Newton from 'its own nature, [time] flows equably without relation to anything eternal ... the flowing of absolute time is not liable to change' (quoted in Adam, 1990, p. 50; see Coveney and Highfield, 1990, pp. 29–31). Such absolute time is invariant, infinitely divisible into space-like units, measurable in length, expressible as a number and reversible. It is time seen through the metaphor of space, as comprising invariant, measurable lengths that can be moved along, forwards *and* backwards, as with a frictionless pendulum. It is a science that is mostly timeless as pre-twentieth-century science examined the very small, the very cold, the very hot, the very brief and so on (see Adam, 1998, pp. 39–41).

A.N. Whitehead provided early reflection upon how *twentieth*-century physics was transforming such notions of time and space (see Harvey, 1996, pp. 256–61). He rejects the idea that time is *outside* the very relations between objects (and subjects). Time and space are 'internal' to the processes by which the physical and social worlds operate. His 'internal relations' conceptualization leads to the thesis that there are multiple times of nature (see Adam, 1998; Capra, 1996; Casti, 1994; Coveney and Highfield, 1990; Hawking, 1988; Prigogine, 1997). Einstein indeed had shown that there is no fixed or absolute time that is independent of the system to which it refers; and that time and space are not separate from each other but are fused into a four-dimensional time-space curved under the influence of mass. Quantum physicists describe a virtual state in which electrons seem to try out instantaneously all possible futures before settling into particular patterns. Quantum behaviour is mysteriously instantaneous where cause and effect no longer apply within a microscopic indivisible whole. And chrono-biologists have shown that rhythmicity is a crucial principle of nature, both within the organism and in the organism's relationships with the environment. Humans and other animals are not just affected by the passing of time but are inescapably temporal beings (Adam, 1998, ch. 1).

More generally, the 'complexity sciences' of non-equilibrium processes and unstable systems show the irreversible flow of time (Prigogine, 1997, p. 2). Rather than there being time-symmetry and a reversibility of time as in classical physics, a clear distinction is made between past and future – an arrow of time results in a future that is unstable, relatively unpredictable and characterized by various possibilities, the 'end of certainty' (Prigogine, 1997). It is the '[I]rreversibility [of time] that brings order out of chaos' (Prigogine and Stengers, 1984, p. 292). The clearest example of irreversibility is seen in the expansion of the universe through the cosmological arrow of time following the singular event of the 'big bang'. There are many mundane examples of irreversibility: coffee always cools, organisms always age, spring follows winter and so on. There can be no going back, no reabsorbing of the heat, no return to youth, no spring before winter and so on. Laws of nature are historical and *contra* Einstein imply pastness, presentness and futureness (Prigogine, 1997, p. 165). As Eddington says: 'The great thing about time is that it goes on' (quoted in Coveney and Highfield, 1990, p. 83).

Complexity involves repudiating dichotomies of order and disorder, of being and becoming. Physical systems do not exhibit and sustain enduring structural stability without change. The common-sense notion that small changes in causes produce small changes in effects is mistaken. Rather there are deterministic chaos, dynamic becoming and non-linear changes in the statistical properties of systems as a whole. Time can be highly discontinuous and there are many non-equilibrium situations in which abrupt and unpredictable changes, or bifurcations, occur. Following a perfectly deterministic set of rules, unpredictable yet patterned results are generated. The classic example within chaos theory is the butterfly effect, where minuscule changes at one location iteratively produce, in very particular law-like circumstances, massive weather effects elsewhere.

Since the individual and statistical levels are not equivalent, complexity investigates the physics of populations and their emergent properties (Prigogine, 1997, p. 35). Such systems are necessarily unstable, with an array of possible outcomes, what Prigogine terms 'a world of irregular, chaotic motions' (1997, p. 155). Consider a pile of sand: if an extra grain of sand is placed on top it may stay there or it may cause a small avalanche. The system is self-organized but the effects of local changes can vary enormously (Cilliers, 1998, p. 97). There is 'self-organized criticality' (Waldrop, 1994, pp. 304–6). The heap will maintain itself at the critical height and we cannot know in advance what will happen to any individual action.

Complexity theory uses mathematical formulae and powerful computers to characterize the enormously large number of iterative events that occur in systems, such as a pile of sand. In particular experiments, examining increases in the reproduction patterns of gypsy moths showed, through resulting changes in population size, dramatic non-linear changes in the quality of the system. Changes in the parameter resulted in transformations in the system; in certain contexts, order generates chaos (Baker, 1993, p. 133).

The emergence of a certain patterning within an overall disorder results from 'strange attractors', the space to which the trajectory of any system is attracted through millions of iterations taking place over time (Byrne, 1998, pp. 26–9). Such attractors are immensely sensitive in the effects that they generate to slight variations in their initial conditions; as iteration occurs time and time again, so a patterned disorder develops.

Thus complexity emphasizes how complex feedback loops exacerbate initial stresses in the system and render it unable to absorb shocks to re-establish the original equilibrium. Very strong interactions occur between the parts of a system and there is presumed to be a lack of a central hierarchical structure. In particular, complexity theory analyses systems as unstable, dissipative structures, thermodynamically open and capable of assimilating large quantities of energy from the environment and converting it into increased structural complexity (Reed and Harvey, 1992, pp. 360–2). But simultaneously systems dissipate into their environment high levels of residual heat. Such dissipative systems reach points of bifurcation when their behaviour and future pathways become unpredictable and new higher-order structures emerge. Dissipative structures thus involve non-linearity, a flowingness of time, no separation of systems and their environment, and a capacity for the autopeitic re-emergence of new order (Capra, 1996, p. 187).

Interestingly, those working at one of the leading complexity centres, the Santa Fe Institute in New Mexico, themselves developed some implications of such complex adaptive systems for thinking through the nature of especially global sustainability (Waldrop, 1994, pp. 348–53). In the rest of this chapter I too consider how complexity may illumine what we call the 'global'.

The globalization paradigm

Indeed, way beyond the Santa Fe Institute, almost all the non-physical sciences have gone global in the past decade. Even by the mid-1990s over one hundred books per year were emerging with global/ globalization in the title, while such articles now run into the thousands (Busch, 1997). Here I consider how this rapidly emerging paradigm of globalization authorizes certain complexity-ways of think-ing (I have treated chaos and complexity as a single paradigm; recent social science applications include Byrne, 1998; Cilliers, 1998; Eve *et al.*, 1997; Hayles, 1999).

It seems that a certain 'structure of feeling' gave rise to complexity within the physical and biological sciences, from the late 1970s onwards, and to globalization within the social and cultural sciences, a decade or so later (Thrift, 1999). Partly such a structure of feeling has been generated by the recent 'internationalization' of scientific com-munities, of constant travelling, of instant electronic communication and of the mediatization of science (Rabinow, 1995; Thrift, 1999, pp. 40–41; Waldrop, 1994). Indeed, the Santa Fe Institute is described by its organizers as a far-flung series of global networks, a 'global family' that has effectively disseminated complexity through various networks across the world, and very much beyond 'science' itself, to business schools, management gurus, New Age practitioners, architects, literary theorists, ecologists, philosophers, novelists, consumer objects and so on (including Chaos scent; see Thrift, 1999). So certainly global networks have promoted complexity as a way of thinking; and around 1989 and the globally staged demolition of the Berlin Wall complexity came to take on a global hue in the social sciences. What kinds of thinking did globalization authorize?

First, there is the notion that events happening in one place may impact in important ways upon other places. Giddens defined global-ization as: 'the intensification of worldwide social relations which link distant localities in such a way that local happenings are shaped by events occurring many miles away and vice versa' (1990, p. 64). Or we put this by saying that globalization brings out how there are non-linear interdependencies between peoples, places, organizations and technological systems across the world, interdependencies that prob-lematize the notion that global systems can be said to reach any state of equilibrium.

Moreover these interdependencies are productive of emergent proper-ties. Global analysis interrogates emergent phenomena, rejecting expla-nations that reduce phenomena to their constituent elements. What happens in one place or even one society (unless maybe the USA!) cannot explain the emergent global level, such as global environmental crises or the worldwide spread of representative democracies (see Held *et al.*, 1999). Indeed, complexity-researcher Chris Langton maintains that: 'From the interaction of the individual components emerges some kind of property – something you couldn't have predicted from what you know of the component part. And the global property, this emergent behaviour feeds back to influence the behaviour of the individuals that produced it' (quoted in Thrift, 1999, pp. 33–4). Specifically within sociology globalization would seem to 'solve' the holism–individualism debate by the discovery of a new holist level, the global, that possesses properties not possessed by individuals, places, organizations or individual societies (Waldrop, 1994, p. 329).

Globalization thus brings out the non-linear character of relationships in the social world. As two or more elements are added together, this may result in dynamically different outcomes as the elements interact together in a non-additive fashion. Global analyses also bring out how relationships are extremely sensitive to initial conditions. Small changes in one country (the equivalent of the butterfly's wings) can move the system into a completely different phase, a system-bifurcation. Byrne describes such big and non-linear outcomes as 'the last straw [that] breaks the camel's back', that can produce radical regime change such as the dramatic implosion of the Soviet system following the pulling down of the Berlin Wall in 1989 (1998, p. 170; and see Casti, 1994, pp. 90–91).

Finally, globalization authorizes examination of how social processes can involve not only negative feedback but also positive feedback, not only decreasing returns to scale but also increasing returns (see Waldrop, 1994). So over time the global order bears no tendency to move towards equilibrium. Positive feedback can escalate change over time to increasing movement away from any tendency to equilibrium, such as that between the earth and its environment where global climate change shows no sign of abating. Increasing (rather than diminishing) returns to scale can produce extraordinary escalations of economic wealth, as with the Internet revolution produced by the 'small' change of the first Web browser that appeared in 1994.

Global hybrids

I have outlined some ways in which globalization has authorized analyses that capture elements of complexity. However, I now turn complexity against such analyses, suggesting that much work done on globalization is insufficiently 'complex'. Globalization studies are often too static, regional and focused upon conditions of equilibrium.

In particular the globalization paradigm insufficiently interrogates the iterative character of systems. Partly this stems from the conceptual divide within sociology between so-called structure and agency. The millions of individual iterative actions are largely subsumed under the notion of 'structure' (such as 'globalization' or the 'global structure') that does not require further examination. It is 'ordered' and will be reproduced through continuous iteration. The concept of structure solves the problem of iteration for sociology. But of course social systems do in fact change, and the sociological trick draws on the concept of agency to argue that some sets of agents can escape this structure and change it. Certain authors have seen the limitations of this formulation: Giddens (1984) for example analysed the 'duality of structure' in order to account for the recursive character of social life. He advances the ways in which we understand how 'structures' are both drawn on, and are the outcome of, countless recursive or iterative actions by knowledgeable agents over time. However, there is in his account insufficient examination of the 'complex' character of these iterative processes. Although there is recurrence over time, such recurrent actions can result in non-equilibrium, non-linearity and, if the parameters change dramatically, a sudden branching of the social world. Complex change may have nothing to do with agents actually seeking to change that world. The agents can simply keep carrying out more or less the same recurrent actions. But through iteration *over time* these can generate unexpected, unpredictable and chaotic outcomes, often the opposite of what the human agents involved sought to realize (see Urry, 2000).

Zohar and Marshall (1994) capture something similar in their concept of the *quantum society*. They describe the collapse of the old certainties of classical physics based upon the rigid categories of absolute time and space, solid impenetrable matter made up of interacting 'billiard balls', and strictly determinant laws of motion. In its place there is 'the strange world of quantum physics, an indeterminate world whose almost eerie laws mock the boundaries of space, time and matter' (Zohar and Marshall, 1994, p. 33). They particularly develop analogies between the wave/particle effect and the emergent characteristics of social life:

> Quantum reality ... has the potential to be both particle-like and wave-like. Particles are individuals, located and measurable in space and time. They are either here or there, now and then. Waves [by contrast] are 'non-local', they are spread out across all of space and time, and their instantaneous effects are everywhere. Waves extend themselves in every direction at once, they overlap and combine with other waves to form new realities (new emergent wholes). (1994, p. 326)

I suggest somewhat analogously that we should analyse various global *waves* that through iteration over time generate 'new emergent wholes'; while noting that such waves are constituted of countless individual *particles*, that is, humans, social groups and networks that are resolutely 'located and measurable in space and time'. Such a metaphor of the wave breaks with a certain immobile and fixed notion of the global.

The sociological concept of society is normally organized around the metaphor of a *region*, namely that 'objects are clustered together and boundaries are drawn around each particular cluster' (Mol and Law, 1994, p. 643). Thus there appear to be different societies with their clustering of social institutions, and with a clear and policed border surrounding each society as region. Now one way to study globalization is through seeing it also as a *region* and as involved in interregional competition with each 'society'. Globalization could be viewed as the replacing of one region, the bounded nation-state society of the 'West', with another, the global economy and culture. And in the fight between these two regions, the global region seems to be winning (see Robertson, 1992).

However, this is a limited way of understanding globalization. The notion of *region* involves a too unified and finalized set of processes. It implies some notion of a global equilibrium. It suggests a clearcut structure of the global order. Game (1998) critiques such a view-point: 'this sort of project is remarkably static and governed by a desire for stasis. Globalisation theorists attempt to produce systems and grids that will take account of all possible cases' (p. 42). Seeing the global as regional is to spatialize the global and to ignore the ways in which various times are profoundly folded into diverse global entities. Complexity shows that there is no distinction between structure and process, structure and action. I suggest that globalization should rather be conceived of through Mol and Law's (1994) metaphors of *network* and *fluid*, both of which are hybrids of the 'social' and the 'material'.

First then there are global *networks*, sets of interconnected nodes, the distance between social positions being shorter where such positions constitute nodes within a network as opposed to those outside. Networks are to be viewed as dynamic open structures, so long as they are able to effect communication with new nodes and to innovate. Network does not mean here purely *social* networks since they can involve complex and enduring connections across space and through time between peoples *and* various objects and technologies (see Castells, 1996, Law, 1994 p. 24; Murdoch, 1995, p. 745). Numerous 'global' enterprises, such as American Express, McDonald's, Coca Cola, Microsoft, Sony, Greenpeace, Manchester United and so on, are organized through such non-failing global networks (see Ritzer, 1992; 1997). Such a network of technologies, skills, texts and brands ensures that the same product is delivered in the same way across the world. Products are predictable, calculable, routinized and standardized. These organizations have generated very effective global networks with few 'failings'. They enable the brand and associated products to roam more or less instantaneously along the various scapes of the contemporary world (Urry, 2000). So global networks constitute one category of global hybrids.

Second, there are global *fluids*. These are the flows or waves of people, information, objects, money, images, risks and networks moving across regions in heterogeneous, uneven, unpredictable and often unplanned shapes (see Deleuze and Guattari, 1986; 1988; Mol and Law, 1994; Shields, 1997). Such global fluids move in particular directions at certain speeds and different levels of viscosity with no necessary end-state or purpose; they result from people acting upon the basis of local information, but where these local actions are, through countless iteration, captured, represented, marketed and generalized within multiple global waves; they may escape (rather like white blood corpuscles) through the 'wall' of particular scapes into surrounding matter; and they move according to certain novel temporalities as they break free from the linear time of existing scapes. Such fluids could be said to 'channel[s] the messy power of complexity'; I mention five examples of such fluids, each characterized by a distinct temporality (Kelly, 1995, p. 26).

First, there is the system of world *money*, what Strange (1986) calls a 'casino capitalism', detached and self-organizing beyond both individual national economies and world production and trade (Thrift, 1996). Foreign exchange dealings based upon 24-hour trading are worth $1.3 trillion per day – 60 times greater than the value of world exports. Money is traded for money especially in terms of its future values; this global hybrid is organized around calculations of, and bets on, hugely uncertain commodified futures.

Second, the *Internet* emerged out of the distributed system of American defence intelligence designed to prevent nuclear attack. Plant (1997) argues, following the small change of the first Web browser in 1994, that an irreversible autopeitic system has emerged:

No central hub or command structure has constructed it ... It has installed none of the hardware on which it works, simply hitching a largely free ride on existing computers, networks, switching systems, telephone lines. This was one of the first systems to present itself as a multiplicitous, bottom-up, piecemeal, self-organizing network which ... could be seen to be emerging without any centralized control. (p. 49; and see Castells, 1996)

Third, more generally there is the global fluid of *information* that, through its digitalization, adopts patterns and modes of mobility almost wholly separate from any material form or presence that it might take (Featherstone, 2000; Hayles, 1999, pp. 18–20). Such information travels instantaneously along the fluid network of global communications, described by Imken (1999) as a: 'non-linear, asymmetrical, chaotically-assembled new artificial life-form of the global telecommunications *Matrix*' (p. 92).

Fourth, there is *automobility*, the spreading across the globe of the car, its awesome infrastructure and a vast array of other objects, technologies and signs that it both presupposes and reproduces. Automobility could be seen as a 'virus', beginning in the USA and Western Europe and then virulently spreading into, and taking over, every part of the body social. Automobility is a vast self-organizing non-linear system constitutive of social life organized around the juggling of tiny amounts of highly fragmented moments of time spent in cocooned movement (see Sheller and Urry, 2000).

Fifth, environmental and health *hazards* travel both geographically and temporally in non-linear fashion. BSE takes between 5 and 20 years to incubate, nuclear accidents can affect generations not yet born, nuclear radiation can survive thousands of years, hormone-disrupting chemicals appear to affect all species living in all parts of the globe. As such hazards, which often start locally, roam over the globe individual consequences are un-measurable and invisible in time–space (see Adam, 1998, pp. 25–7, 35). Colborn *et al.* (1996) summarize how: 'We design new technologies at a dizzying pace and deploy them on an unprecedented scale around the world long before we can begin to fathom their possible [long-term: author's addition] impact on the global system or ourselves' (p. 244).

I have thus mentioned five highly mobile fluids that roam the globe. These hybrids intersect with each other in complex, unpredictable and temporally–spatially distanciated forms. Each involves novel ways in which different times, of intensively commodified future, nanosecond instantaneity, the hyper-fragmentation of time and awesome longevity, have come to be folded into, and operate through, these roaming hybrids.

Conclusion

Such 'global complexity', the non-linear, unpredictable and interacting global hybrids that irreversibly roam the globe, leads us to consider just what this emergent level of the global amounts to. First, it is partially self-organizing through an enormous array of interdependent organizations: the United Nations, World Bank, Microsoft, World Trade Organization, Greenpeace, CNN, BBC, News Corporation, World Intellectual Property Organization, International Air Transport Association, Federation of International Football Associations, World Health Organization and so on. This is an emergent global order. There are also many signifiers of this emergent global level, such as the blue earth, Nelson Mandela, Princess Diana, the Amazon rain forest, tigers and elephants and so on, which have the effect of partially and imperfectly generating a global imagined community (see Urry, 2000, ch. 7).

Such an emergent level is transforming states, whether national or regional, into what elsewhere I term, reinterpreting Bauman, as the shift from a gardening to a gamekeeper state (Urry, 2000, ch. 8). The gamekeeper is concerned with regulating mobilities, with ensuring that there is sufficient stock for hunting in a particular site but not with the detailed cultivation of each animal in each particular place. Animals roam around and beyond the estate, like the roaming hybrids that currently roam in and across national borders. States are increasingly unable or unwilling to garden their society, only to regulate the conditions of their stock so that on the day of the hunt there is appropriate stock available for the hunter.

How though is this emergent level being generated? Baker (1993) elaborates on the relationship between 'centre' and 'periphery', the 'centriphery', and the ways in which it creates both order *and* turbulence in social life. The centriphery acts as a strange attractor, the space to which the trajectory of any particular system is attracted over time (Byrne, 1998, pp. 26–9; Cilliers, 1998, pp. 96–7). In this case the centriphery is a dynamic pattern that is repeated at many different levels, involving flows of energy, information and ideas that simultaneously create both centres and peripheries. The trajectory of social systems is irreversibly attracted to the centriphery. Baker further notes that with globalization: 'the exchange of goods and services binds and lubricates a dynamic relationship between the center and the periphery. As centering progresses, it deepens the periphery. Because centering and peripheralizing involve the transformation of energy and information and, thus, the creation of entropy, the process is irreversible' (1993, p. 140).

I suggest that the specific form that is now taken by centriphery is the 'glocal', whereby there is a parallel irreversible process of globalization–deepening–localization–deepening–globalization and so on. There is a dynamic relationship, as huge flows of resources move backwards and forwards between the two. Neither the global nor the local can exist without the other. They develop in a symbiotic, irreversible and unstable set of relationships, in which each gets transformed through billions of world wide iterations. Small perturbations in the system can result in unpredictable and chaotic branching of such a system. The trajectories of all social systems world wide are increasingly drawn to the attractor of 'glocalization'.

Barber (1996) has explored one aspect of glocalization when describing the emergent global order as locked in a conflict between consumerist 'McWorld' on the one hand, and the identity politics of the 'Jihad' on the other. There is a 'new world disorder' resulting from this strange attractor in which McWorld and Jihad depend upon, and globally reinforce, each other in a spiralling global disequilibrium that threatens public life and democratic forms. World money is a second example of how glocalization functions as a strange attractor. Thrift (1996) argues that, as the global financial system has become progressively disembedded from place, so its very universalism forces a new set of local particularisms (and see Boden, 2000). He describes the re-embedded spaces that result from the need to cement relationships ever more intensely because of the especially fragile and symbolic communities being formed within electronic money-space. Intense meeting-places become nodes of reflexivity and resonate back over time and millions of iterations to the globally organised and fragile electronic spaces.

Such 'globally complex' systems can thus be summarized in terms of a number of characteristics (adapted from Cilliers, 1998):

- there is an enormous number of 'global' elements which render formal means of representation inappropriate;
- over hugely different temporalities, such elements interact physically and informationally under, over and across much of the earth's surface;

- such interactions are rich, non-linear and move towards the attractor of 'glocalization';
- globally complex systems involve positive feedback loops that render the global level far from equilibrium, on the edge of chaos;
- while elements respond only to 'local' sources of information, this produces, through iteration over time, roaming networks, global fluids and gamekeeper states;
- global networks and fluids interact dissipatively with their environment and have a history which evolves irreversibly through time and where their past is co-responsible for their uncertain futures;
- while all times are irreversible, there are various temporalities that are folded into these global processes, as I have begun to sketch out.

Acknowledgements

I am very grateful for the comments of various Lancaster colleagues on this paper: Anne Marie Fortier, John Law, Mimi Sheller and Andrew Sayer. I am also grateful for comments from colleagues at the BSA Annual Conference and the Portuguese Sociological Association Conference, both held in April 2000.

3

Service Regimes and the Political Economy of Time

Jonathan Gershuny

Introduction

At the very heart of that now rather unfashionable book by Karl Marx, *Capital*, is a political economy of time. The definition of the central concept, the rate of exploitation, was expressed straightforwardly in terms of the ratio between the time necessary for the production of a good and the actual amount of labour extracted from the workers. The longer the hours of work, the greater the rate of exploitation and the higher the profits. Of course we are none of us Marxists now, and we are all *in favour* of profits, and that book finds itself in the dustbin of history.

I do not advocate a return to the specifics of Marx's political economy. Nevertheless, in his attempt to found a political economy on those universal denominators of human activity, the minutes of the day, instead of financial instruments, he had an infant idea that, in a more empirical form, may be of vital importance for the understanding of post-industrial societies. We should not throw away that baby when we lose that book. Time is at the heart of many of the problems facing modern economies. There is the growing class-type polarization between work- (and money-) rich–time-poor, and others (for example the unemployed, or those unable to work because of disability or age) with free time but too little money. There is the strongly gendered issue of the 'time bind'; women in good jobs may still be left with, in effect, a second job at home, caring for young or old people, with not enough time to do both. And there is the question of what exactly work *consists of*, in the age of e-commerce and the World Wide Web. What sort of consumption do we find in a successful service economy?

To confront these problems adequately, we need to include that counterpart to production which Marx left out of his great book altogether: the nature and the distribution of time in activities *outside* paid work. We need to put together our understanding of *production* with that of *consumption*. And we can best draw together these two intermeshing classes of activity in terms of their common denominator, *time*. The political economy of post-industrial society is, in essence, the political economy of time.

My starting-point in this chapter, however, is not the future, but the recent past. I will show some of the empirical evidence of how time-use patterns have been changing in the developed world. And then I return to the future, discussing some of the moving principles of this political economy of time and dramatizing these through a contrast between two 'ideal types' of post-industrial society. Post-industrial societies certainly are, as Daniel Bell told us a generation ago they would be, service economies. But there is a wide range of ways of organizing a service economy. Hence the title of this chapter: by service 'regimes' I mean something similar to what Esping-Andersen (1990) meant by welfare 'regimes': particular patterns of regulation of the conditions of service consumption and production, reflecting some coherent underlying view of how societies should be organized. The alternative 'service regimes' represent alternative ways of resolving the problems at the heart of the political economy of time.

Historical change in time use

This chapter uses evidence from a multinational longitudinal dataset, including thousands of respondents in some 35 separate surveys, from 20 different countries (see Table 3.1; more extensive discussion of this evidence, and the arguments of this chapter in general, may be found in Gershuny, 2000). It puts together, for developed countries, a comprehensive account that covers all daily activities, paid work, unpaid work, leisure or consumption time, and sleep. What the 35 surveys have in common is the use of a 'diary' methodology. Respondents give sequential accounts of all the activities of a day (or a week). For the analysis that follows I have taken just respondents of 'core working age', and the days have been reweighted to make the samples representative of the national population, and of the days of the week.

I start by demonstrating *three convergent trends* in time-use patterns: by nation, gender, and 'class' (though strictly, what is discussed is not class at all but merely the position of individuals, or their households, in a system of social stratification or differentiation). As an expositional device, consider the triangle graph, which allows us to plot three

Table 3.1   The cross-national longitudinal time-use dataset

	1961–70	1971–77	1978–82	1983–90	1991–
Canada	1,828	1,845	8,138	6,351	–
Denmark	2,365	–	–	2,389	–
France	2,898	4,633	–	–	–
Netherlands	–	960	2,161	2,348	–
Norway	–	4,309	3,410	–	–
UK	1,702	1,901	–	1,996	1,211
USA	1,790	1,753	–	2,268	–
Hungary	1,989	4,663	–	–	–
West Germany	2,137	–	–	–	–
Poland	2,863	–	–	–	–
Belgium	1,938	–	–	–	–
Bulgaria	–	–	–	14,834	–
Czech Republic	1,668	–	–	–	–
East Germany	1,550	–	–	–	–
Yugoslavia	2,227	–	–	–	–
Finland	–	–	8,309	10,277	–
Italy (Turin)	–	–	2,116	–	–
Australia	–	1,276	–	–	–
Israel	–	–	–	3,126	–
Sweden	–	–	–	6,178	–
Total N of cases (aged 20–59)					121,407

categories simultaneously (Figure 3.1). Take three different categories of time use: paid work, unpaid work and leisure or consumption time. There is a fourth, from this point of view a residual, category, sleep, which is, for any social group, to within very few minutes per day a constant over historical time. So without much loss of information, we can express the first three categories in terms of proportions of the waking day, and then plot change in time-use patterns within the triangle. The three apexes of the triangle represent respectively, time spent entirely in unpaid work (bottom left), time spent entirely in paid work activities (bottom right) and time spent entirely in leisure (top). Within the triangle, a historical sequence of points that shifts upwards, denotes an increase in leisure time over the period (and since sleep is effectively a constant, this means an *absolute* increase); a shift to the left denotes a proportional increase in unpaid work relative to paid; and a shift to the right means that an increasing proportion of the work is paid work.

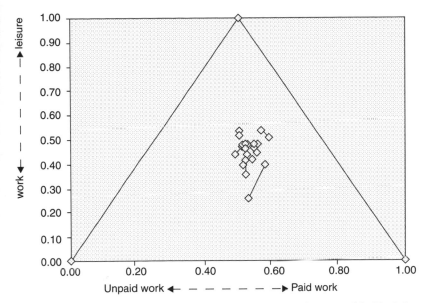

Figure 3.1 The virtuous triangle: work and leisure in the second half of the twentieth century

The first of the three trends is the *national convergence*. Figure 3.1 only includes the 9 countries for which we have two or more surveys; the arrow indicates the historical sequence. It shows, over the latter half of the twentieth century, a small shift in the balance towards paid from unpaid work. There is a general increase in leisure (ie a decline in the total of paid plus unpaid work), though some of the richer countries, towards the end of the century, show a small overall decline in leisure time.

Figure 3.2 plots men's and women's positions separately for all 20 countries. We see a convergence towards somewhere just to the right of the centre of the triangle. This is the second of the trends: without exception in every country for which we have the evidence, there is a *gender convergence*. Women, in each country, and throughout the period, do on average much more domestic work and much less paid work than men do. And the majority of men's work is certainly paid work, so the women's plots will always be found to the left-hand side of the triangle, the men's to the right. And generally the total balances of work versus leisure, for men and women, in any

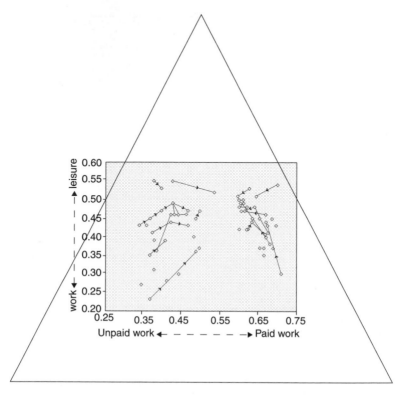

Figure 3.2   The changing work/leisure balance, 1960s–90s

country and at any point in history, are approximately the same. But over time the balances change. The women come to do absolutely more paid, and absolutely less unpaid work. The men do generally less paid and increase their unpaid work.

The third of these trends is slightly more complex: for each sex, over this historical period, we see a reversal of the relationship between educational level (which I take for this purpose as an indicator of social stratification) and leisure time. To simplify the presentation I have put all the countries together, and shown just the positions for each of the educational groups, across the countries, over the successive time periods – but the same trends emerge when we look at the countries separately. Straightforwardly, the previous leisure *advantage* of the more (educationally) privileged is reversed, becoming a *disadvantage*. This emerges with great clarity if we change the pictorial convention;

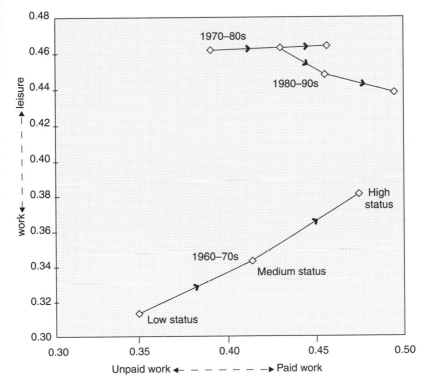

Figure 3.3   Women: a reversed status/work gradient

in the final pair of figures, rather than using the arrow to indicate the historical sequence, it now points from the position for the lowest educational status groups to that of the highest (Figures 3.3 and 3.4).

For both men and women, we see that in the period 1960–75, there is a positive gradient; for the period 1975–85 the line is approximately level; and for the period after 1985 there is a negative gradient. There no space here to investigate precisely why the long-standing positive association between class position and leisure time, identified so clearly by Veblen at the end of the nineteenth century, disappeared so abruptly at the end of the twentieth century. But we can certainly speculate that the apparent contradiction between my previously discussed generally 'increased leisure' finding, and the popular conception of *declining* leisure time, relates quite closely to the gradient reversal. After all, the writers of the popular literature presumably belong precisely to that high-status group that has so recently lost its relative leisure advantage!

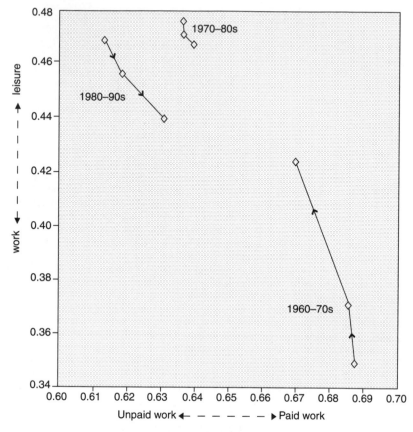

Figure 3.4   Men: a reversed status/work gradient

The convergence in patterns of daily life both across status groups and sexes, and amongst the developed societies, is quite striking. But nevertheless, when we think about time use in the future, there emerges a rather different theme: of *alternative* patterns of development within the general scheme outlined above. There is continuing potential for some really rather substantial divergences between societies.

The political economy of time

I start this section with a few words on what I have in mind as the political economy of time. For Marx this was straightforwardly about subjection of the time of workers by their capitalist masters.

Exploitation consisted of extra work time – extra in the sense of being beyond that necessary to reproduce their own labour – spent by the subjected group, to produce profits for the exploiters. So for Marx, that central plank of the nineteenth-century Left political programme, the reduction of the hours of paid work, was not, fundamentally, motivated by any desire to increase leisure – simply, fewer hours of work meant a reduction in the 'rate of exploitation', hence reduced profits, and the onset of the final crisis of capitalism.

What I have in mind, however, is altogether much less confrontational. It concerns interdependencies rather than conflicts. Rather than coercion of the time-use patterns of one part of the society by another, it concerns, in effect, collaboration. But in more general terms it still sees, just as Marx did in *Capital*, an intimate interconnection between patterns of social stratification and the distribution of work and leisure time. I will illustrate the scope of this new political economy of time with two examples.

The first concerns dynamics of gender differentiation, as they operate within households. Let us assume a certain range of household operations that must be carried out on a daily or weekly basis – childcare, shopping, cooking, cleaning and so on. These tasks might be carried out, in a heterosexual couple, by the male or the female partner, or by both. But different circumstances constrain the range of choice. For example, consider a couple in a long-working-hours culture such as the UK or the USA. A full-time job may involve 43 or 45 hours per week. In such a country, those not able to do this amount of paid work, or more, may be suspected of having insufficient commitment. Suppose also that this society has relatively low levels of publicly provided childcare services. The result is that to fulfil their household obligations, either both partners work part-time and both lose out in career stakes, or one works full-time, the other part-time or not at all. And once the female partner – for it *is* generally *she* – *has* dropped out, even for a short time, she is marked as a less-than-totally committed worker, her promotion is retarded, and the gap between her wage and that of her partner further increases, providing still more incentives for gendered choices in the labour market. In short, the long-working-hours culture carries within itself dynamics that lead to gender polarization.

Now contrast these dynamics with those within a short-working-hours culture – with a standard working day of say 36 or 38 hours – with good public childcare and other services. Simply, sharing the household operations under these circumstances is much *easier*. To continue the example, the couple adopt a limited degree of staggering of their work hours, one takes the child to crèche, and starts work later, the other finishes earlier and collects the child. Neither is regarded as an inferior worker as a result. So the dynamics of gender differentiation operate much less viciously.

The second, more macro-sociological, example concerns the balance among *production* and *consumption* activities. Consider again that first society with long hours of work, particularly for the most highly qualified workers, and an extreme of gender polarization. What does leisure look like? For the overworked élite: high pay but little time to spend it in. For the rest of the society, those in work are also *over-worked*, but with not too much money, and they are therefore pushed in the direction of debased, speeded-up, service consumption of the McDonald's type. And of course a society in which McDonald's provides the model for mass service consumption is also a society in which the model for service employment is the 'Mc-job'. Clearly, in addition to gender differentiation, these issues of working hours and leisure activity patterns are also closely intertwined with occupational employment patterns, class distributions, and matters of social stratification in general.

High and low value services, production and consumption

The divergences between the alternative service regimes rest on a crucial choice, between the consumption of high- and low-value-added final services. The simplest examples are in traditional services. Consider traditional 'grand' opera: the opera house seats an audience of say three thousand, the orchestra, principals and chorus total 150 people, and the same number again provide ancillary services. Let us say that an hour's performance takes ten hours of rehearsal and other preparation, then *each hour's consumption time by an opera-goer calls for an hour of someone's production time.* Contrast this arithmetic with that of a TV soap opera. There is a cast of 15, the labour of 50 others – perhaps 1,500 person hours of production time per hour of prime soap; there are, say, 15 million viewers – here the ratio could be 1,000 or more hours of consumption time for every hour of production time.

Or take fine food as against fast-food services. In the traditional French restaurant, the proprietor and chef visit markets, supervise purchases and taste the food, the apprentices chop and stir, the waiter advises us what to eat and drink. Contrast this with the fast-food establishment: the food is mass produced in a remote factory, transported frozen, and the major unmechanized labour is shared between essentially untrained cooks and checkout operators, and customers are self-trained to select and carry disposable food containers. To judge by the prices, high-value eating out might easily involve a ratio of paid labour to consumption time which is five or ten times that of the low-value-added equivalent.

The particular examples of high-value-added services may seem somewhat elitist and rather old-fashioned. But consider that sports (both participatory and spectator), adult and continuing education, fine arts and crafts, counselling and advisory services and so on, all fall into the same category. All of these involve the paid work of skilled workers in combination with the consumption time of people who are able to pay for them. And in addition to these are those services which may act as substitutes or supplements for unpaid caring activities in the home, childcare services, care of chronically sick and elderly; all these again require trained, often highly trained, workers. Plainly, which sorts of leisure services people spend their time consuming is of very great importance for the evolution of the wealth and welfare of the society. The society may devote its production and consumption time to low-value or to high-value services. Prospects for 'progress' depend on what sort of service economy develops.

Alternative service economies

This distinction between high- and low-value-added services finds a macro-reflection at the level of the state. Different mixes of the different sorts of service provision are associated with different sorts of society. There is a wide range of possible patterns of leisure service consumption. But, to concentrate our minds on the implications of the choice of the consumption mix, let us just consider two polar alternatives: one a type of society whose pattern of consumption is skewed towards high-value leisure services, the other, skewed towards low-value services. Let us, for the sake of a clear discussion, draw a binary ideal-type distinction between social democratic and liberal market states. (I should say that, though the names are similar, I do not necessarily subscribe to the precise system of regime classification developed by Esping Andersen, 1990). We would expect that there should be a correspondence between the nature of the state's regulatory activities and its pattern of leisure consumption: social democratic states tending towards high-value service consumption, liberal market states towards the low-value pattern.

The high-value service-consuming social democratic state benefits from a virtuous circle of income flow. The more high-value service producers, the more potential consumers of high-value services; the more doctors and members of other skilled caring professions in the society, the more potential restaurant customers and opera-goers, and high-value-added sports participants. This is in part a matter of disposable income, and is also a result of education and other factors which give people the capacity to enjoy consumption. And in turn the highly trained, well-paid, professional providers of leisure and other similar services themselves constitute further demand for medical and other caring services.

We cannot all be doctors. If the paid work in the society is to consist increasingly of high-value-added production *and* grow in volume, the society must develop *different sorts* of high-value- added consumption. The society, as it develops, needs more sophisticated tastes, more sophisticated skills in consumption. We must, as a society, go to the opera in sufficient numbers that we can afford to pay opera singers well enough to motivate their lengthy training. And this in turn presumably requires that we provide appropriate educational patterns for children and adults, so as to recruit future opera patrons as well as opera singers. And of course, as well as opera, there are other forms of high-value production and consumption, other performance art, sports, crafts, and caring services. And presumably, as part of this high-value production package, there must be a recognition that some members of the society, who are simply not able to be high-value producers, must nevertheless receive sufficient transfer payments to allow them to live decently and make a social contribution appropriate to their abilities.

The adjustment of gender roles plays an important part in the emergence of this sort of virtuous society. As women cease to provide unpaid caring services (i.e. domestic services at what are in effect subsistence wage levels paid in kind), some of these are substituted for by professional or semi-professional workers. *Some*, but not *all*; just as full-time domestic servants largely (if not necessarily permanently) disappeared from developed societies two generations ago, the large numbers of professionally trained workers and the generally high real wages in the high-value-added society mean that it may be difficult to arrange for domestic cleaning, *ad hoc* household maintenance, irregular or informal child care and similar services. In this sort of service economy, high-value-added services from the market must be complemented by *unpaid work time* devoted to self-provisioning of some of the low-value household services.

This in turn implies a thoroughgoing change in the patterns of men's and women's activities. Men in such societies are forced to change, not merely their household activities, but also their attitudes to paid work. In a high-value-added society, job pressures no longer provide a respectable way for married men to avoid household responsibilities. Their wives now also have high-value jobs and there is insufficient low-wage labour available to substitute for their domestic work. So the husbands ultimately have no excuse for doing other than sharing the unpaid domestic work, alternating with their wives in taking days off work to care for temporarily sick children, to visit schools, to wait for the arrival of household service engineers and so on. (The gender convergence we saw in Figures 3.3 and 3.4 shows the start of this trend.)

The opposite pole is not simply a low-value-added society but, rather, the dualistic liberal market society. This will contain some high-value-added, skilled occupations, doctors, lawyers, engineers, and a limited number of the sorts of skilled cultural and recreational workers found in the social democratic society. But a growing proportion of the workforce in this sort of society is deskilled, often operating the sorts of automated parodies of traditional services represented by the fast-food establishments. This sort of society will specialize in low-value-added services for low-income consumers, together with some cheap(ish) services for the minority of rich consumers. In this dual society there are no very intense pressures for substantial adjustments in gender roles. Only a minority of women, those with particularly high-value skills, find their place in the core workforce, while the others remain specialized in more peripheral, low- or unpaid menial service work.

The liberal market society is likely to be poorer than the social democratic society. The wealth of any society is the sum of wealth generated by its members. A society that engages on average in the production and consumption of low-value-added services must (*ceteris paribus*) have a lower GNP than societies that specialize in higher-value services (so the dualistic society is less likely than the other to find resources for transfers to the least well-off). It is of course possible to oversimplify and exaggerate the contrast between these two sorts of society. There is a continuum of service jobs from the lowest wage and lowest skill levels to the highest, and there is an infinite range of possible mixes among them. And both sorts of society have in common the basic gain from modernization, the shift of time away from provision of the more basic wants; all that differs is the range and quality of those services above the subsistence level.

Conclusion

Obviously there is much more to be said. For a start, there are more than just my two archetypal states: in addition to the 'Nice North' social democracy and the 'Wild West' liberal market societies, the old East European command economy is clearly a distinct type of service economy. And whether the forced and rapid replacement of this by liberal market *theories*, in the absence of the *economic culture* and well-established and strongly regulated financial *institutions* possessed by the USA and the UK, leads to an extreme Eastern version of the Wild West, or something even more sinister, remains to be seen. And there is insufficient space to explore the evolution of the more global time balance between the developed North and the less developed South. Just to take one of the many variants: migration of low-skilled domestic service labour from Eastern Europe or Asia might encourage gender equality among privileged groups in the West, while at the same time increasing *in*equality among ethnic groups in those same societies.

There is a need for a great deal of new social theorizing. At the micro-level we need theory about the determination of individuals' activity sequences through the day, and about how these sequences are coordinated with other members of the same household, and with the temporal rhythms of the locality and of the society as a whole. And at the macro-level, there is need for an understanding of the societal balance between the time necessary for production and consumption in different sorts of service society. The English saying 'We can't all take in each other's washing' is a neat expression of the essential constraint on the development of service economies. If the great bulk of all material goods are produced in automated factories or on other continents, then full employment in a society requires both production and consumption of a really very wide range of services. There is no reason why economies should not work on this basis; in many places they already do work in exactly this way. But making them work requires some careful thinking about patterns of public regulation.

For example, we saw, in the triangle graphs, that now the financially best-off people also work the longest hours. But *because* they work the longest hours these people, who have the *most money* to pay for services, have the *least time* available to consume them. There are complex arguments here, and it would be easy to devote all the pages available to me in this volume to a discussion of the extension of Gary Becker's famous micro-economic model of time allocation (Becker, 1965), and Bourdieu's not dissimilar 'distinction' model, to deal with this macro-sociological issue (Bourdieu, 1984). But the simple conclusion that emerges is: there is a prospect for increasing service employment if those with jobs reduce their working hours and spend their extra free time consuming services.

This, incidentally, brings us back full circle to that book we consigned to the dustbin of history: the Marxian policy of reducing working hours to provoke the final crisis of capitalism, now re-emerges in a post-industrial context as the mechanism that *saves* capitalism. And this line of argument is in fact widely accepted across the social democracies of the European Union, though not yet in Europe's Wild West, the UK. This is just an example. I end with a more general proposition. The political economy of early industrialization may have been dominated by issues of paid work time and its relation to exploitation. The political economy of post-industrial societies will certainly be dominated by the more general issues of the allocation of *all* of societies' time, production time *and* consumption time. It is this *new political economy of time* that will enable sociologists to come finally and fully to grips with the problem of creating wealth while at the same time reducing inequalities associated with class, gender and life stage.

4
Politicizing Time: Temporal Issues for Second-Wave Feminists

Mary Holmes

Introduction: if only we had time

Much sociological analysis of time understands it as a resource and focuses on the increasing dominance of capitalist temporality (e.g. Nyland, 1986). These works trace the commodification and standardization of time within industrial capitalism and the increasing control of capital over temporality. Roy (1990) has documented how workers cope with their lack of control over their work time through the use of humour and by interrupting work time with a fractured series of ritualized 'times' such as 'coke time'. These and other instances (see Inglis and Holmes, 2000) may be said to represent forms of resistance to capitalist control of time, but are not an overtly politicized resistance. In fact, the issue of resistance to capitalist 'control' of time is underdeveloped in sociology because there has been little investigation of the connections between politics and time. In this chapter, I focus on time and feminist politics.

Feminist[1] politics have been concerned, among other things, with women's lack of time. To say women lack time is to assume that it is a quantity of which some have more and some have less. But what are the assumptions behind seeing time as a quantity? Sociologists have tended to distinguish between different types of time, such as astrological time, clock time and social time (see Hassard, 1990). This chapter engages primarily with social time, beginning from a definition of it as expressing 'the change or movement of social phenomena in terms of other social phenomena taken as points of reference' (Sorokin and Merton, 1990, p. 58). Common understandings of some people having more time than others are socially referential. But in analysing such understandings time must be thought of as a resource *and* as a social meaning (Hassard, 1990, p. 14).

I use temporal issues within second-wave feminist politics to illustrate the benefits of understanding time as both resource and meanings. I draw my examples of feminist struggles with temporality from
the self-produced writings of New Zealand feminists between 1970 and
1984; but Jackson and Scott's (1996) discussion of feminist debates
about sexuality makes some similar points about feminism and time in
the UK. I also make comparisons with the work of Sasha Roseneil
(2000) on Greenham women's uses of time. While acknowledging
certain particularities I argue that New Zealand examples are broadly
representative of second-wave feminist social movements within
Western liberal democracies, and illustrate general points about politics
and time.

The documentary sources I have analysed also raise methodological
issues about studying time. Documentary sources both transcend and
'freeze' time, in the longevity of the written (and especially 'published') account and its fixedness. This fixedness was important to me
in my research, because I wanted to analyse how feminists represented
themselves during that period of intense political activity, rather than
how they represented themselves when interviewed 15 to 20 years
later. This seemed appropriate because the often-stated political intention of the writings I looked at was to keep a record of the feminist
movement. The result was a wonderful range of sources, yet the small-
ness of New Zealand made it possible for me to look at almost all that
was still available. Most of the sources had an ongoing life and permanence, rather than being ephemera (though I was aware of that
through its reprinting in less transient publications). *Broadsheet* magazine, for example, had a very wide circulation and was the longest-
running feminist publication, produced virtually throughout the
period I studied (it began in 1972) and beyond. Other publications
were more temporary, some newsletters or magazines (such as *Juno*)
running for only a few issues. These nevertheless provided important
representations of feminists with particular political, sexual and/or geo-
graphical locations. In other cases I consulted 'one-off' publications
such as conference reports, or submissions by feminists to the 1975
Parliamentary Select Committee on Discrimination against Women,
because I wanted to see how feminists represented themselves to wider,
if sympathetic, publics, and to 'the State'. The fact that the submissions
were 'one-off' says something about the difficulty of engaging the state
in ongoing political dialogue. The range and variety of sources used
also allowed me to assess feminist activity as varying from the ongoing
intense involvement of some individuals to the less frequent, but

perhaps also intense contributions of others (cf. Roseneil, 2000). Part of the point for me, and for second-wave feminists, is that not all women had the time to be extensively politically involved, but they were still involved.

Women's problems with finding time for politics are related to the gendered division of public versus private time. Eviatar Zerubavel's (1990) work on public versus private time may offer a starting-point for considering the gender politics of temporality and the temporality of gender politics. His assessment of bureaucratization as making increasing demands on the time of workers is useful, and it may be true that the (capitalist) workplace shows the most obvious temporal segregation of public and private, but this leads him to ignore a proper analysis of gender and of private time. As a result he does not recognize the impact of gender and status differences between the doctors and nurses in his study. He maintains that doctors are still almost always expected to be available to patients, while nurses are much stricter about not working when they are officially 'off-duty'. Zerubavel fails to consider that at the time of his study nurses were most likely to be women with lower pay and domestic work to do after their paid work.

The gendered consideration of private and public time has so far been largely related to the public world of work, but politics is also an important public arena. Glucksmann's (1998) study of women in Northern cotton-weaving communities is useful, however, because she highlights how time is not simply gendered but constitutes public and private structures in different ways for different groups of women. Women in relatively stable well-paid jobs are able to demarcate 'private' time for themselves by paying for the time of casual women workers (to child-mind, for example), a strategy similar women have used to find time for political activity. But women's political activity has been hampered by understandings of public politics as opposite to and separate from the private sphere (Pateman, 1989, p. 90). This includes domestic life, the family and personal relationships, all of which have been considered as 'natural' and less subject to the rationalized timekeeping of capitalism. Social meanings of time construct the private sphere as having a timelessness associated with nature and reproductive cyclical time, which supposedly disconnects it from politics.

Feminism was partially constituted by the gendered nature of social constructions of temporality, but it has also constituted a challenge to those social constructions (see Forman and Sowton, 1989; Kristeva, 1981; Massey, 1993, pp. 146–51). Second-wave feminists implicitly and sometimes explicitly challenged understandings and uses of time within the society around them. Teleological, individualistic and disembodied time practices were in various ways taken to task (Kristeva, 1981). I begin with the problem of women's lack of time for feminism, then consider how feminists 'made time' for politics, and also how they challenged dominant discourses on time.

Women have no time

Discursively speaking, women do not have time. Time is constructed as masculine, dynamic and inherently political, as opposed to space, which is coded as feminine, static and apolitical (Kristeva, 1981, pp. 15–16; Massey, 1993). Women have routinely been thought more closely associated with a cyclical 'natural' time, rather than the rational clock time of modern society.[2] But it is doubtful whether there is something that can be identified as 'women's time', and simplistic to oppose 'women's time' to 'men's time' as commodified market time (Adam, 1995, pp. 8–9). Nevertheless, it is possible to speak of a privileging of commodified time over time-giving and generating activities that fall outside 'the time economy of employment relations' (*ibid*, p. 95) and are more often performed by and associated with women (Davies, 1990).

Women's engagement in time-giving and generating means they also lack control over time as a resource within male-dominated capitalist society. In theorizing issues of political participation, time constraints have been identified as a barrier for women. For example, Anne Phillips (1991, p. 127) argues that an emphasis on meetings effectively excluded many women, making feminism less representative. My research offers the evidence Phillips notes she lacks to support this and surrounding arguments, but I emphasize the extent to which feminists were active despite 'lack' of time.

It was apparent to second-wave feminists that women's symbolic association with, and practical ties to the private often made political action difficult (Phillips, 1991, pp. 96–7). Conventional prejudice still saw married women as responsible for childcare and domestic chores, and research in the 1960s and 1970s suggested that most New Zealand women conformed to those roles (Novitz, 1978, pp. 79–82). For some women even becoming politically aware continued to be considered a major hurdle, as their domestic roles made leisure time meaningless. Christine Dann noted this (1976, p. 7) in interviewing Maori activist and feminist Donna Awatere for *Broadsheet* magazine. It was argued that it was difficult for Maori women to become politically aware when that involved 'precious leisure time which many Maori women do not have'. They lacked time because '[i]n their private lives, most Maori women had accepted oppressive systems, such as the Pakeha [white] marriage system, and such systems were now trapping them'. But improvements in birth control did make it possible for more married women to delay childbearing or to manage it so that they had more time and energy to give to feminism (Novitz, 1978, p. 78). Many heterosexual and lesbian feminists had children, as both the texts and data collected at some feminist gatherings indicate (Coney, 1973, p. 61; United Women's Convention Committee 1979, pp. 124–30; *Women '74*, 1975, p. 127).[3] Sasha Roseneil (2000) has also recorded that many Greenham women managed their involvement in the camp around family commitments. It was not birth control alone that suddenly made feminist political activity possible, but the condition and quality of women's private lives determined, to a large extent, the time they had for public political involvement. This was more obvious when they engaged with conventional political processes, such as when making submissions to the Parliamentary Select Committee on Discrimination against Women in 1975. Donna Hedgland (1974) (whose submission was printed in a feminist newsletter) clearly expressed these difficulties:

> Having been a full time housewife again for the school holidays I have found it impossible with small children around to write anything. My brief attempts have been made when I arranged for a friend to mind my pre-schooler and while the baby was asleep. This can only be arranged occasionally and you can appreciate is [sic] not the best of conditions to write sustained, well organised and documented arguments ...
>
> Holding the committee so early in the year with the closing date for submissions the 31st January is quite ridiculous as most women who have a family are involved in the extra household preparations for the festive season and then usually have to organise the family holidays and cleanup afterwards and then arrange for the children going back to school so that like this sentence there is no space to breathe let alone write submissions until February. (p. 3)

She also wondered how women could get their submissions typed and duplicated. Providing the required 27 copies must have been a difficult and time-consuming task given that this was before the widespread availablity of photocopiers. She wondered how women could complain when most could not meet the committee's primary conditions (*ibid*, p. 3). Other feminists also described the difficulties preventing many women from engaging in politics.

> A New Zealand mother could not leave her children with her husband for a week while she shot off to Parliament. And even women without children would probably have considerable difficulty leaving their husbands to go to Parliament, let alone embark on an active political campaign. (Kedgley, 1972, p. 19)

Despite the difficulties, many women did become politically active and worked around 'private' constraints. The difficulty of trying to label women's temporality as either simply 'private' or 'public' (Davies, 1990) is clear in one example from a feminist who wrote of the problems she was having printing a feminist newsletter on old Gestetners. She explained that she was typing the stencil at home, but was not a professional typist, and the uncorrected mistakes were due to the fact that she did not have time to run to the shop to get correcting fluid (Anonymous, 1975, p. 4). Despite her lack of time she participated in producing the newsletter, and the time constraints were acknowledged as part of her politicized reflections. Feminists made time to act politically in a variety of ways.

Making time to act

Women could use political action literally and symbolically to distance themselves from familial temporality. Four conference participants specifically stated in response to a survey that the conference meant a weekend away from home (*Women '74*, 1975, p. 134). Such time 'away' was easier for those who, like the women weavers Glucksmann (1998) studied, could make time by buying the time of others. The organizers of the 1979 United Women's Convention (UWC) were such women. Marcia Russell (1979, p. 21) attended one of their monthly planning meetings, held at a committee member's beach house, where '[e]veryone brought food and wine (delicatessen exotica without a hint of a home-baked scone)'. Russell's reference to the lack of scones designates these women as different from the stereotypical (white?) kiwi woman/wife, up to her elbows in flour and never without her Edmond's cookbook.[4] She implies that these women are too busy with political activity to have time to bake scones. The contrast constructs the scone-baking 'private' woman as not political. Russell's account also indicates that the committee was probably composed of middle-class women, with access to a beach house and the resources and inclination to buy 'delicatessen exotica'. They bought the time of those who produced the delicatessen food in order to make more time for politics. In this sense they could 'afford' to separate themselves from the traditional role of women.

If not all women could buy time for politics, many could make more time for feminism by devoting less time to men (cf. Jackson and Scott, 1996, pp. 12–17). As Val Cole (1976, p. 12) argued, the feminist movement was about self-determination for women, meaning that women had 'neither the time nor the energy to worry about men's problems'. One 'group of Auckland lesbian feminists' stated that they saw improving men as 'a hopeless de-energising waste' and confirmed their orientation towards defining themselves as lesbians and women (quoted in Ray and Lloyd, 1979, p. 18). There was often criticism of those women who worked politically with men (Allen *et al.*, 1976, p. 11; Juno Collective, 1977a, p. 3). In fact, feminist political power could be evidenced by the ability to create a male-free space and time. Some lesbians claimed such power after they had forced the last male reporter to leave the 1977 UWC and compelled media women to decide whether their loyalty was to their profession or to other women (Johnson, 1979, p. 5). Women's liberation was thought to require rejecting 'what oppresses women' (Cole, 1976, p. 13); thus rejecting men could be seen as a prerequisite for women to become independent, and self-sufficiency in political action was promoted. For instance, at the inaugural WSA Conference, Julia Seule (1978, p. 6) was shocked to discover men present at the social, and critical of the fact that three men videotaped the opening address. At the 1978 Women's Studies Conference Claire-Louise McCurdy (1979, p. 6) even wondered whether men doing the chores was a good idea.

Temporal struggles occurred not only with men but between feminists. These struggles recognized time as integrated with space and space/time as relational (cf. Massey, 1993). Lesbian feminists, for example, had to fight for space/time to express themselves and their politics. Linda Evans made a speech to the 1977 convention only after lesbian feminists had demanded time from the convenors, which was then given up by the guest speaker (Browne *et al*, 1978, p. 81). One of the best-known feminist struggles around time and space was the split between heterosexual and lesbian members of the *Broadsheet* collective in 1978. The lesbian Circle Collective (1978, p. 74) claimed the split was partly due to disagreements over whether to share new premises with the Women's Art Collective (WAC)[5] (see also *Broadsheet*

Collective, 1978). This and Christine Dann's editorials (which were critical of lesbian politics) led to four lesbian *Broadsheet* members resigning. The resigning members criticized declining a sharing of space which could have made the magazine more accessible. Lesbian time and energy were withdrawn from *Broadsheet* until the political significance of lesbianism was properly acknowledged (Circle Collective, 1978, pp. 76–80)[6]. Greater openness was thereby called for.

Openness was an important feminist ideal, but involved problems with time. The openness of the United Women's Conventions, for instance, caused difficulties:

> The involvement of more conservative women's groups at the Wellington convention had advantages and disadvantages. On the one hand it brought in many women who might otherwise never have considered attending a feminist convention. On the other hand it delayed any real progress, because issues that had been dealt with at the first convention – like abortion, homosexuality, the media and the presence of men – had to be fought out all over again. It was a bit like going back to square one. (Russell, 1979, p. 20)

Openness also extended to attempts to achieve equal and democratic divisions of labour within feminism, but these were time-consuming (Phillips, 1991, p. 126). Sharing and rotating tasks made sure that skills were passed on, but could waste women's talents and time. Julie Thompson (1975) noted that '[a]ll energy and concern is expended in ensuring that once a woman has learnt skills and developed her talents in a particular area she passes these skills onto somebody else. The inevitable result is that the group is forever looking inwards and is not able to use the abilities of individual members to further the aims of feminism' (p. 9).

One way of trying to overcome the temporal problems openness caused was to focus on the importance of commitment. Roseneil (2000) has also argued that despite efforts not to make distinctions based on the time women devoted to Greenham, commitment did play a crucial role in negotiations over power. I would argue that com- mitment became the basis of power, especially when a group had par- ticular tasks to do. Feminist groups pared themselves down to 'that informal group of friends who were running things in the first place' (Freeman, 1972, p. 159). Changes in the Broadsheet Collective illus- trated this. By 1980 it had become 'a closed collective which means there has to be a unanimous decision to invite a new person onto the collective and that person must be a radical feminist who's shown a commitment to the magazine and who's worked on it for a while'. This differed from the early days when anyone involved with the magazine could be in the collective (Broadsheet Collective, 1980, p. 15). Nevertheless, 'knowledge' and 'commitment' (presumably of and to feminism) had always been seen as desirable capital for women to bring to political processes (Coney and Cederman, 1975, p. 32; see also Broadsheet Collective, 1980, p. 15). Most of the other magazine-producing collectives also stressed the crucial importance of commitment (Juno Collective, 1977b, p. 6; Woman Collective, 1977, p. 2), as did other feminists with tasks to complete, like the coordinators for UWC 1977 who 'pledged themselves to put the Convention first at all times' and 'realised the amount of work that would be needed' (Browne *et al*, 1978, p. 7). The commitment of time and energy from its members was the 'primary (and often only) resource' of the women's movement (Calvert, 1981, p. 32), but those with less time could therefore feel marginalized or all feminists feel obliged to do more and more. The expectation of high levels of commitment could make the temporal routines of individual feminists punishing. Many feminists juggled participation in a number of political groups and activities (see Anonymous, 1983, p. 34; Victoria University Wellington Feminists, 1978, p. 1). Also, feminists often combined paid work with their political activities and collectives were often restricted to meeting in the evening. Even then feminist meetings often took around three to four hours (Broadsheet Collective, 1980, p. 15). Those without this amount of time to devote could not participate as key, powerful collective members. But this focus on commitment was part of the feminist challenge to dominant forms of temporality.

Challenging time

Within second-wave feminism 'linear temporality has been almost totally refused, and as a consequence there has arisen an exacerbated distrust of the entire political dimension' (Kristeva, 1981, p. 19). Questioning the teleological temporality of liberal democratic politics was a crucial part of feminism. Melucci (1989) has argued that feminist challenges to the political illustrate how means became the ends for new social movements. I would rather say that feminists took apart the dichotomy between means and ends – process and goals were entwined. Working collectively emphasized process as goal, but could be lengthy and difficult. In a 1983 article *Broadsheet* admitted it had 'taken months for this issue on collectives to come together. This illustrated some of the difficulties in working collectively – reaching consensus, the slow process of decision-making, who takes responsibility' (Broadsheet Collective, 1983, p. 28). In this article the New Plymouth Women's Centre, among others, reported temporal difficulties, as they 'often spent half an hour deciding on something, then scrapped it in the last five minutes' (cited in Broadsheet Collective, 1983, p. 30).

Feminists invested time because they felt that their work processes should reflect their political beliefs (Broadsheet Collective, 1980, p. 15). Feminist recognition of the importance of process and of relationships meant feminists continued to try to make decisions 'by consensus rather than by voting no matter how much longer it takes' (Coney and Cederman, 1975, pp. 31–2). Many feminists felt time spent in process was worth it and satisfying (Bitches, Witches and Dykes Collective, 1980, p. 2), but others became frustrated. At a radical feminist caucus, Joy Allen was disappointed that after lengthy discussions everyone 'seemed so paralysed by the problems of structurelessness that [they] could not even make a decision on whether to discuss decision making' (Allen *et al*, 1976, p. 13). The Wellington Women's Liberation Front also experienced the 'process/product' conflict. The group was deliberately unstructured, and although this kept discussions free and open, some talked much more than others, there was apparently considerable confusion, and it made decisions difficult. However, the group pursued these methods because they were determined to avoid developing a hierarchy (cited in Brownlie, 1970, p. 26). Feminist processes also ideally allowed attention to relationships through continual assessments of intra-group conflicts and tensions, and by encouraging 'support and caring for individual people to guard against "burn-out" from overwork' (Broadsheet Collective, 1980, p. 15). But for collectives trying to organize action there was not always the leisure to attend to relationships. For instance, *Broadsheet* had a monthly deadline, which if not met could damage credibility and sales. This made it 'hard to find the time to devote to the process of working' (Broadsheet Collective, 1980, p. 15). Some (Juno Collective, 1977a; Poulter, 1977, p. 11) read this lack of devotion to process as a failure to be sufficiently radical or even feminist.

Process as talk could also be suspect because talk/analysis/theory were sometimes characterized as male preserves that could not represent women, and time was therefore better spent in political 'action'. Daphne (1974, p. 4) of Wellington Women's Workshop felt that 'after one and a half years of discussing the same problems about women and groups functioning, [she] wanted to go beyond repetitious verbal-izing'. Three women left the Bitches, Witches and Dykes Collective (1980) before even producing their first issue, because they wanted action and more immediate results. 'They didn't see talk as action' (p. 3). Those who remained felt 'that talking is important; it is impor-tant to go beyond gut feelings, to analyse and gain perspective about those feelings' (*ibid.*). If feminism was politically and culturally to rep-resent women in their diversity, then time to talk and listen was important. Feminists were not merely promoting the message of differ-ence as acceptable, as Melucci (1989) suggests. They were negotiating how to represent differences. Val Cole (1976, p. 13) wanted a pluralist movement. She hoped that directions would be thought out in terms of feminist aims and ways of doing things, and that this would include analysis, discussion and possibly confrontation where necessary. But confrontation, or any significant differences between collective members, could cause problems for feminist processes.

Ultimately, second-wave feminists dealt with the temporal problems that difference posed for collectives by working with women like them-selves. When being a feminist collective meant using consensus deci-sion-making, this was an understandable response. If any action the group took depended on its members being able to agree, then differ-ences that made agreement difficult made action difficult. But the way in which processes were redefined led to a broader, more ongoing, sense of action. Yes, differences may have made things difficult, but despite faults, feminist processes worked. Gatherings were planned, magazines were produced. And importantly, feminist activity both challenged distribution of time as a social resource and indicated that there were alternative ways of understanding time.

There is not a monolithic and complete understanding of time that could be defined as 'feminist'. Neither can women's bodies, *as* or *in* space and time, be simply defined as feminist. Feminists frequently represented time and space as relational and interwoven and created understandings of women to counter dominant associations of women with static, unchanging space (Kristeva, 1981; Massey, 1993). Feminists were independent and progressive – going forward in time; while men were described as 'an anchor dragging the movement down', as having stayed still (Kedgley, quoted in Ray, 1982, p. 18). Indeed, femi-nists frequently politicized space and time as not opposed but integral. They created space/time where embodied women could supposedly be free from the distortions of patriarchy. Problematic in this vision was the tendency to assume that there was a true femininity, which could be discovered. Separate 'female' space/time, according to writers of a lesbian 'herstory', needed to be recognized as an issue for 'all women seeking liberation from male rule'. The expulsion of the male media at the 1977 UWC was seen as some recognition of this (Eagle and Argent, 1978, p. 11). 'Female' space was supposedly based on 'the power of female solidarity, emotion and wisdom' (*ibid.*). Such space/time was seen as part of the time of feminist politics, which meant 'a continuous process of peeling back layers of patriarchal lies and false concessions to women' and of trying to discover 'women's true reality' (Livestre, 1979, p. 6). Alyn Thompson (1979, p. 51) wrote of a women's culture that she argued had its own 'different underlying system of beliefs and values' perhaps based on 'a matriarchal system of values that was maintained over centuries and handed down from mother to daughter'. But even such separatist rhetoric (not always lesbian) was not a straightforward 'essentialist' discourse because it often implied that 'female' temporality and spatiality were produced by women's social positions within patriarchy (cf. Forman, 1989).

Feminist consciousness-raising was a definite attempt to use the shared experiences of women to understand what it meant to have a woman's body in the time/space of patriarchal culture. Foucault (1992, p. 321) states that experience, in modern thought, links 'the space of the body and the time of culture'. This may explain why embodied experience became the privileged basis of feminist knowledge and sexuality was central in debates on when the personal was political. Some lesbian feminists felt that being 'truly feminist' meant choosing to give emotional and sexual, as well as political, energy to women (cf. Jackson and Scott, 1996). Lesbianism could then be seen as a form of political action. For example, there were lesbian feminists who preferred to exist on irregular or low incomes rather than working at jobs which might 'prop up institutions that oppress women etc.'. This potentially left lesbian feminists with more available energy for political action and more time to put into personal relationships – time they argued was needed because they rejected heterosexual models for relationships (Juno Collective, 1977b, p. 5).

Valuing time devoted to relationships and to all caring for others was another way in which feminists challenged conventional understandings of time and space based around capitalist production. Time-giving activities (Adams, 1995, p. 95) were appreciated. For example, feminists nearly always carefully acknowledged the importance of the cleaning, childcare and other support work that was a crucial part of feminist political organizing (see also Roseneil, 2000). For example, in the 1975 UWC booklet it is recorded that:

Deidre Milne organised extra buses and trains to cope with the closure of the airport [due to bad weather]. Hundreds of Wellington people responded to Rose Lovell-Smith's radio appeal for billets. And Barbara Stephen didn't stop working till Monday night when the show building was cleared, even though she and her team had been there from 5 a.m. every day doing everything possible to make the physical arrangements work well. (Meikle, 1976, p. 9)

Recognizing the relational aspects of space–time challenged individualistic conceptions of space and time, but feminists struggled to dissociate the relational from the privileging of presence. In the emphasis on experience and on face-to-face meetings feminism became a politics of the present (cf. Melucci, 1989). Those who were 'there' knew best and exercised most power, although this power was often unacknowledged because of feminist ideals prohibiting leaders and formal structures (Alba, 1980, p. 4). Thus there were tensions between openness and continuity in feminism that hampered efforts to involve and represent a range of women. Yet the very relationality inherent in feminist processes and in thinking on time-giving disrupted notions of a self-identical subject in the present. To understand 'others' as exterior, and not to be incorporated, was an important struggle within feminism. As Cornell (1995) has argued, if this understanding can be combined with an understanding of 'the temporality of the subject of history', then the philosophy of presence can be challenged. Feminism can then offer the possibility of representing sexual difference 'beyond accommodation to the limits of the masculine symbolic' (p. 152). In making time for others, and in seeing process as important, feminists resisted the self-serving and end-profit-oriented 'logic' of male-dominated capitalist societies.

Time enough?

Whether women can be said to have time depends largely on the constructions of women's history and of women as subjects. Crucial in these constructions are gendered divisions of time associated with public versus private social spheres. If second-wave feminists began from the assumption that time was something women did not have, then part of their political action was aimed at demanding a redistribution of time, as they demanded a redistribution of other social resources.

Women had varying access to time as a social resource, but there were opportunities within feminism for varying levels of participation.

Many women with domestic duties managed to participate in at least some feminist events, even if they could not be active in groups that met frequently. Feminist activity could provide temporal escape from domestic roles, but women with access to money were more able to 'buy' time for politicking. Other women were more likely to make time for political thought and action by devoting less time to men, or by negotiating and struggling among each other for time and space to represent themselves and their varied interests.

Feminists struggled and experimented with using temporal resources and understanding time. Not all feminists were unified in their understandings of what 'women' meant or needed. They were not involved in philosophical debates about the nature of time. Nevertheless feminists implicitly and sometimes explicitly challenged understandings and uses of time within the society around them. There was an appreciation of time as an ongoing commitment to process and to care, rather than as a quantity, or a marker of difference. These feminist re-evaluations of space/time were hampered, to a degree, by the privileging of presence. Not to have been 'there' is to not know. Simultaneous presence allows a particular form of relationality that can encourage dialogue and participation, but it can make it difficult to assimilate the past and to move towards the future. Without such movement political change for women can feel like always covering the same ground. Had feminists been concerned only with time as a social resource that they needed more of, this might have been the end of the story. But feminists have struggled to understand the politics of time as requiring both a redistribution of temporal resources and a recognition of alternative definitions of temporality. These struggles provide an example of how politicizing time both as a resource and as social meaning can resist dominant forms of temporality within patriarchal capitalism.

Now that mass collective feminist activity has largely dissipated, feminist resistance to dominant forms of temporality has become increasingly focused on symbolic aspects of time. Whether feminism was ever unified is debatable, but resistance to male domination has certainly changed. The continuance of feminism by different means is not a tale of dominant temporalities becoming reasserted. I would argue that since the 1980s the institutionalization of many feminist ideas (and feminists) within state bureaucracies, parliamentary and local politics and academia make policy, public political debate and academic research not new but newly articulated sites from which alternative visions of time and space can challenge and change. Other sites and styles of temporal resistance are awaiting further investigation.

Notes

1. I use 'feminist' rather than 'women's liberation' so as not to exclude less radical women who were nevertheless important in the broader struggles.
2. Ironically this supposedly more 'natural' temporality has been thought to make women more suited to the routine repetitive tasks resulting from the rationalization of capitalist production (Game and Pringle, 1984, pp. 28–9).
3. The results of the 1973 questionnaire given to convention participants suggested that the 'average woman' at the conference 'had 2.8 children, was married and living with her husband, worked part-time, cared for 3.5 people, belonged to 2.7 organizations' (Coney, 1973, p. 61). At the 'Women '74' convention, the questionnaire responses suggested that 71 per cent were married (*Women '74*, 1975, p. 127). Five years later at the 1979 United Women's Convention, 58 per cent of participants had children, and most also lived with a husband. Forty-nine per cent of the women had pre-school or school age children and were in paid employment, with a variety of child-care arrangements (United Women's Convention Committee 1979, pp. 124–30).
4. 'New Zealand's greatest selling cookbook', according to the back of my 1985 edition. By 1985, over 3 million copies had been sold: the population of New Zealand in 1985 was just over 3 million.
5. Other factors mentioned were that '*Broadsheet*'s middle class heterosexist reformist feminism proved incompatible with the more radical philosophy of lesbian separatist feminism'. The four lesbians who resigned made a statement outlining what happened. This was produced in a statement only delivered to subscribers of *Broadsheet*, but the split was also discussed in the issue of *Circle* cited.
6. Finally, in May 1980, *Broadsheet* made a statement that seemed to satisfy these demands (see *Broadsheet* 79, May 1980, p. 2).

5
Time and Speed in the Social Universe of Capital

Michael Neary and Glenn Rikowski

Economy of time, to this all economy ultimately reduces itself.
(Karl Marx, *Grundrisse*, 1858, p. 173)

Introduction

In contemporary society it appears that speed and the 'tyranny of time' (Reeves, 1999) are forces gathering increasing strength in all areas of social life. Matthews (1999) notes that, subjectively, we experience this as a sense of acceleration in our daily lives (p. 44). These effects, notes Luke (1998), are 'global in their scope and impact' (p. 163). The *speed of life* has increased throughout society: objectively, as all social processes are subject to an increasing 'Need For Speed' (Matthews, 1999) as we try to 'save time', and subjectively, as we experience the sensation of speed in social life (Gleick, 1999). For Luke, the speed of life in contemporary society has now reached such intensity that it 'recreates the world as humans have not known it' (1998, p. 165). Davis and Meyer (1998) assure us that we are not imagining things when we experience life as 'blur' – the sum of electronic connectivity, speed and intangibles, which are the 'derivatives of time, space and mass' (p. 6). These three phenomena in combination are inexorably 'blurring the rules and redefining our businesses and our lives' (*ibid.*).

Existing accounts of the tendency for increased speed and the exhaustion of time in contemporary society typically posit a 'fast capitalism' (Agger, 1989) or 'turbo capitalism' (Luttwak, 1999), but without providing an explanatory dynamic of the social drive for increased speed in social life. This chapter provides such an explanatory dynamic. It unfolds a theory of the speed of life in capitalist society. This theory rests upon illuminating the significance of Karl Marx's concept of socially necessary labour time for exploring the *social form* of time in capitalist society. It is necessary to indicate how this theory is grounded within a more expansive understanding of the social universe of capital. This involves analysis of certain forces at work in this social universe: value, surplus value, labour and capital. It also involves delineating two structuring concepts: totality and social form. After this initial exploration, the chapter proceeds to develop a theory of the speed of life in capitalist society through the writings of Marx, but also drawing upon the work of Moishe Postone (1993) and especially Albert Einstein's conception of the physical universe.

We are concerned primarily with uncovering a *theory of social time*, as opposed to developing a social theory of time. We will demonstrate the significance of our approach by counterposing our work against two exemplary social theories of time: the work of Barbara Adam (1990, 1995) and of Philip Turetzky (1998).

Adam acknowledges that time is a 'fact of life', and seeks to develop a concept of *social* time that 'encompasses its multiple expressions' (1990, p. 24). Her starting-point us that time is fundamentally a social construction. However, she argues that merely stating this proposition is insufficient; it does not dissolve the enigma of time – time as transcendent, i.e. a phenomenon that cannot be reduced to either social convention or a method of regulating social life. Thus Adam has a complementary position where 'the source of time must not be ignored since it is central to an adequate interpretation of time in social theory' (1990, p. 43). However, this sets up a natural/social time distinction as a form of *interactive dualism* – where the concepts of natural and social time are implicated in the explanation of each other, but a dualism none the less. Adam notes that when social and natural scientists search for the *source* of time then it 'is found to represent a multitude of phenomena' (p. 43). From this, Adam concludes that it is impossible to hold that *all* time is a social construct, and goes on to maintain that natural time is 'intimately tied to the conception of social time' (p. 48). On this basis, theories of natural time need to be 'recognized as an important focus for social science enquiry' (p. 49), a position we endorse for time studies in this chapter in relation to Einstein's theory of relativity and its consequences for developing Marx's labour theory of value. Adam also holds that the social theory of time incorporates different conceptions of *natural* time existing in historical eras and in different societies. At the end of *Time and Social Theory* (1990), Adam is still wrestling with the natural/social time distinction. On the one hand, she holds that her *Time and Social Theory* has demonstrated that 'the characteristics identified with natural time are in fact an *exclusively human creation'* (p. 150, our emphasis). On the other hand, she also maintains that her study of time indicates that 'natural time is *very different* from its social science conceptualizations' (pp.150–51, our emphasis), implying limits to social constructionist explanations of natural time, and opening up natural time as a transcendent, a-historical constant. Still dissatisfied by dualities (p. 153), Adam leaves the problem of dissolving the social/natural time dualism to her next book, *Timewatch*.

In the opening chapter of *Timewatch*, Adam (1995) nails her colours to the mast. She starts out from a discussion of 'my time', 'our time' and 'other time', and this provides rich social content. This attempt to dissolve the social/natural time dualism invokes a savage relativism (and temporal solipsism) that provides time sociologists with an infinite research and writing programme: the comparison of different social/personal 'times'. Throughout her first two books (Adam, 1990, 1995), Adam holds on to abstract clock time as one of an infinite number of 'times'. She asserts the need to dissolve dualisms, but clings to the social/natural time dualism, to the last.

Turetzky (1998), on the other hand, illustrates the opposite of Adam's work. He has a strong sense of the *form* of time in his neo-Deleuzian theory of becoming-time. Turetzky develops a three-stage theory of becoming-time based on interconnected syntheses that 'connect successive instants as past and future' (p. 212). This points towards the *flow* of time. The aim of the theory is to uncover the 'conditions under which something new is produced' (p. 221) and in such a way that the theory reflects how we actually experience time. However, at most, this is an abstract psychology of time with minimal social content.

Taken together, Adam's (1990, 1995) and Turetzky's (1998) texts incorporate elements that our theory of time and speed seeks to avoid. In the case of Adam, the movement from social constructionism to subjectivism ends in a relativism (and ultimately solipsism) that negates explanation of the subjective feelings of time exhaustion. In the latter case (Turetzky), the polar opposite dangers are uncovered: a-historicism, essentialism, reification, naturalism and an extreme formalism. On the one hand, Adam's (1995) work provides rich social content (but fails to indicate an adequate social *form* for its analysis). On the other hand, whilst Turetzky's theory of becoming-time incorporates a strong sense of form, it provides inadequate social *content*, which ultimately results in the reification of time.

The theory of social time advanced here pursues the question of the *social form of time* in capitalist society. Hence we seek to develop an explanation of the nature of social time whose content is given by its incorporation within a specific and historical space: the social universe of capital. This chapter explores this social universe, and social form of time therein, through the writings of Marx – especially his notion of socially necessary labour time. Our examination of the form of time within the social universe of capital brings Marx into contact with that great theorist of physical space-time: Einstein.

The speed of life

Marx develops his ideas on the temporal aspect of capitalist society through the concept and reality of socially necessary time. A commodity has value only because of the abstract labour that has materialized in it. This is measured by the quantity of the value-forming substance that the object contains. Marx's great leap out of classical political economy was to recognize that this quantity was a direct result of the amount of time taken to produce the commodity. He realized that this time could not be based on direct, concrete time, as this would clearly cause insurmountable theoretical problems due to reconciling the different speeds at which people work. For example, one consequence of focusing on concrete time was that the lazier the worker, the more labour time it would take to produce a commodity, hence the greater that commodity's value, with the opposite result for the speedy and diligent worker. This results in equivalence problems when the units of labour time are unequal on the basis of labour powers of varying quality and intensity. Rather, Marx posited the quantity of time involved in producing a commodity as a social fraction or social *average* of the total amount of time that labour power was expended in society. Although composed of 'innumerable individual units', each unit of labour time is not a discrete, disconnected period of time but serves as a social average of 'one homogeneous mass' of the 'very developed totality': 'Socially necessary labour time is then the labour time required to produce any use value under the condition of production normal for a given society and with the average degree of skill and intensity prevalent in that society' (Marx, 1867, p. 129).

What Marx is explaining is that while the amount of value in society remains constant during the period when this value is being produced, the amount of socially necessary labour time needed to produce the commodity is reduced. As the pressure is constantly to expand the amount of surplus value being extracted, there is corresponding pressure to reduce the amount of socially necessary labour time in the production of commodities. What is being recognized is not simply the quantity of use values – an increase in productivity will increase the quantity of things – but, rather, the fact that decreases in socially necessary labour time change the magnitude of value of the individual commodities produced and not the total value produced per unit of time.

The crucial point in this process is not the amount of value produced; it is rather the magnitude of (surplus) value that is recoverable. This is not then simply a quantitative equation, but is a *regulatory* device as to what constitutes the socially accepted standard for the expenditure of human energy (labour power). This reduction redetermines the normative social labour unit. Thus, what is socially defined is not simply the quantity of social labour, *but the standard of what constitutes social time.* Whilst the abstract measurement of time remains the same, and this process is set within the framework of abstract time (days, hours, minutes, seconds etc.), there is a change in the normative social labour hour.

The effect of this relation is both dynamic and directional, imposing a law-like quality independent of human will. Socially necessary labour time becomes the measure of the speed of human activity: *the speed of life.*

The demand to increase the extraction of surplus value leads to the creation of clock time, the utilization of the clock time to the maximum (absolute surplus value) and finally the redetermination of the social labour hour (relative surplus value). However, this leads to a paradox. In his *Time, Labour and Social Domination*, Postone (1993) explores the redetermination of the labour hour: the standard by which value is attributed to labour. When pursuing this question he discovers that time appears to be constant and non-constant. It is constant at the point at which it is constituted through abstract labour as truly social time, but variable as the labour hour is reduced on the basis of changes in labour productivity flowing from the social drive to increase relative surplus value. Postone argues that this paradox cannot be explained within the Newtonian theory of absolute and linear time. Rather, he notes, 'it implies another sort of time as a superordinated frame of reference' (Postone, 1993, p. 192). For Postone, the paradox is explained by what he calls the relation between 'abstract independent time' and 'historical time'. Abstract independent time represents clock time and is constant. The redetermination of the standard of time through the workings of socially necessary labour time within which time units go through a process of densification is non-constant. This non-constant redetermination of the standard of time is not reflected in abstract independent time.

In order to try to make headway with the paradox, Postone introduces the notion of historical time, as another sort of concrete time. Historical time is a reflection of the relationship between the redetermination of the standard of time (the non-constant variable) and abstract independent time (the constant variable). Through the redetermination of the standard of time the position of each new time unit is changed. It is as a result of this change in position that the constant and non-constant variables are moved forward. It is this forward motion that constitutes historical time. Postone is clear that this is not a movement *in* time, but rather a movement or flow *of* time in space. While this is a sophisiticated social theory of time, it lacks a spatial dimensionality. Postone's posited solution to the time paradox that he has identified does not incorporate a theory of the immanent relation between time and space, i.e. space-time.

Any account that raises unexplained paradoxes in Newton's theory of time must make reference to Einstein. And yet Postone does not make the move. Einstein dealt with the paradoxical nature of time in his Special Theory of Relativity (of 1905). In this formulation, both time and space (space-time) are, in fact, the result of the relationship between two frames of reference. These two frames are the speed of light, which is constant at all times, and the speed at which an object is travelling. The faster an object is travelling, the slower time will run. There is no absolute time; time exists only at the point at which it is being measured, and, as a consequence, there is no absolute space. This is not to say that everything is relative, as time is measured against the absolute measure of the speed of light. But, while this explanation works for objects travelling at constant speed and in a straight line, a more developed account was required for accelerating objects and with changing velocities. The answer was encapsulated by Einstein's theory of gravity contained in the equation $E = mc^2$ (1905) and the General Theory of Relativity (of 1915).

A fully elaborated theory of social space-time would then connect the theory of Einstein with Marx. This link has already been established. In a discussion about the relationship between political theory and the natural sciences, Kay and Mott (1982) point out the link between the way in which advances and failures in the natural world are recorded as political theory. They argue that the concept of natural equivalence in political economy, in which equal exchange was based on the apparent equivalence of labour, was the counterpart of Newton's symmetrical space, providing the principle through which all movements in society were made comprehensible (Kay and Mott,

1982, p. 76). Kay and Mott suggest that by challenging the principle of natural equivalence of labour Marx moved beyond the concept of symmetrical space and anticipated relative or curved space. For Marx, space was non-symmetrical, depending on whether the commodity took the relative or the equivalent form of value. It was neither homogeneous nor isomorphic, neither empty nor endless, as it had been for Newton. On the contrary, for Marx, space was directionally oriented; and, rather than mysterious forces acting at a distance across space from one object to another, force, object and space-time were united in a single concrete formulation whose structural principle was discontinuity. Kay and Mott argue that Marx was anticipating Einstein's theory of relativity. Indeed, they argue, had Marx written *Capital* only 40 years later, the theory of relativity would have provided a more adequate language for his thought, which was well in advance of the science of the day (Kay and Mott, 1982, p. 76).

This is a dramatic juxtaposition that Kay and Mott develop no further. Writing on only the first section of Marx's first volume of *Capital* (of 1867), their focus is on consequences of the exchange relation and is restricted to Einstein's Special Theory of Relativity. This enables them to make a very useful intervention. However, in order to bring out the full significance of the connection it is necessary to examine the relationship between Marx's law of value and the way that Einstein developed his Special Theory into a theory of gravity through his equation $E = mc^2$ and his General Theory of Relativity (1915).

The social universe of capital: *M–C–M′* meets $E = mc^2$

Both Einstein and Marx revolutionized the way in which we understand the basic laws of the physical and social universe. Both radically disrupted common-sense notions of time and space, and yet neither left us with a finished work. Even so, their work forces us to reconsider the nature of the physical and social worlds. A review of Einstein's work reveals striking similarities between the way in which Marx formulated his labour theory of value and Einstein's formulation of his theory of gravity. Marx maintained that the law of value that he elaborated was like the law of gravity. However, the law of gravity to which he was alluding was set within a Newtonian perspective on the laws of physics. What Marx could not know was that his elaboration of the law of value was, in fact, in advance of the science of the day. It anticipated the revolutionary ways in which Einstein's theories of relativity and gravity recomposed our notions about the relationship between time, space, matter, mass and energy. While the links between Marx's critique of political economy and Einstein's cosmology have been made elsewhere (Kay and Mott, 1982), systematic connections between Einstein's law of gravity and Marx's law of value have yet to be made.

We live in the social universe of capital. This is the social universe that was the focus of Marx's three volumes of *Capital*. The substance of this social universe is value (Neary, 2000; Neary and Taylor, 1998; Rikowski, 2000a). Capital is value in motion (Kay and Mott, 1982). Value is not a 'thing'. In its first incarnation in the capitalist labour process it inheres within some material 'things', in commodities; though it can also be created within immaterial commodities too (Burford, 2000; Lazzarato, 1996). Thus value, as the substance of the social universe of capital, should not be thought of as some kind of 'stuff', some material substratum (Rikowski, 2000a). It is, after all, a *social* substance. Value can be viewed as being social energy that undergoes transformations, its first metamorphosis being its constitution as capital in the form of surplus value. As Ana Dinerstein (1997) notes, 'social energy is permanently being transformed' (p. 83), and created too. Value is a multi-dimensional field of social energy – a social substance with a directional dynamic (expansion) but no social identity. It is the matter and anti-matter of Marx's social universe. The cosmological character of Marx's exposition can be fully drawn out by comparing Marx's law of value with Einstein's theory of gravity.

In the social universe of capital, value takes on the identity of things in the material world: it is objectified in the form of money (M), commodities (C) and capital (M'). Money and commodities, therefore, are materialized forms of social relations. The basis for the social relation is human energy in a particular form of labour in capitalism – or the imposition of capitalist work.

In capitalist society, labour takes on two forms: as use value and as value. This two-fold nature of labour is specific to labour in capitalist society, one of its defining features. In the capitalist labour process, labour is expressed in two modes. First, commodities incorporating utility, or usefulness, are produced as *use value*. Second, labour is expressed in the form of value. The labour process in capitalist society is also a valorization process – the production of value and surplus value, the latter being value over and above that required for the reproduction and maintenance of the labourers and their dependants – the labourers of the future – as expressed in the wage. As Marx notes (1867), it is not the case that there are two types of labour going on, one that produces useful things (use values) and the other value. Rather, the *same* labour exists in two modes, and is expressed in two forms.

The main point is that *labour in capital* has two social dimensions: it exists as direct mediation between man and nature, a truism of little conceptual significance, *and* the social context within which that mediation is grounded. Marx regarded the discovery of this duality as his most important theoretical discovery (in his *Capital*, 1867). In this arrangement, labour does indeed appear as if the direct mediation (use value) aspect of the dimension exists without reference to anything other than itself and the substance of the social context (value) is not discernible to bourgeois social theory. In fact, the duality of labour presents social scientists with a dimension that they are conceptually unable to deal with and forms the basis of what Marx called 'commodity fetishism' (1867, pp. 163–177).

Labour, then, is the basis of all social life in capitalist society, but labour in capitalism is itself constituted as a form of value (the value form of labour). Therefore, it is value, not labour, that is the foundation of all social life. Value is *the* category of social totality. In order to explain this it is necessary to unravel the particular form of interdependence that this peculiar arrangement presupposes. The two dimensions of labour are the result of the unique form of social interdependence, i.e. within capitalist society workers do not consume what they produce. Rather, workers work in order that they may consume what others have produced. Here, a further duality of labour in capitalism is involved. Workers are involved in the production of use values and the production of exchange value. The quality of the use value is specific to the kind of work they are engaged in, while exchange value is abstracted from any specific content or, rather, its content is the social relation that it constitutes. On this basis, the product of any form of labour can be exchanged, in definite proportions, against the labour of any other worker. The product of ten hours of the labour of either Neary or Rikowski might be equivalent to only one hour of the intense labour of soccer player David Beckham, for example. Some such equivalence sticks. This is the form of equality socially validated on the basis of value (i.e. *capital*, as surplus value in its emergent form).

This is a real process of abstraction and not simply a conceptual event in which 'Labour grounds its own social character in capitalism by virtue of its historically specific function as a social mediating activity. Labour in capitalism becomes its own social ground' (Postone, 1993, p. 151). It is this process of abstract social mediation that Marx refers to as abstract labour which, as the ground of its own social relation, constitutes a unique form of social totality. The social totality is non-empty social space; it is value as a *field of social energy or force* that constitutes a specific field of social being, the social universe of capital. Abstract labour is the social substance through which matter in this social universe moves and is constituted as commodities. In such a situation, labour is not recognized, validated or rendered equivalent as a result of any intrinsic capacity or social need. Labour is socially validated only to the extent that it forms a part of this social generality: 'as an individuated moment of a qualitatively homogeneous, general social mediation constituting a social totality' (Postone, 1993, p. 152). Or, what happens is that objects materialize within this space as forms of the social relation out of which they are derived. Objects materialize as congealed quantities, in the form of labour materialized, not only as *C–M–C* (Commodities–Money–Commodities), but also as a set of institutional forms that exist to resolve the contradiction in the duality: *the state.*

This is a historical as well as a logical process. The history is implicit in the reformulation of *C–M–C* into *M–C–M'* (Money–Commodities –Money Plus Surplus Value). Indeed, the historical dynamic for this process is incorporated within the relation between the concrete and abstract character of the commodity form examined as a non-identical unity. The existence of the commodity presupposes the expansive logic of capital, understood as *value in motion.* Motion is derived from the increases in productivity that are required to maintain expansion. In the drive for surplus value, the abstract social dimension of labour in capitalism formally rearranges the concrete organization of work so that the maximum of human energy can be extracted (absolute surplus value: *C–M–C–M–C–M'–C*). This results in, among other things, the social division of work, the organization of the working day, which includes the invention of machine time (the clock). When the limit of this process has been reached, the abstract social dimension of labour in capitalism can only increase the production of surplus value by enhancing the general productivity of labour (relative surplus value *C–M–C–M–C–M'*). Through large-scale industry the worker becomes a part of the machine and is forced to change his or her nature and become something other than human: *the human as capital, humanity capitalized, human–capital* (Rikowski, 1999, 2000b). In this process, the concrete material character of labour is no longer recognizable or feasible as an independent form of existence; it is completely overwhelmed by the abstract–social dimension. Marx refers to this as the process of *real subsumption.* This real subsumption does not simply imply revolutionizing the organization of work in the factory, but it becomes the organizing principle throughout capitalist society. Postone (1993) reminds us that Marx argues that real subsumption heralds a qualitative change in history. Only with real subsumption does capital become truly *totalizing* and the whole process intrinsically capitalist, and only then does labour become the constituent source of its own domination. It is at this point that the logic of production escapes human control, the machine (large-scale industry) has taken over and human powers are constituted in an alien form; workers become a particular mode of existence which accumulates the constituted powers of humanity in an alienated form. The duality of labour has materialized at the level of society. This is a theory not simply of time but of the objectification of spatiality.

For Newton, gravity was the result of an invisible force that pulled objects instantaneously across empty space at a force that was related to their mass. Although borne out by mathematics and its ability to predict celestial events, Newton's law could not explain its own basic presuppositions and was eventually undermined by Einstein's theory of relativity. For Einstein, the universe was not empty space. It was composed of the relationship between mass and speed that existed as a totalizing field of energy and objectified as matter: congealed quantities of speed and mass, or frozen space with a specific energy that could be calculated through the famous equation, E (energy) = m (mass) c (*celeritas*: the speed of light[2]). Within this formulation, mass and energy are not simply interconvertible; they are identical (Calder, 1979, p. 33). Gravity therefore is not a force acting between bodies but an energy field of space-time distorted by its own materialized objects whose effect is expressed by the level of the density of these objects. Where matter exists, so does energy, with the greater the mass, the greater the energy and the more intense the gravitational distortion of space-time. The denser the material, the more disruption is caused to the energy field. The distorted effect, or energy field, creates trajectories within which non-linear movement occurs. Movement is the way in which materialized objects maintain themselves in a solid state. When confronted with strongly distorted space-time a materialized object loses rest-energy, i.e. the energy needed to create matter in the first place, and, therefore, must exhibit another form of energy to maintain itself. According to Einstein, the way an object maintains its materialized integrity, its solid state, is to *accelerate*. It is in the nature of the process to *devalue* the rest-energy of matter in an object nearing a source of strong gravity (Calder, 1979, p. 53). Therefore, for Einstein, gravity was a function or *field* characteristic of matter itself, with its effects being transmitted between contiguous portions of space-time (Clarke, 1973, p. 199).

As characterized in the preceding two sections, Marx's theory of value is decidedly 'Post-Newtonian'. In Isaac Newton's world, relations between objects are governed by force (gravity) acting at a distance between them (Hey and Walters, 1997, p. 23). Forces repel or attract objects. In positing capital as a totality of relations, and as a totalizing force, Marx's theory of value pointed the way forward towards *value as a field of social energy*. In Newton, the force (gravity) acted between objects. This was true for relations between social phenomena in Marx's theory of value too: capital as a *social relation*. However, Marx went further than Newton by positing capital as a totalizing social force, a force existing not just *between* social phenomena (in relation), but as the very substratum for the relation itself. This insight remained underdeveloped in Marx, not surprisingly, as Marx did not have access to the Einsteinian theory that could have generated a view of the social universe as *a field of social force (energy) whose substance was value*.

A theory of social time

A social theory of time is not able to get beyond the paradoxes established in the work of Adam and Turetzky. Caught between the dualism of natural and social time, Adam's preoccupation with different times degenerates into a theory of relativism that is not resolvable by Turetzky's theory of abstract and absolute flows of time. A theory of social time is better able to conceptualize the relationship between the natural–social/abstract–concrete worlds not by conflating the opposites into each other; but, rather, by recognizing the way in which social space-time is derived. This can only be done by a critical political cosmology which involves the radicalization of Marxism through an engagement with the work of Einstein which is then in turn radicalized through a re-engagement with the social theory of Marx.

Einstein's universe is a four-dimensional space-time continuum. Within this continuum gravity is not a force acting between bodies through empty space, but is itself a totalizing energy field created by the densification of matter, which is itself the product of congealed quantities of speed and mass. The energy fields are in fact distortions of the space-time continuum, creating trajectories along which the densified matter moves and accelerates to maintain itself in a solid state. The denser the matter, the greater the distortion and the stronger its gravitational effect. The logic of the process, described by the equation $E = mc^2$, is such that it overwhelms the material world in the form of black holes (Hawking, 1993). The power of Einstein's universe is then not an *external* force as it had been for Newton; it is locked up in a material form within the objects that constitute the universe. What Einstein's logic also implied was that this power could be released in the form of nuclear energy and/or the nuclear bomb (Bodanis, 2000; Clarke, 1973; Strathern, 1997).

Marx's social universe is a five-dimensional space-time continuum. Although not normally conceived in this manner, the commodity form is a peculiar relationship between space–matter–energy–speed. The denser the space-time unit, or socially necessary labour time, the greater the distortion of social space. In order to maintain its integrity, congealed forms of matter (human energy) must accelerate and increase their productivity. The logic of Marx's social universe, described in the formula $M–C–M'$, is that the production of immateriality (abstraction) will overwhelm the material world, and this occurs either in the form of environmental destruction or explodes as the nuclear bomb. Postone clearly recognizes the overwhelming logic of the production of immateriality. He argues that:

> Material wealth is constituted by (concrete) labour and nature, but value is a function of (abstract) labour alone. As self-valorizing value, capital consumes material nature to produce material wealth and then moves on characterized by a movement towards boundless expansion. The dream implied by the capital form is one of utter boundlessness, a fantasy of freedom as the complete liberation from matter, from nature. This 'dream of capital' is becoming the nightmare of that from which it strives to free itself – the planet and its inhabitants. (Postone, 1993, p. 383)

However, Marx has an extra (fifth) dimension within his social universe that creates the space for a socio-political critique of Einstein's four dimensions. The social power of the social universe is not a mysterious force or an 'invisible hand'; it is the social power of the social universe locked up in the commodity form. Marx's theory implies that this social power can be unleashed to produce another form of human society. Marx's formulation contains within it the possible for an entirely new social dimension, or in cosmological terms there is the possibility for the discovery of a new form of human life in the universe.

PART II
Work Time

6
How Many Hours? Work-Time Regimes and Preferences in European Countries

Colette Fagan

Introduction

The length of the 'working week' is now shorter than in earlier historical periods, but there are signs that working time is creeping up again in some parts of the economy. Furthermore, a growing proportion of the employed are living in busy 'dual-earner' households, where the combined paid and unpaid workloads of women are heavier than those of men. A number of authors have argued that the time pressures experienced by the employed are increasing as a result, contributing to the more general quickening pace of life in contemporary societies, and captured by notions such as the 'time bind' (Hochschild, 1997), 'overworking' (Shor, 1991) or 'harriedness' (Linder, 1970).

This chapter opens by reviewing working-time trends and summarizing the explanations for why weekly working time may be lengthening. The second section discusses gender, job and international differences in the number of weekly working hours. In the third section results from a recent European survey are analysed, which reveals that large proportions of the workforce want to trade reduced earnings for shorter hours, and conclusions are drawn together in the final section.

Working-time trends and pressures in contemporary societies

The amount of time that is absorbed by work has fallen when assessed from a long historical perspective. Working time[1] increased as capitalism developed in the eighteenth and nineteenth centuries (see Bienefeld, 1972; Shor, 1991) because employers installed a new 'time-discipline' in wage-labour contracts (Thompson, 1967). Working time then fell from the late nineteenth century as weekly full-time hours of work were reduced and holiday entitlements extended, with some of the largest reductions achieved in Europe after the Second World War (Matthews *et al.*, 1982; Price and Bain, 1988). Subsequently, the expansion of part-time work has further contributed to the reduction in the average weekly hours of the workforce. However, the long-term trend of reductions in full-timers' working hours slowed and stalled in many European countries in the 1980s and 1990s (CEC, 1996), and in some parts of the economy full-timers' hours of work are now expanding, particularly in the managerial and professional grades (Golden and Figart, 2000).

Trends in women's workloads must also be taken into account. The labour market participation rate for women rose throughout the twentieth century after falling in the second half of the nineteenth century (Hakim, 1996; Scott and Tilly, 1980). Since the 1950s, the 'male bread-winner' arrangement has been eroded and the 'dual earner' has become the usual arrangement for couples. While this often means part-time work for women in many countries, 'dual full-time' arrangements are becoming more common (Rubery *et al.*, 1999). Thus a growing proportion of women are combining employment with the 'second shift' (Hochschild, 1990) of childcare and domestic work, whether in dual-earner or lone-parent households.

The content and organization of this 'second shift' has not changed sufficiently to offset women's increased working time in employment. From a historical perspective, many domestic chores have become less onerous due to innovations in domestic technology and market services. However, changing expectations about child-raising, domesticity and larger houses have placed new demands on the time, skills and money involved in running a home (Cowan, 1983; Shor, 1991). In addition, women have fewer domestic servants or children (depending on their class position) to help them with housework than at the turn of the twentieth century. Employed women purchase 'time-saving' market substitutes (e.g. ready-made meals, childcare and domestic services), particularly those with high incomes (Anderson, 2000; Brannen *et al.*, 1994; Gregson and Lowe, 1994; Hochschild, 1997). They also have more help from men, who are doing more housework and child-care in a process of 'lagged adaptation' in response to the spread of women's employment (Gershuny *et al.*, 1994). However, with the exception of childcare, the amount of 'time-saving' goods and services purchased by households is more to do with income levels and the consumption norms of the period than the actual time demands of women's employment (Horrell, 1994). Men's contribution to housework remains small, and women retain responsibility for organizing and delegating domestic tasks (Brannen *et al.*, 1994).

Overall, time-budget studies show that when more of women's time is taken up with employment less time is spent on housework. During the early decades of the twentieth century a sharp decline in the amount of time spent on housework coincided with a rising number of women in employment, and in contemporary society women spend less time on housework when they are employed (Seymour, 1988). However, this only partly offsets the increase in the time absorbed by employment so that women's total (paid and unpaid) work time increases, and in dual-earner households women's total work time exceeds that of their male partners. This pattern holds cross-nationally (Gershuny *et al.*, 1994; Kiernan, 1991; Shor, 1991; Spain and Bianchi, 1996). Women manage this time squeeze by sleeping less, and with the more intense and complex daily schedules of a harried lifestyle (Daly, 1996; Horrell, 1994).

So, the long-running trend of a steady fall in working hours appears to have halted. On top of this a growing proportion of the employed live in busy 'dual-earner' households where women also carry the 'second shift' of domestic work. At the household level the aggregate weekly workloads of the employed are increasing, in contrast to the experience of the growing number of underemployed 'no-earner' households. There are two related sets of reasons offered for why the work time of the employed is developing in this way: economic and political changes which have made it more difficult to introduce collective working-time reductions in companies, and changes in cultural norms that have influenced individuals' preferences for time use and consumption.

The main mechanism for reducing working time in companies are regulations set by collective agreements and legislation. Changing economic and political conditions have made it more difficult for unions and other campaigning movements to get these regulations introduced. Most of the previous collective reductions have been secured in periods of rapid economic growth when productivity rates, wages and living standards were rising (Bienefeld, 1972; Hinrichs *et al.*, 1991). In this economic context employers are more willing to concede reductions and employees' rising real incomes makes them more predisposed to accept lower wage rises in exchange for shorter working hours. However, regulated reductions – whether in government policy or collective agreements – have been more difficult to negotiate due to a combination of slower rates of economic growth, increasing competition in globalized markets, changes in work organization and reduced trade union bargaining power (Bosch *et al.* 1994). Instead, the pace of work has become more intense and pressures to work longer hours have increased (European Foundation, 1997) as faster and more responsive 'flexible' production systems, '24/7' operating hours, and lower staffing levels as firms 'downsize' have become common features of contemporary employment. The diversification of working schedules to obtain more flexible work practices, particularly the expansion of part-time work, may have reduced the pressures for collective reductions in full-time hours as well, for those who want shorter hours have the option of looking for part-time work.

The second set of reasons indicates that cultural norms have shifted, time-use preferences have changed and individuals do not want shorter full-time hours. One cause is that if real income is only rising slowly or not at all, then employees are less willing to trade lower wage rises for shorter hours (Bienefeld, 1972), particularly since the worse excesses of long hours have been removed in Europe by the recent history of negotiated reductions. Another is the 'work–spend–work' ratchet, whereby advertising, rising personal debt ratios and competitive consumption to keep up with the material living standards of peers create the context in which people prefer to maintain or raise their earnings rather than reduce their working hours (George, 2000; Shor, 1991). A different type of cause rests on the status, job satisfaction and other non-financial rewards gained from employment (Rose, 1994). The 'time bind' may result in some men and women working long hours in their jobs because they feel more competent and appreciated in this role than in their family roles (Hochschild, 1997), or because the job demands are such that the amount and quality of their leisure time deteriorates, and leisure becomes devalued (Shor, 1991). Conversely, people with a low commitment to their employment career may opt for part-time work (Hakim, 1996).

Given these working-time trends and debates, the rest of this chapter identifies who works the longest weekly hours and examines the extent to which the number of hours that people work align with their preferences.

Who works the longest hours?

Who works the longest hours? The first part of the answer is men. The working time regime in every EU member state bears the familiar imprint of a 'male-breadwinner' arrangement of gender relations, which assigns men the family role of primary earner and women the role of running a home and caring for family members. Hence women's employment rates fall when they are mothers, although women are taking fewer and shorter breaks from employment for child-raising than was the case for their predecessors (Rubery *et al.*, 1999). Employed mothers with young children work shorter hours than men and childless women. Care responsibilities for elderly or incapacitated adults also have an impact on women's labour supply (Bettio and Prechal, 1998). Fatherhood has little effect on men's employment rates or hours of work (Fagan *et al.*, 2001).

This gender differentiation in work time is the product of both the division of labour within the household and processes of gender segregation within the labour market (Rubery *et al.*, 1996). From the supply side, women typically seek out jobs with shorter hours when they have time-consuming domestic responsibilities. From the demand-side, employers generally presume that women prefer shorter hours and that men are more available to work long hours because of the 'male-breadwinner' arrangement, and this influences their working-time policies. For example, employers make more use of part-time contracts when they have a female-dominated workforce or when they are trying to increase their recruitment of women (Beechey and Perkins, 1987; Horrell and Rubery, 1991). Thus full-time hours tend to be shorter, and part-time work more common in the jobs that are largely filled by women.

Long hours of work are associated with a number of job characteristics. One consistent pattern is that in every EU country the self-employed work longer average hours than employees, particularly the self-employed men. The hours worked by the self-employed are not regulated by collective agreements or protective legislation. While some may choose to devote their lives to their work or are compulsive workaholics, others may have little choice but to work long hours for their business to be viable. Comparisons by sector show that agricultural employees typically work longer hours than other employees in every country. The hotels and distribution and the transport sectors also involve long hours of work for male employees in many countries. Hours are generally shortest in the public sector. Managers and manual supervisors work longer hours than other employees. Micro-firms with fewer than ten employees make the greatest use of both very short part-time and very long full-time hours (Fagan *et al.*, 2001; Rubery *et al.*, 1997).

However, country differences are also important. There is now a large body of research that has documented international differences in the employment patterns of women with young children and in the number of hours worked at the sector or occupational level (e.g. Anxo and O'Reilly, 2000; Bosch *et al.*, 1994; Boulin and Hoffman, 1999; Lehndorff, 2000; Rubery *et al.*, 1997, 1998, 1999). Thus operational requirements influence but do not determine the working-time schedules in different jobs. A clear example is the distribution and catering sector. In some countries work is organized mainly around long full-time hours, while others make more use of part-time workers, and the UK uses both arrangements (Rubery *et al.*, 1998).

A number of societal institutions influence the number of hours people work and the extent to which care responsibilities result in reduced working hours or exits from employment for women. These institutional arrangements vary between countries and impact on the types of arrangements sought by employers (labour demand) and the workforce (labour supply). A major influence on the number of hours worked are the working-time regulations set by national legislation and collective bargaining. These regulations set a ceiling on the number of hours that full-time employees work, and it is within these frameworks that employers develop their firms' working-time practices. There is a clear impact of regulations on the average number of hours worked by full-timers, and in the EU the shortest working week is established in regulations in Denmark, the Netherlands, France and Belgium (Rubery *et al.*, 1998).

A second influence on working hours is present in the earnings structure and fiscal system, which vary between countries. Wage levels and differentials between higher- and lower-paid groups, and the structure of earnings and hours thresholds for different tax rates in the systems of personal taxation and employers' social security contributions, create financial incentives and disincentives that have some influence on rates of part-time work and the number of hours worked in part-time and full-time jobs. The unemployment support system may also create incentives or hurdles to part-time work (Doudeijns, 1998).

A third set of institutions are those that shape the availability of women for waged work when they also have care responsibilities to attend to. International differences in women's employment patterns have been linked to different 'welfare state regimes'. Esping-Andersen's (1990) influential study argued that the 'Social Democratic' regime of the Nordic countries provided more inducements for women to participate in employment than either the 'Conservative' or 'Liberal' regimes. Feminists criticized this typology for its focus on the income security of wage earners and the neglect of other benefits and services that are important to women in their roles as carers (e.g. Lewis, 1993; Orloff, 1993). As one alternative Lewis (1993) draws a distinction between 'strong', 'modified' and 'weak' male-breadwinner states to highlight the extent to which state policies encourage women's employment.

The development of state policies in the Nordic countries since the 1960s have produced 'weak breadwinner' states, where the expectation is that all men and women of working age are members of the work-force. Here state policies, including extensive childcare services and family leave provisions, make it easier to combine employment with care responsibilities than in other countries. 'Modified breadwinner' states have some policies that help women to combine employment with motherhood – whether intentionally or not – such as the extensive childcare system in France and Belgium.

In 'strong breadwinner' states there is less state support to facilitate women's employment, and the policy regime either discourages women's employment, for example through tax subsidies to married men, or channels them into part-time jobs as a modification of the breadwinner arrangement. The 'part-time' model for mothers has developed most in the Northern 'male breadwinner' states (Austria, Germany, Ireland, the Netherlands, the UK), due to a combination of quite different constellations of state policies and market developments in each country. In contrast part-time work has not developed to the same degree in the Southern member states (Portugal, Italy, Spain and Greece), and a number of other shared features structure women's employment patterns in a particular way in these countries, including more extensive systems of family-based welfare than in Northern member states, larger informal economies and agricultural sectors, and more self-employment and family-run businesses.

These national differences in working-time regimes are exposed in the employment patterns of women with young children. The highest employment rates are found in the Nordic countries, Eastern Germany and Portugal. The extent of part-time employment also varies, and full-time employment for mothers is particularly rare in the UK, the Netherlands and Western Germany (Rubery *et al.*, 1999, fig. 3.5).

Turning to those who are employed, the number of hours worked also varies between countries (Table 6.1). The longest hours are worked by employed men in Greece and Austria, who work an average of five hours more per week than men in six countries where men's average

Table 6.1   The weekly working hours of employed men and women by country

(a) Employed men

	% whose current weekly working hours are ...					Average hours (mean)	Standard deviation
	<35	35–39	40–49	50+	Total %		
Greece	9	6	44	42	100	47.6	14.3
Austria	6	11	47	36	100	46.6	11.7
Ireland	11	17	39	33	100	45.1	12.9
Portugal	5	16	52	27	100	44.4	11.5
UK	12	19	37	32	100	44.3	13.5
Germany	9	18	44	29	100	43.7	12.4
Finland	4	20	55	21	100	43.1	10.4
Sweden	10	8	59	23	100	42.4	11.5
Spain	8	17	55	20	100	42.2	8.6
Italy	10	21	47	22	100	41.8	10.6
Norway	9	33	38	20	100	41.8	9.8
Belgium	9	33	41	17	100	41.6	10.4
France	8	41	36	15	100	41.5	9.6
Netherlands	18	17	39	26	100	41.1	14.2
Denmark	11	39	32	18	100	39.8	10.6
EU15+N	9	22	44	25	100	43.0	11.7

hours fall below 42 per week (Italy, Norway, Belgium, France, the Netherlands and Denmark). Long full-time hours of 50 or more per week are particularly common in Greece, Austria, Ireland and the UK, where at least 30 per cent of employed men have this schedule. Short full-time hours (35–39 hours) are particularly common in Norway, France, Belgium and Denmark, while the highest proportion of men working part-time hours (under 35) is in the Netherlands.

Employed women work an average of 34–35 hours in six countries, ranging up to just over 40 hours in Greece and down to 26 hours in the Netherlands. More than half of employed women work at least 40 hours a week in Greece, Portugal, Austria and Spain, compared to less than a quarter of employed women in France, Denmark and the Netherlands. Short full-time hours (35–39 hours) are most common in Finland, France and Denmark. Short part-time hours (less than 20) are particularly common in the Netherlands and the UK.

These national differences indicate the powerful influence of societal institutions on the working-time regimes in the EU member states. The

Table 6.1 The weekly working hours of employed men and women by country
cont.

(b) Employed women

	% whose current weekly working hours are ...						Average hours (mean)	Standard deviation
	<20	20–34	35–39	40–49	50+	Total %		
Greece	7	19	5	41	28	100	40.5	15.1
Portugal	6	14	24	46	10	100	37.7	10.9
Finland	5	10	41	39	5	100	37.5	8.5
Austria	8	22	17	43	10	100	36.5	12.4
Spain	6	20	21	46	6	100	36.1	11.3
Sweden	6	32	16	39	7	100	35.0	10.0
Ireland	10	24	31	27	8	100	34.9	11.7
France	8	25	41	21	5	100	34.9	10.0
Italy	8	24	27	35	6	100	34.7	10.3
Denmark	8	26	42	20	4	100	34.2	10.3
Belgium	11	28	34	20	7	100	34.0	11.7
Germany	17	25	22	29	7	100	32.6	13.2
Norway	16	25	32	20	7	100	32.5	12.6
UK	20	28	26	19	7	100	31.3	13.0
Netherlands	34	32	14	18	2	100	26.0	12.5
EU15+N	14	25	26	28	7	100	33.5	12.2

Note: The countries are ranked by average hours. Luxembourg is not shown due to sample size limits, but it is included in the overall figure for all countries (EU15+N).
Source: analysis of the European Foundation's 1998 Employment Options Survey.

next section explores the extent to which current working hours fit with working-time preferences.

How many hours would men and women prefer to work?

To what extent do people's current hours of work diverge from their preferences? Some answers to this question can be obtained from the 1998 *Employment Options Survey* (Intratest Burke Sozialforschung 1998), which is a representative European survey of 30,000 working-age people (16–64) from the 15 EU member states plus Norway, providing information on the number of hours that both the employed and 'job-seekers' would prefer (the latter group including all those who are not employed but would like a job now or within five years). This survey was commissioned by the European Foundation for the Improvement of Living and Working Conditions (a tri-partite research institute

funded by the European Commission) and the Norwegian Royal
Ministry of Labour. Computer-assisted telephone interviews were
carried out in each country using a standardized questionnaire in 1998.
The sample was drawn by random dialling methods to contact households, and *within* household by random selection of eligible persons.
The number of interviews conducted in each country varied according
to the population size, ranging from 822 interviews in Luxembourg up
to 3,000 interviews in the UK, Spain and France. The sample was
weighted using population and labour force statistics to produce a representative survey of individuals in each country and to adjust for the
country size. The fieldwork was coordinated by Intratest Burke
Sozialforschung (1998), which also prepared the technical reports and
first analyses of the findings.

People's preferences do not provide a 'hard' or accurate measure of
how they would behave in some future situation, for what they do is
affected by the constraints and opportunities that they face, and other
considerations and priorities. However, people's working-time preferences do influence their plans, decisions and behaviour. More generally this information gives an indication of how people feel about their
current hours of work, and provides some insight into the kind of
developments in working-time policy that the population would like.

Nearly two out of three employed women and men would prefer to
work a different amount of hours to their present arrangement.[2] Half
(51 per cent) would prefer to reduce their hours, whether traded for
lower current earnings or against future pay raises. Another 12 per cent
would like to work longer hours. Employed men are even more likely
to want to reduce their hours than employed women, 57 per cent compared to 44 per cent (Table 6.2). Conversely, women are more likely to
be underemployed, for 16 per cent of employed women would prefer
to work longer hours, as would 9 per cent of employed men.

Overall, employed men are slightly more likely to have a preference
to adjust their hours than employed women. In other words, they are
less able to achieve their preferred volume of working hours – which
for most is shorter hours – in a gender-segregated labour market where
'men's jobs' are constructed as full-time. However, another part of the
explanation is that women are more likely than men to exit the labour
market to manage care responsibilities if they require less time-
consuming jobs but are unable to secure this preferred arrangement.

Preferences for adjustments to hours are clearly related to current
hours of work. Very few full-timers want to work longer hours, and the
proportion who want to reduce their hours rises with the number of

Table 6.2 The preferred adjustment to the number of hours worked by the current weekly hours of employed men and women

(a) Employed men

% who want to …	Current weekly working hours are …					All
	Under 20	20–34	35–39	40–49	50 +	
Reduce their hours by 15 or more	1	1	6	8	55	19
Reduce their hours by 5–14	3	9	16	43	25	29
Reduce their hours by less than 5	1	5	19	10	..	9
Keep the same number of hours	34	48	49	36	18	35
Increase their hours by less than 5	8	2	5	1	..	2
Increase their hours by 5–14	12	21	5	3	1	4
Increase their hours by 15 or more	41	15	1	1	..	3
Total %	100	100	100	100	100	100

Table 6.2 The preferred adjustment to the number of hours worked by the current weekly hours of employed men and women   *cont.*

(b) Employed women

% who want to ...	Current weekly working hours are ...					
	Under 20	20–34	35–39	40–49	50 +	All
Reduce their hours by 15 or more	1	3	12	15	60	12
Reduce their hours by 5-14	5	10	30	45	23	25
Reduce their hours by less than 5	2	4	11	9	..	7
Keep the same number of hours	42	56	42	30	17	40
Increase their hours by less than 5	6	3	3	..	..	3
Increase their hours by 5–14	23	16	2	1	..	8
Increase their hours by 15 or more	21	8	..	..	..	5
Total %	100	100	100	100	100	100

Note: .. = less than 0.5%.

Source: as for Table 6.1.

hours that they currently work. This fits with the results from other research for the UK that has shown that those who work long hours are the least satisfied with the amount of time that they have for family and leisure pursuits (Fagan, 1996), and that preferences for hours reductions are highest in couples with the longest combined hours of work (Dex *et al.*, 1995, p. 25). Part-timers, particularly those in short-hour jobs (20 or fewer) are the most likely to want to work more hours. The underemployment of people with short part-time hours indicates that many of these jobs are designed to meet employers' requirements rather than labour-supply preferences.

The amount of adjustment that most people want to make is substantial, particularly when considered as a proportion of their current volume of work. Over half of those who work 40–49 hours want a reduction of at least five hours, while a reduction of at least 15 hours is preferred by over half of those working 50 or more hours. Forty-six per cent of the employed who work under 20 hours want to work at least five more hours. These preferences for adjustments indicate an overall general tendency to exit the extremes of very short or very long hours of work and move into the middle ground of long part-time/short full-time hours in the 20–39-hour range. The minority of men who work part-time are even more likely to want to work longer hours than women part-timers, while women full-timers are even more likely to want to reduce their hours than men full-timers.

However, there are some employed men and women who currently occupy this middle ground who also want to move, mainly switching between short full-time and part-time hours. Large proportions of employed men and women who work short full-time hours (35–39) would prefer to reduce their hours, mainly to move into the long part-time-hour range (a reduction of 5–15 hours). Of those working long part-time hours (20–34 hours) at present, around 15 per cent of men and 17 per cent of women would prefer to work shorter part-time hours, while 36 per cent of men and 24 per cent of women would prefer to work at least another five hours.

The net picture is that on average men would prefer a 37-hour week and women a 30-hour week (Table 6.3). This translates as an average reduction of six hours a week for employed men and three and a half hours for women. The standard deviation indicates that the spread of preferences around this average is wide for both sexes,[3] indicating diversity in the precise number of hours that they would prefer to work. However, it is clear from Table 6.3 that the general picture is that

Table 6.3 The distribution of actual and preferred number of weekly working hours

Weekly hours	Employed men		Job-seeking men prefer ...	Employed women		Job-seeking women prefer ...
	Actual	*Preferred*		*Actual*	*Preferred*	
			% distribution of actual and preferred weekly hours of work			
Under 20 hours	3	4	5	14	11	9
20–34	6	19	21	25	44	44
35–39	22	34	26	26	26	19
40–49	44	34	43	28	17	27
50 +	25	9	5	7	2	1
Total %	100	100	100	100	100	100
Average	43	36.7	35.3	33.5	30.2	30.4
Standard deviation	11.7	9.9	9.9	12.2	10.0	9.6
Base number	10682	10484	2365	7702	7604	3668

Note: the analysis is based on the people who provided information about their actual and or preferred hours. Job-seeking men and women are those who want a job immediately or within the next five years.

Source: as for Table 6.1.

more employed women and men would prefer to work shorter full-time (35–39) hours or long part-time (20–34) hours than currently do so. If this adjustment took place, then one result would be a smaller gender difference in the volume of waged working time than exists currently. On average, job-seekers have similar working-time preferences to the employed, although a larger proportion of them would prefer full-time hours in the 40–49-hour range.

The longest average hours are worked by the self-employed, followed by white-collar employees with managerial responsibilities (Table 6.4). Compared to the occupational differences in current hours, there is less variation in preferences. As might be anticipated from the previous analysis in Table 6.3, a higher proportion of the self-employed and managers wanted to reduce their hours compared to those in other employment positions, associated with their longer average hours of work. In contrast, manual employees were the most likely to want to increase their hours of work. This is driven by financial considerations, for manual jobs tend to be the lowest paid. Other analyses have shown that it is people who are low paid or in financial difficulties who want to work longer hours and are the least willing to exchange lower earnings for shorter working hours (Fagan, 2001; Fagan *et al.*, forthcoming).

It is common knowledge that women are less likely to be in employment if they have young children, and when employed they work in jobs with shorter hours, often increasing their hours as their children grow older. In contrast, men's hours vary little with fatherhood. Both patterns are shown in Table 6.4, alongside the more novel data on preferences. This shows that fatherhood has little influence on men's working-time preferences. In contrast, employed women prefer shorter hours if they have young children, shadowing the current pattern of actual working hours. The comparison of employed and non-employed women according to the age of their youngest child shows that the working-time preferences of non-employed women are similar to the preferences of employed women.

The marked national differences in the length of the working week were discussed in the previous section, and Table 6.5 examines the average preferred hours for employed and job-seeking women and men in the member states. In every country men and women would prefer shorter hours than the current practices. For men the picture is very similar across countries, for in 11 countries the preferred average is 35–37 hours, with the overall range running between an average 34 hours for men in Denmark to just over 38 hours in Austria and Portugal.

Table 6.4 Average actual and preferred weekly volume of working hours for men and women by job status and parental status

| | Employed men: average weekly hours | | Employed women: average weekly hours | | Job-seeking women |
	Actual	Prefer	Actual	Prefer	Prefer
Self-employed	51.6	38.7	39.4	32.5	n.a.
Managers	44.6	36.8	37.2	31.7	n.a.
Other non-manual	38.7	34.9	32.1	29.7	n.a.
Manual supervisors	42.0	37.5	32.3	30.0	n.a.
Other manual	37.8	35.8	29.5	28.7	n.a.
Childless	42.5	37.4	35.9	32.6	32.4
Child < 6	44.6	37.5	29.9	26.8	27.9
Child 6–14	44.1	37.0	32.4	29.2	28.2
Child aged 15 plus	44.3	37.5	34.0	30.8	29.5

Note: n.a. = not applicable.

Source: as for Table 6.1.

Table 6.5   Average preferred weekly volume of working hours by gender and country

	Preferred average number of weekly hours of work – people who are employed or job seeking			
	Men		Women	
	Average	Standard deviation	Average	Standard deviation
Austria	38.4	11.9	30.9	11.1
Portugal	38.2	9.5	33.9	8.4
Ireland	37.4	10.0	29.6	10.1
Spain	37.0	6.9	34.1	8.5
Italy	36.9	9.3	30.1	9.8
Greece	36.7	13.2	34.9	10.8
Germany	36.6	10.0	29.1	10.5
UK	36.6	11.8	27.7	10.5
Sweden	36.2	9.2	32.5	7.9
Belgium	35.8	11.8	30.6	10.6
Finland	35.6	9.9	32.1	9.5
France	35.6	8.4	31.5	8.5
Netherlands	35.5	10.3	24.9	10.2
Norway	35.0	8.7	29.1	10.5
Denmark	34.3	9.2	29.5	8.7
EU15+N[1]	36.5	9.9	30.1	10.1

Note: EU15+N includes all 15 member states plus Norway. Luxembourg is not shown separately due to sample size limitations. Job seeking men and women are those who want a job immediately or within the next five years.

Source: as for Table 6.1.

For women the preferred average varies more markedly between countries than is the case for men. By far the shortest hours are preferred by women in the Netherlands (24.9), where women's hours are already the shortest. Under 30 hours is also the preferred average for women in Ireland, the UK, Germany, Norway and Denmark. The average preferences of women in the other member states are for longer hours, with national averages in the range of 30–35 hours. This suggests that women's preferences are more influenced by the societal context than is the case for men, and that much of this variation is attributed to whether the social norms and childcare facilities endorse full-time or part-time employment for mothers. However, the national differences in women's working-time preferences are not as large as might be expected. For example, on average Danish women would prefer a working week that is only two hours longer than that of women in the UK, despite quite different systems of childcare, other welfare state provisions and employment regulations.

Conclusion

There is a growing time pressure in contemporary societies, particularly for employed parents with young children. More mothers are in employment than in previous generations, and this extra work has not been offset by an equivalent redistribution of the time demands of domestic work and childcare. Time pressures are also growing for many full-timers to work longer hours in response to workplace pressures for more flexible and intense working practices, in the context of high unemployment and growing job insecurity.

Differences in current working hours are more pronounced by gender and by country than by occupation or sector. Working-time preferences vary by gender, but most clearly according to current hours. The overall picture is that many full-timers would prefer substantially shorter hours, reducing their wages accordingly, and many part-timers want to increase their hours. The preferred arrangements generally fall in the range of substantial part-time (20–34 hours) or short full-time hours (35–39 hours).

Those who are unprotected by working-time regulations are particularly vulnerable to a lengthening of their working hours. Long hours are particularly acute in managerial and the higher-level professional jobs. Working time in these jobs is generally considered to be self-determined, and there is less collective and statutory regulation of working time than at other occupational levels, including exemptions from the EU Working Time Directive. However, the low paid are also vulnerable to having to work long hours through overtime or multiple job-holding, and financial pressures to maintain a basic standard of living make them the least willing to consider a wage-adjusted reduction in working hours.

This analysis has shown how existing working-hours schedules are clearly out of step with many people's preferences. Many people want shorter hours and say that they would trade this for lower income, which indicates that at least some elements of the 'cultural shift' explanation are dubious. Conversely, there are some indications in this survey that people's inability to reduce their hours were as much to do with workplace pressures and employers' resistance as with wage considerations (Fagan *et al.*, 2001). However, further research is needed to understand the priorities which women and men attach to working-time reductions and the trade-offs against wages or work reorganization that they would make in exchange. It is difficult for people to convert their preferences into actual working-time reductions through individual negotiations with current or alternative employers. Public debate and collective action are needed to broaden the politics of time. Such actions are occurring in some societies where there is an established tradition of regulating working time. For example, the state has intervened to regulate a reduction in full-time hours in France, and in the Netherlands full-time hours are falling alongside an expansion in part-time work as a result of state policies and collective bargaining (Boulin and Hoffman, 1999). But in some countries such as the UK the debate has barely started, and it is there that the 'time squeeze' is most in danger of growing.

Notes

1. For the sake of brevity and convention, the term 'working time' will be used to refer to time absorbed by employment, although this does not include the time spent on domestic work and other types of work.
2. The analysis was derived from questions 55 and 56: 'In total, how many hours per week do you work at present – on average?'. 'Provided that you (and your partner) could make a free choice so far as working hours are concerned *and* taking into account the need to earn a living how many hours per week would YOU prefer to work at present?'
3. The standard deviation indicates that approximately two-thirds of both populations fall within the range of plus or minus ten hours, that is 27–47 hours for employed men and 20–40 hours for employed women.

7
Gendered and Classed Working Time in Britain: Dual-Employee Couples in Higher/Lower-Level Occupations

Tracey Warren

Introduction

Working time in Britain remains weakly regulated. As a result, there is wide variation in the number of hours and times of day worked and in the types of employment contracts available. Importantly, there are both gender and class dimensions to this variation. In terms of gender, at an individual level there is a gendered polarization in typical working weeks, with women over concentrated in short-hours jobs, and men over concentrated in longer full-time work. At a household level, these hour differences have been mutually reinforcing. If a couple have children, men's longer hours have meant that many mothers, if they are in jobs, have tended to work short hours to provide child care and, likewise, women's reduced hours have meant that fathers worked longer hours to supplement this wage loss. The notion of a male-breadwinner model has been developed to express such a prevalent societal gendered division of labour in which women caring for children or other dependants are located at one end of a breadwinner–carer working scale, whilst men are more likely to spend their working lives nearer to the opposite, breadwinner, pole (Warren, 2000).

Despite its prevalence, substantial variety has been detected in the strength of this male-breadwinner model over time and place (Crompton and Harris, 1999). As a result, typologies have been formulated to depict similarities and differences in gender contracts. Lewis (1992), for example, proposed that there are three major variations of male-breadwinner system operating in Europe: strong, weak and modified. Pfau-Effinger (1998), on the other hand, has argued that rather than talking about variation in one male-breadwinner model, we need to accept that there are many sub-variants of gender relations models. For example, she labelled the 'gender arrangement' of Britain as male-breadwinner/female part-time carer, and of some Nordic societies as dual-breadwinner/dual-carer.

Clearly then, mapping variation *between* societies has been key in the development of different gendered models. Increasingly, there are also moves to identify heterogeneity *within* societies in the prevalent gender contract. This heterogeneity includes regional-based differences in gender arrangements (Duncan, 1995), and also any class-based variation in the degrees to which men are the main breadwinners of the household associated with class-based variation in working time (Warren, 2000). In terms of class, at an individual level, the longest employment hours in Britain are worked by men in the very highest- and very lowest-status occupations, and women in low status occupations are most likely to work short part-time hours, often at unsocial times of the day. The outcome of these household-level differences, that class variations occur in the strength of the male-breadwinner/female-carer model, has led to suggestions that a dual-breadwinner model is more widespread for professional/managerial couples. Indeed, there has been a growing interest in whether such couples are time-poor, characterised by longer working hours and an intensification of time pressures (Sullivan, 2000). Yet given the typical employment arrangements experienced by working-class couples, this chapter asks whether they too are likely to be experiencing family-unfriendly working schedules.

Stimulated by the moves to examine heterogeneity within breadwinner/carer models, this chapter explores the gendered and classed working patterns of women and men in couples in Britain. It questions to what extent they fit the societal-level male-breadwinning/female-caring typology and asks, given class-based heterogeneity, how useful are societal-level breadwinner/carer models for depicting variation in the ways in which couples juggle their home and working lives? The chapter concludes that the male-breadwinner/female-carer gender arrangement demonstrates well that, in general, men remain the main earners of the household and women remain the main carers, but it fails to identify the disparate conditions under which the everyday experiences of balancing caring and breadwinning are being carried out.

Data

The chapter is based on an analysis of the respondents who gave a full interview in the fifth wave of the *British Household Panel Survey* which was conducted in 1995. A sub-sample of over 3,000 female employees of standard working age (between 18 and 59, excluding full-time students) was constructed. Sixty-two per cent were in employment and had data available on their working conditions, including their wages and hours of work, and on their household characteristics such as family circumstances and employment details of any partners. A couple data set was then constructed containing the women who were married or cohabiting, and their working age (18–64) male partners. To explore in more detail how women and men distribute their paid and unpaid caring labour, the chapter focuses on couples where both partners are in employment. This selection process necessarily reduced the sample size, and a final sample of around one thousand couples resulted.

Part of the research was to indicate the relative amount of time the couples spent in what could be termed breadwinner work, and also the time when employees were unavailable for private unpaid caring work within the home. The 'public work' measure, therefore, includes total usual hours (normal and over-time hours, paid and unpaid overtime) employees spent in employment – in a first or additional job – and also the hours spent travelling to work. Given the rather general working-time questions in the *BHPS*, some qualifications about the data should be provided. For example, an issue which can arise in allocating time to public, private or indeed other categories is how to deal with workplace breaks such as lunch hours. They are not incorporated into the measure of public work here. It is difficult to categorize this time as we do not know what the respondents were actually doing in their breaks, if indeed they had any. For some a lunch break should no doubt be classed as public (unpaid) working time as they work through and/or don't leave the work place (Roberts, 1998). For others, a lunch hour can be a time for leisure – be it shopping for pleasure or playing sports. For many, and particularly the most time-pressured, lunch may be an opportunity for a quick burst of intensive caring work – whether a rush home to clean the house and/or care for children or time for a dashed grocery shop.

Even with these problems, for most workers, indicating the time they dedicate to public work is no doubt much easier than estimating their caring hours (but see Steward, 2000 on tele-homeworkers' problems differentiating home time from paid working time). Many workers have an hours-specific contract, and even those without can usually estimate the hours they dedicated to work in the previous week, and whether these were typical. Hours spent on unpaid caring work are more of a private matter not subject to outside assessment, and are less commonly estimated in everyday life. To measure private work – time spent on unpaid caring work – respondents in the *BHPS* are asked to estimate the hours they spend a week on housework, and are guided to consider 'time spent cooking, cleaning and doing the laundry' (Taylor, 1999). Estimated number of hours a week spent caring for a dependent child are not asked specifically (and, of course, it is debatable how useful a simple hours measure is, if we want to indicate *quality* of care work). Neither are respondents asked about hours spent in 'caring' work outside the home such as grocery shopping (although they are asked for details of any caring work they provide for a sick or elderly relative). Given these problems, to indicate further who provides the main unwaged work in the couple, information is used from a number of questions asking respondents to estimate who is mostly responsible for certain household tasks (themselves, their partner, or whether the responsibility is shared or someone else has it). Of course, 'most' or 'mostly shared' do not indicate the time taken, but this additional task-based approach to the domestic division of labour can be used to begin to indicate who dominates caring work and to reveal the carer side of the breadwinner/carer typologies.

Gendered and classed working time

Distinct gendered and classed dimensions to working time remain apparent in Britain. A clear gender pattern which persists is that women are much more likely to work part-time and for short full-time hours than men, whilst men are much more likely to work very long full-time hours (especially when overtime is included in the calculations). Alongside these gender patterns, there are marked differences in typical hours for women and men in different level occupations. In the data, working part-time – particularly for very few hours – was much more prevalent for women in lower-level jobs. At the same time, the longest usual hours were worked by female full-timers in professional occupations, and also in craft and plant operative posts once paid overtime was added in. Hours were similarly longest for male full-timers at the top and bottom of the occupational hierarchy. If the aim is to trace working-time extremes, then, we need to take into account dimensions of both gender and occupational class. To go on to examine the central theme in the breadwinner/carer models – how this work is distributed between women and their male partners – it is essential to see how these gendered and classed differences play out at a couple level. First then, to what extent can we classify the couples as dual, male or female breadwinner?

Dual breadwinners?

If any couple type can be seen to be approaching the gender equality implied within the notion of dual breadwinning, then we would surely expect it to be dual employees. Although they are a minority of households it is important to stress that dual employees are not a marginal group. The majority (70 per cent) of women aged 18 to 59 in the individual sample were married or living as a couple and the largest couple type (around 50 per cent) were dual employees. Of course, dual wage earning does not mean dual breadwinning, and so to map the extent of male (and female) breadwinning within the sample, a range of breadwinner-type couples was created based on their relative earnings. Reflecting both Lewis's notions of strong/moderate/weak male breadwinners and Pfau-Effinger's dual-breadwinner gender arrangements, five breadwinner categories were produced (see Figure 7.1). Using this measure, three-quarters of couples could be classed as male breadwinner, just under 20 per cent were dual breadwinners and half as few

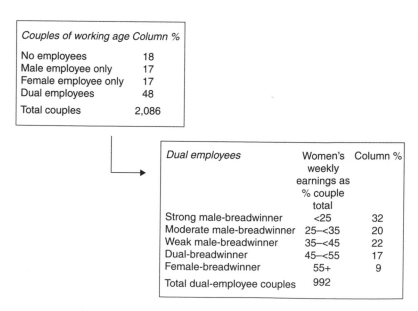

Couples of working age	Column %
No employees	18
Male employee only	17
Female employee only	17
Dual employees	48
Total couples	2,086

Dual employees	Women's weekly earnings as % couple total	Column %
Strong male-breadwinner	<25	32
Moderate male-breadwinner	25–<35	20
Weak male-breadwinner	35–<45	22
Dual-breadwinner	45–<55	17
Female-breadwinner	55+	9
Total dual-employee couples	992	

Figure 7.1   Constructing couples' breadwinner typologies
Source: *British Household Panel Survey* (*BHPS*), Wave E, 1995.

again were female breadwinners, an almost identical distribution to that produced by Arber (1999) in her analysis of General Household Survey data from 1992 to 1995.

Even within the select group of couples that dual earners represent, diverse models of breadwinner working were in operation. This chapter will show that, in addition, there were distinct class differences in typical breadwinner arrangements. The higher status the woman's occupation, the more likely she was to be in either a dual- or female-breadwinner couple (Table 7.1), and so class was evidently shaping to which breadwinner category the couples would be allocated. It was also impacting on couples' experiences *within* each typology. (Knowing the man's occupation did not throw light on the couple's breadwinner type to any great extent. In couples in which the man was either a professional/managerial or manual worker, around one-third were strong male breadwinners, for example.)

Male breadwinners

Beginning with the largest breadwinner category, it is clear that the male-breadwinner model dominated even for these dual-employee couples. Having said that, however, a number of distinct differences emerged. First, there was variation in the degree of male breadwinning amongst the couples, ranging from strong male breadwinners, in which women were earning less than a quarter of couple wages, to moderate male breadwinners, where women were earning up to 44 per cent. Second, there was marked variety between couples in their actual working hours. Behind the strongest male-breadwinner typology, for example, lay a picture of couples in which women were concentrated in part-time jobs (averaging 20 hours a week – see Table 7.2)

Table 7.1 Couples' breadwinner typologies by women's occupation, dual-employee couples of working age

	Strong Male BW	Moderate Male BW	Weak Male BW	Dual BW	Female BW	N of couples
Women's occupation						
Prof/assoc. prof/ managerial	14	16	22	30	17	316
Clerical	30	20	29	16	6	318
Manual	51	22	16	6	5	358
All	32	20	22	17	9	992

Source: British Household Panel Survey (BHPS), Wave E, 1995.

Table 7.2 Breadwinner typologies and the division of labour, dual-employee couples of working age

	Median gross wages Weekly		Hourly (£s)		Weekly Public hours		Weekly Private hours		Paid work schedules	N of couples	% with children
	Women's % share	Couple (£s)	Women	Men	Couple median	Women's % share	Couple median	Women's % share	% conflicting/ complimentary		
Strong male BW	14	487	4	9.3	74	30	24	85	39	324	69
Female P/Male P	17	675	6.5	13.8	75	28	25	84	31	(10)	72
Female P/Male M	17	467	5.4	9.4	64	31	32	83	31	(4)	77
Female CM/Male P	15	564	4.3	11.5	77	29	24	86	23	(35)	61
Female CM/Male M	15	409	3.6	7.2	72	29	24	85	52	(51)	73
Moderate male BW	30	503	5.1	7.7	85	41	22	78	36	196	53
Female P/Male P	29	811	8	13.1	92	39	14	73	18	(20)	62
Female P/Male M	29	514	5.8	8.2	81	43	22	77	42	(6)	75
Female CM/Male P	31	537	5	9.7	87	38	22	80	23	(25)	39
Female CM/Male M	29	404	4.3	6	81	42	24	80	49	(49)	54
Weak male BW	40	552	5.9	7.7	90	46	16	72	30	219	26
Female P/Male P	42	796	8.8	11.5	95	42	14	67	30	(23)	34
Female P/Male M	40	572	7.9	8.8	89	48	18	78	37	(9)	42
Female CM/Male P	39	560	5.8	8.1	89	46	15	75	12	(24)	19
Female CM/Male M	39	472	5.3	6.3	87	47	17	71	38	(45)	23
Dual BW	48	584	7.7	7.1	94	49	17	67	27	170	36
Female P/Male P	51	763	10.3	10.2	98	47	15	61	18	(39)	31
Female P/Male M	48	541	6.9	6.5	91	47	18	72	48	(18)	52
Female CM/Male P	48	550	7.1	5.8	96	49	16	62	19	(9)	44
Female CM/Male M	50	458	5.9	5.3	89	49	18	67	28	(34)	32

Table 7.2 Breadwinner typologies and the division of labour, dual-employee couples of working age *cont*

	Median gross wages				Weekly Public hours		Weekly Private hours		Paid work schedules	N of couples	% with children
	Weekly Women's % share	Couple Weekly (£s)	Women Hourly (£s)	Men	Couple median	Women's % share	Couple median	Women's % share	% conflicting/ complimentary		
Female BW	62	563	8.8	5.2	94	51	15	67	27	91	27
Female P/Male P	63	739	10.4	6.2	97	51	14	64	30	(30)	26
Female P/Male M	63	580	9.7	5.6	94	53	17	50	29	(32)	39
Female CM/Male M	61	457	7	4.2	91	49	15	67	24	(36)	18

Note: P = professional/associate professional/managerial; C = clerical; M = manual.

Source: British Household Panel Survey (BHPS), Wave E, 1995.

whilst their male partners were working long hours. Central to this model, then, is the notion that women's public working hours are reduced, no doubt to cope with the greater caring work associated with having dependent children. Indeed, almost half the couples with dependent children could be described as strong male-breadwinner (compared with only one-fifth of couples without children).

Women's reduced contact with the labour market in strong male-breadwinner couples plainly impacts on couples' income levels. In a sense, the degree of reduction which occurs may be related to the ease with which the man can shoulder the extra breadwinning burden. The men in strong male-breadwinner couples, for example, were working slightly longer hours than other men, had higher hourly wages and were more likely to be in the highest occupational grouping. In effect, these couples may have been able to afford for one member to work reduced hours. This could suggest that strong male breadwinners were actually in the best financial positions of the working couples and that, perhaps, the women were able to exert more choice in reducing their paid working (see Hakim, 1991). What is clear, however, is that the men's higher hourly wages were not making up fully for women's reduced earnings because strong male breadwinners were the lowest waged of the five broad couple types. As these couples were more likely to have dependent children too, their financial positions were likely to be even more strained. Furthermore, a strong class element lies behind this picture of potentially chosen breadwinning/caring arrangements. Men in strong male-breadwinner couples who were working in professional occupations had such high wages that they took the couples comfortably up the wage hierarchy and well above average couples' earnings. The reduction in women's earnings, which is part of the adoption of the strong male-breadwinner contract, clearly has different ramifications depending on the waged income of the male breadwinner.

Despite its prevalence and usefulness for depicting the gendered division of breadwinning work, the strong male-breadwinner categorization did not pick up on some key divisions amongst the couples. By definition, in all cases, the women had similarly proportionally lower earnings than their partners with correspondingly shorter paid working weeks, but the strong male-breadwinner couples varied substantially in their actual levels of earnings. Some were faring quite badly and for around half, those who could be termed working-class couples because both the woman and man were in the lowest-level occupations, total couple wages were very low indeed. It is important to stress that their wages were low despite the fact that, in an average week, they were working 11 hours more than their dual-professional strong male-bread-winner counterparts, but for around £250 less.

Working-class strong male-breadwinner couples were not only working long hours for low pay, they were also characterized by very particular employment schedules. In just over half, the female and male partner were working in the labour market at different times of the day or night. Their work schedules meant that, in effect, the couples would have had little shared time to be used for joint caring work and/or for pooled leisure. In a sense, their work schedules can be termed conflicting because they are incompatible with such joint time, but partners who work different times of the day like this are typically doing so to fit around each other and to facilitate a household juggling of caring and breadwinning work (Fagan, 1996; van den Broek, Breedveld and Knulst, Chapter 13 in this volume). In this sense, such scheduling can be termed, alternatively, as complementary. Whatever the label, such schedules signify a strong and negative impact on any shared time the couples may have.

These simultaneously conflicting/complementary work rotas, with their associated reduction in shared time, were most prevalent for working-class couples in the strong male-breadwinner category. They were common too for couples across the male-breadwinner category and up to the dual-breadwinner typologies particularly if the man was a manual worker (Table 7.2). This is no doubt because around two-fifths of the men in manual jobs were working shifts and/or were employed mainly in the evening or at night (compared with only 15 per cent of non-manual workers). Attention has been devoted, deservedly so, to the negative impact on family life and on joint caring or leisure time which can result when dual high-status couples work very long hours. Yet clearly, it is important to recognize too that because of their conflicting work schedules, working-class couples may also have little opportunity for joint time. Moreover, they have fewer economic resources to ease their juggling of caring and breadwinning work.

Dual breadwinners

Moving on to the most gender-equal breadwinner model, in 16 per cent of the couples women and men were bringing home very similar wages and working very similar hours in the labour market. It is important to point out here, because dual breadwinning was calculated by examining proportional earnings, that dual breadwinners emerged because women were adopting typical male-breadwinner working patterns and not because men were reducing their paid working to short full-time or part-time hours. As a result, dual breadwinners were working some of the longest weeks and had the highest overall wages of all the couples. Yet class-related differences were substantial for these couples too. Around 40 per cent were dual professional workers, whilst approximately a third were dual low status, and a corresponding wide divergence in the couples' wage levels was apparent. The polarization of earnings of the professional and low-status dual-breadwinner couples adds support to the above argument that, whilst we do need to examine women's working and earnings relative to their male partner to begin to examine gender divisions within the home, it is vital to combine the within-couple approach with an awareness of variations between couples in their economic positions.

Female breadwinners

Given the combination of men's longer hours in Britain and the male hourly wage advantage, it is little surprise that female breadwinners accounted for only a small proportion of working couples (9 per cent). What marked these couples out from the majority were women's longer working weeks, their higher hourly wages and the particularly low hourly wages of the men. Reflecting McRae's (1986) findings on cross-class couples, the men in female-breadwinner couples here were overconcentrated in low-paid clerical, and craft and related, occupations. The women were more likely to have reached the highest ranks of manager and professional worker and this is no doubt in part because they were less likely than other women to have dependent children (Table 7.2).

Dual carers?

The above analysis of breadwinner working time showed that the gendered division of wages and working time can be represented by variation in breadwinner models, but it is important also to recognize class dimensions to the gender division of labour. The next issue is to examine the carer side of the gender contracts in order to question whether female-, dual- or male-carer gender contracts prevailed. Indeed, a key question in the analysis of breadwinner models is whether dual breadwinning is part of a gender-equal dual-breadwinner/dual-carer gender arrangement. Previous research has tended to suggest that in Britain, although dual-breadwinner households have been emerging, the carer side of the gender arrangement remains more firmly female-dominated. Women retain responsibility for the bulk of unpaid domestic work even if they are in dual-earner couples, even if they work full-time and even if they are in professional-couple households (Speakman and Marchington, 1999). Further, it is not just that women do most of the housework, but they are also seen to *own* many household tasks, especially cleaning and washing and ironing clothes. There is evidence of increased equity amongst younger couples, especially when women's wages approach men's (Crompton and Harris, 1999; Gershuny, *et al*., 1994; Gershuny, Chapter 3 in this volume), but still a marked discrepancy in the domestic division of labour persists. This section examines how true this is of the different breadwinner couples in the sample.

An equitable allocation of couples' workloads would mean that the stronger the male-breadwinner contract, the stronger the female-carer side of the 'bargain', and vice versa. It would appear from the data that women's shares of caring work were indeed lower for couples with weaker male-breadwinner arrangements (Table 7.2). However, women's share of caring work in dual- and female-breadwinner couples had fallen only to an average of 67 per cent: they were still providing two-thirds of the work. Indeed, for no group of women did their share of caring work fall below 50 per cent and it actually fell to this low figure only for the small and very particular group of female-breadwinner couples in which women were in professional jobs and their partners were manual workers. It was not, then, that as women increased their breadwinning to equal that of their male partners, their male partners increased their caring to equal that of the women.

Another management strategy which was apparently being employed was an overall reduction in the hours spent on housework by weaker female-breadwinner, dual- and female-breadwinner families, even though substantial minorities had dependent children. (The presence of dependent children was associated with somewhat longer private work hours, and also reductions in women's relative shares in dual- and female-breadwinner couples.) We will see below that the couples' fewer housework hours were seldom boosted by another person. Behind this reduction lies a complex picture of less time spent on food preparation, supplemented with greater expenditure on eating out or on pre-prepared food, and perhaps reduced housework standards or the intensification of housework into a shorter time-frame.

A similar persistence in gendered patterns of caring work emerged when examining which partner was mostly responsible for domestic work (we focus here on women's answers to the household tasks questions: overall, the majority of men and women agreed that women took major responsibility for these tasks, but men were consistently more likely than their partners – about 10 per cent more – to have said that tasks were mostly joint responsibilities). Five household tasks of cleaning, cooking, washing/ironing, grocery shopping and caring for a child were focused upon. Women retained major responsibility for most of the jobs, although there were differences in their degrees of dominance related to their degree of breadwinning and the specific task (Table 7.3). The work where responsibility was most likely to be shared was childcare and, in addition, grocery shopping. If we were to try to identify those jobs into which men had made greatest inroads and taken over from women as the major responsible partner, for most couple types it would be such food-related work as grocery shopping and cooking. Yet even here, it was still only a very small minority of couples where the man was the main person responsible for shopping/cooking. Childcare, cleaning, and washing and ironing clothes remained the areas where most men had least sole responsibility, although men in female-breadwinner homes had taken on more. Overall, then, if the woman was not mainly in charge of the tasks, the responsibility tended to be shared; it was rare for the man or someone else (either paid or unpaid) to take it away from her.

The gender dimension to the domestic division of caring labour remains unmistakable. There were some class dimensions to the couples' distributions of care work too, but it is difficult to identify any clear patterns across all the household tasks and all couple types. Cleaning was the only job in which another person figured, aside from members of the couple, and having a paid cleaner is closely determined by levels of economic resources. Attention has been paid to the increasingly marketized nature of certain caring tasks within the home and, in particular, the provision of childcare by nannies and the employment of cleaners by income-rich/time-poor families (Gregson and Lowe, 1994; Hardill *et al.*, 1999). Yet whilst employing a cleaner was certainly more common if both partners were professional workers, especially when women were doing more breadwinning work, this was still true for only a small minority of these couples.

To summarize this section, if we want to typologize the carer side of the gender arrangements of the working couples, we need to recognize the persistence of women's domination of caring work. Compared with the strong, weak and moderate male-breadwinner categories which were constructed earlier, the main carer categories here were strong and moderate female-carers. There was little evidence of dual-carer, male-carer or even weak female-carer gender arrangements. And

Table 7.3   Who takes major responsibility for household tasks, dual-employee couples of working age

	Grocery shopping				Washing/ironing				Cooking			
	Mostly woman	Mostly man	Shared	Other/ paid	Mostly woman	Mostly man	Shared	Other/ paid	Mostly woman	Mostly man	Shared	Other/ paid
Strong male												
BW	67	8	25	0	90	1	7	1	80	5	15	0
Female P/ Male P	75	6	13	3	88	0	6	3	78	0	16	3
Female P/ Male M	77	15	8	0	77	8	15	0	77	8	15	0
Female CM/ Male P	61	11	28	0	91	2	5	1	81	7	11	0
Female CM/ Male M	68	5	26	0	91	1	8	1	79	4	17	0
Moderate male BW	50	11	37	1	75	2	20	2	65	10	23	1
Female P/ Male P	54	13	33	0	64	5	31	0	62	18	21	0
Female P/ Male M	67	17	17	0	92	0	8	0	67	8	25	0
Female CM/ Male P	51	8	41	0	84	0	15	0	76	8	16	1
Female CM/ Male M	46	12	39	1	73	2	18	4	62	9	27	0

Table 7.3 Who takes major responsibility for household tasks, dual-employee couples of working age   cont.

	Cleaning				Child-care			
	Mostly woman	Mostly man	Shared	Other/paid	Mostly woman	Mostly man	Shared	Other/paid
Strong male								
BW	82	1	13	3	73	2	25	0
Female P/ Male P	78	0	6	13	100	0	0	0
Female P/ Male M	77	0	23	0	78	0	22	0
Female CM/ Male P	84	1	11	4	82	0	18	0
Female CM/ Male M	82	1	16	1	63	4	33	0
Moderate male								
BW	64	5	26	4	57	1	40	1
Female P/ Male P	56	8	23	13	76	0	24	0
Female P/ Male M	83	0	17	0	67	0	33	0
Female CM/ Male P	69	4	27	0	53	0	47	0
Female CM/ Male M	63	4	28	3	46	3	49	3

Table 7.3 Who takes major responsibility for household tasks, dual-employee couples of working age   *cont.*

	Grocery shopping				Washing/ironing				Cooking			
	Mostly woman	Mostly man	Shared	Other/ paid	Mostly woman	Mostly man	Shared	Other/ paid	Mostly woman	Mostly man	Shared	Other/ paid
Weak male												
BW	45	11	43	1	74	4	20	2	65	8	27	0
Female P/ Male P	50	12	36	2	58	2	36	4	70	10	20	0
Female P/ Male M	53	16	32	0	89	0	11	0	53	16	32	0
Female CM/ Male P	38	8	54	0	67	8	25	0	62	10	29	0
Female CM/ Male M	44	11	43	1	84	3	11	2	67	5	28	0
Dual BW	46	9	44	0	65	5	28	2	54	15	30	1
Female P/ Male P	48	9	42	0	57	6	33	3	52	16	28	1
Female P/ Male M	66	14	21	0	86	0	14	0	69	10	21	0
Female CM/ Male P	31	13	56	0	63	6	31	0	50	13	38	0
Female CM/ Male M	39	7	54	0	65	5	28	2	51	16	33	0

Table 7.3 Who takes major responsibility for household tasks, dual-employee couples of working age   *cont.*

	Cleaning				Child-care			
	Mostly woman	Mostly man	Shared	Other/ paid	Mostly woman	Mostly man	Shared	Other/ paid
Weak male								
BW	68	6	21	5	60	0	40	0
Female P/ Male P	56	10	24	10	64	0	36	0
Female P/ Male M	68	5	11	16	57	0	43	0
Female CM/ Male P	73	4	21	2	78	0	22	0
Female CM/ Male M	71	6	21	2	47	0	53	0
Dual BW	57	5	30	7	38	2	60	0
Female P/ Male P	61	4	19	13	50	0	50	0
Female P/ Male M	66	7	28	0	23	0	77	0
Female CM/ Male P	44	0	56	0	75	0	25	0
Female CM/ Male M	53	7	35	5	29	6	65	0

Table 7.3 Who takes major responsibility for household tasks, dual-employee couples of working age   *cont.*

	Grocery shopping				Washing/ironing				Cooking			
	Mostly woman	*Mostly man*	*Shared*	*Other/ paid*	*Mostly woman*	*Mostly man*	*Shared*	*Other/ paid*	*Mostly woman*	*Mostly man*	*Shared*	*Other/ paid*
Female BW/ Female P	43	12	43	1	53	8	34	4	51	20	28	1
Male P/ Female P/	37	22	41	0	63	11	26	0	41	22	37	0
Male M/ Female CM/	57	11	32	0	39	4	50	7	54	14	32	0
Male P/ Female CM/	0	0	100	0	50	50	0	0	100	0	0	0
Male M	39	6	52	3	58	6	30	6	55	24	18	3

Table 7.3 Who takes major responsibility for household tasks, dual-employee couples of working age   *cont.*

| | Cleaning | | | | Child-care | | | |
	Mostly woman	*Mostly man*	*Shared*	*Other/ paid*	*Mostly woman*	*Mostly man*	*Shared*	*Other/ paid*
Female BW	48	8	31	13	30	15	55	0
Female P/ Male P	48	4	26	22	29	14	57	0
Female P/ Male M	36	11	43	11	25	13	63	0
Female CM/ Male P	100	0	0	0	0	0	0	0
Female CM/ Male M	55	9	27	9	40	20	40	0

Note: P = professional/associate professional/managerial; C = clerical; M = manual.

Source: British Household Panel Survey (BHPS), Wave E, 1995.

rather than a gender-equal dual-breadwinning/dual-caring model emerging, a more appropriate typology would appear to be dual-breadwinner/ moderate female carer. Clearly, the breadwinner side of the breadwinner/carer gender arrangement has been challenged by women far more than the carer side has been by men.

Conclusion

Examining working couples in the mid-1990s, this chapter has questioned to what extent they fit the broad male-breadwinner/female-carer societal model or whether more gender-equal contracts are developing. It would appear that applying this model to their experiences was fruitful to an extent, but it was limited by the heterogeneity which emerged in the gender contracts in operation. The chapter focused first on breadwinning work, and identified a definite range of breadwinner couple types. Male breadwinners accounted for the majority of the dual-employee couples, but these ranged from strong male breadwinners – where women contributed very little to the household purse – to moderate and weak male-breadwinner types as women's relative contributions grew larger. There was, in addition, a substantial minority of couples where women and men were either earning very similar wages or the women were the main wage earners. Within one broad societal gender arrangement, then, lay distinct variety in women's and men's relative contributions to breadwinning work.

Bringing in class further complicated the picture of breadwinning. First, there were additional, class-based differences in typical gender contracts; the higher women's occupational status, the more likely couples were to be dual breadwinner. Second, even when couples of different classes could be identified by one gender contract, moderate male breadwinners for example, such a categorization based on proportionality was limited. It did not reveal unmistakable variation amongst the couples in their weekly wage packets. Higher- and lower-status couples within each breadwinner category were clearly in very different structural positions and with vastly different levels of economic resources to draw upon. Breadwinner contracts help us to see who is doing what work within the home. They do not reveal the conditions under which the juggling of family and employment is being managed.

Examining the carer side of the breadwinner/carer gender arrangements, the caring work of dual-employee couples remained firmly female-dominated. Women provided the greatest shares of caring work in couples where the male-breadwinning model was stronger, but men did not fully reciprocate this arrangement when women's breadwinning approached theirs, or even overtook it. As a result, there were fewer variations in caring patterns amongst the couples than there had been in breadwinning strategies and only strong and moderate female-carer gender arrangements emerged. There was very little evidence of dual caring and almost none of male caring, and this was true even when women were the main or dual breadwinners of the couple.

Examining male-breadwinner/female-carer gender arrangements has highlighted the advantages but also some limitations of these gender-based approaches to the household division of labour. Whilst such models do depict the prevalent breadwinner/carer typology of Britain, they fail to emphasize distinct within-society variation. One key element of this variation is related to class. Couples in different occupational classes fit the societal-level gender arrangement to differing degrees and there is also substantial class variation hidden within each gendered typology. The male-breadwinner/female(part-time)-carer gender arrangement may show well that men remain the main earners of the household and that women remain the main carers, but it fails to identify that the everyday experiences of balancing caring and breadwinning are classed. It does not show how couples in similar breadwinner/carer typologies but with different levels of economic resources manage intensifying time pressures in their endeavours to reconcile their working and family lives.

8

Employment Patterns for the Future: Balancing Work and Family Life in two Local Authorities

Mark Smith and Marilyn Carroll

Introduction

Recent trends in employment and the labour market have brought into focus the nature of the interaction between work and family life, especially for those with responsibilities for caring for others, whether for children, or elderly, sick or disabled relatives (Dex, 1999). Women's increased participation in paid employment has led to a rise in the number of dual-earner households, and increasing pressures between the demands of job and family. The 'traditional' family unit, with a woman in the role of full-time carer and a man in the role of full-time breadwinner, is now the exception rather than the rule and this has stimulated an interest in how employment practices and workplace provision can help workers to combine these two areas of responsibility. Employers have had to adjust to the changes in labour supply, although in the UK this has tended to mean offering more part-time work with little change to the working hours of men (Fagan, 1996; Rubery, 1998). Full-time employees in the UK, especially men, work longer hours than in any other EU country (Rubery *et al.*, 1999; Watson, 1994), which has obvious implications for balancing work and family life.

The change of government in 1997 led to increased interest in the area of 'family-friendly' work with, for example, the introduction of parental leave, a national childcare strategy and the establishment of the Women's Unit (now known as the Women and Equality Unit). However, many employers associate part-time jobs with 'family-friendly' employment practices, paying little attention to the fact that such work often involves marginalization and long-term disadvantage in terms of career prospects and pay. Here we interpret this term in a broader context in which 'family-friendly' policies offer potential benefits to employers other than cost-cutting. These benefits include increased commitment from employees, reduced sickness absence, increased productivity, and easier staff recruitment and retention.

Forth *et al.* (1997) have provided evidence of the extent of provision by employers and take-up rates by employees of 'family-friendly' working arrangements. They distinguish between 'flexible' arrangements, which primarily benefit employers, allowing them to respond to product market fluctuations (for example overtime and temporary contracts) and 'family-friendly' arrangements (such as job-sharing and term-time working), which primarily benefit the employee. They also distinguish between 'focused provisions' aimed at particular groups of workers, such as those with childcare responsibilities, and 'unfocused provisions' that may benefit a wider group of employees. They found that only 5 per cent of employers provided 'family-friendly' arrangements in each of four categories (extra maternity benefits, paternity leave, childcare arrangements and non-standard working time). However, 19 per cent provided arrangements in three of the four categories and 65 per cent in two of the four. The most common types of provision were working time arrangements, such as special leave at short notice to deal with family emergencies, and the least common type was assistance with childcare. (Forth *et al.*'s research was conducted before the introduction of the legal right to time off for family emergencies.)

Lewis (1997) divides 'family-friendly' employment policies into those which enable employees to conform to the (male) normative model of continuous, full-time employment (for example workplace nurseries), and those which involve alterations to working-time patterns, enabling them to integrate more easily their care responsibilities with their work responsibilities. This chapter focuses not only on care-related changes to working time patterns but also on care arrangements themselves, since the two are inevitably interlinked. Our research was carried out in two local authorities and examines how employees cope with work and care responsibilities, the impact of care on patterns of work and preferences for working-time changes. We examine evidence of a polarization between groups of carers in terms of their working-time and care arrangements, reflecting their ability to control their working patterns. This ability appears strongly correlated with employment status, measured by both occupation and working-time contract. A further dimension to our study concerns equality of access to care provision and here again we find that both access and preferences for care support vary according to ability to pay and status. Even within the same organization, employees' access to, and expectations of, 'family-friendly' arrangements are shaped and constrained by factors such as job status, occupation and income level.

The case study organizations and the survey

The survey of over 900 employees was carried out in two local authorities in the north-west of England. The City Council is a unitary authority in a large metropolitan area employing over 12,000 people and delivering services to over 200,000 residents in a mainly urban environment. The County Council employs 9,000 employees and delivers services across a large county, with employees distributed across a number of centres in large towns. The rationale for comparing two local authorities was initially to explore differences between carers in urban and rural settings. However, in practice we found little difference between urban and rural employees, while observed differences by gender, occupation and working-time status were common to both local authorities. Within local authorities there is a wide range of different occupational groups which have traditionally had a variety of working arrangements and patterns, including shorter standard weekly working hours and access to flexitime for non-manual workers.

Nearly two thousand questionnaires were sent out to employees across a range of departments. The random sample was achieved in two ways: first, by using a systematic sampling of employees in the larger departments or locations, and second by sampling all employees in the smaller departments or locations. This approach meant that the sampling fraction varied between departments, which were selected according to employee characteristics and the types of service provision. Care was taken to include departments with a reasonable gender balance and some weekend and evening working. Similar departments were chosen in the two local authorities. The final choice of sample departments was social services, cleaning and catering, leisure, development services, corporate services, refuse, education and environment services. The questionnaire was administered and collected through the internal post system of each local authority. The response rate at the City Council was 36 per cent while at the County Council it was higher at 43 per cent (some respondents from the City Council placed their completed questionnaires in the external mail and although some of these were safely received, others went astray, which may explain the lower response rate). Around half the sample had care responsibilities.

The similar grading structures in both local authorities allowed us to make comparisons between grades relatively easily and we categorized the job grades into four groups. The lower grades included Scales 1 to 3, covering occupations such as carers, former manual grades and the lower administrative grades. The medium grades were Scales 4 to 6, and included jobs such as computer officers, social workers and community workers. The senior officer grades (SO1 and SO2) included jobs such as project officers and some lower management positions such as group leaders. The management grades were classified as all those in the professional and management grades PM1 and above and SM1 and above.

Polarization in coping with care responsibilities

Although the distribution of care responsibilities tended to be concentrated upon women, we found similar shares of women and men had care responsibilities for children in both local authorities. However, their impact on working patterns and the type of care arrangements were quite different. There were also strong differences in the care arrangements and their impact on working lives according to job grade and working time, in addition to anticipated gender differences. Other factors such as the age of employees also affected their care profile but occupational grade and working-time status were more important as variables.

Similar proportions of women and men were parents, but a higher proportion of women than men had some form of care responsibilities, 53 per cent compared to 44 per cent. This difference arose from the greater proportion of women with care responsibilities for older, sick or disabled relatives (in these analyses we have prioritized childcare responsibilities over elder care, and elder care over care for a sick or disabled relative). Women were also more likely to have multiple care responsibilities for two or more of the dependent groups.

The division of care responsibilities between women and men and the impact this had on their working lives was quite different. Men were more likely to say that their care responsibilities had an occasional impact on their working day while women were more likely to report a great deal of impact. Around three-fifths of women employees in two-parent households stated that they took at least 80 per cent of the responsibility for their children compared with less than 10 per cent who stated that their partners took 80 per cent or more of the responsibility. (There were 24 female single parents in the sample, nearly all of whom took at least 80 per cent of the responsibility for their children.) Male employees with children seemed to recognize that their partners undertook more of the responsibility for their children but only two-fifths stated that their partners did at least 80 per cent of the work. Only seven women in the whole sample stated that their partners did more than 50 per cent of the tasks. Seventeen per cent of women, compared to 31 per cent of men, stated that they shared the responsibility for the children equally. Either men in local authorities come from households which are more likely to share caring responsibilities equally or there is some discrepancy between the reporting of shared care responsibilities of women and men. Men at the County Council were less likely to say that they shared the responsibility equally and more likely to say that their partners took on most of the responsibility. This reflects the higher share of single-earner households with caring responsibilities in the County Council (see Figure 8.1).

The gender differences in care responsibilities were reflected in the type of care duties reported by employees with different working-time status. The majority of employees on atypical contracts in both local authorities were women, and these women were more likely to be carers than other employees. The majority of atypical contracts were part-time, although there were a few women in job shares (nine),

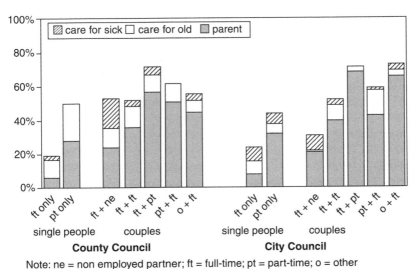

Note: ne = non employed partner; ft = full-time; pt = part-time; o = other

Figure 8.1: Care responsibilities by household working status and type of care

casuals (six) and temporarily reduced hours (five) and we have grouped these together in the 'other' category. There were just seven men in the whole sample working part-time and only one of these had care responsibilities. In both local authorities it was those households with 'one and a half workers', a full-time and a part-time worker, that were the most likely to have care responsibilities (Figure 8.1).

Despite the high share of dual-earner households, the most common childcare provider during working hours was the employee's spouse or partner. Over half of male full-time employees used this option but so did a third of female full-timers and two-fifths of female part-timers (Table 8.1). Closer inspection of these results shows that male full-timers relying on spouse or partner were more likely to have younger children, particularly under three years, while female employees relying on their spouse or partner tended to have children older than three years. It should also be remembered that care arrangements are not mutually exclusive and some employees had multiple care arrangements. Only half of employees using some kind of childcare arrangement used only one method. Female employees were more likely than men to rely on other informal childcare arrangements such as another family member, a friend or another child. Of the more formal arrangements female full-timers were the most likely to use a childminder but the shares using nurseries were similar across gender and working-time statuses.

The type of care arrangements that employees use will be shaped by the type of job they do, both in terms of the demands that this work places on their time and their access to higher income. Both women and men in the higher and management grades were more likely to rely on a spouse or partner than in the lower grades. This finding reflects a number of factors. These employees are older, so there is likely to be a cohort effect for the men living with spouses or partners who are less likely to work. These higher-grade jobs are also more likely to provide an income that can sustain a household. There may also be a measure of greater equality of caring responsibilities between employees further up the hierarchy. We found that workers with high demands on their time, managers and medium-grade workers, do share some care responsibilities slightly more equitably, but the findings for the senior grades (SO1 and SO2) challenged this.

An income effect may also explain the finding that those workers in the lowest grades are the least likely to rely on their spouse or partner for care but record some of the highest frequencies using another family member for care. The proportion of employees using more

Table 8.1 Type of childcare arrangement used by gender, working-time status and grade (per cent using method)

	Spouse or partner	Friend	Childminder	Nursery	Other child	Other family member	After-school club	Share with one care arrangement
Male								
Low	37	*	*	*	*	26	–	*
Medium	48	*	*	*	*	36	*	62
High	46	*	21	*	*	25	*	47
Management	65	10	12	12	*	20	10	51
Full-time	53	9	14	12	8	29	10	47
All	53	8	13	12	8	25	9	51
Female								
Low	33	11	9	6	11	47	6	50
Medium	37	12	19	12	11	47	*	50
High	43	14	19	12	24	31	14	43
Management	44	15	15	15	*	38	24	33
Full-time	34	11	19	10	9	41	12	46
Part-time	42	13	10	10	14	45	7	46
Other	27	14	11	*	18	46	*	53
All	37	12	14	9	12	44	8	47
Total	41	11	14	10	11	39	8	48

Note: Categories are not mutually exclusive.
* represents cells with fewer than five cases, – represents cells with no cases.

formal care arrangements also tended to rise with the grades, reflecting higher income and less family time available to these workers. Women in senior grades and management positions were more likely to use a childminder than those in other grades, while nurseries were used in similar proportions among the medium, high and management grades. However, against this we find that similar proportions of all grades use a friend to help out while at work. The number of different care arrangements across the grades is relatively consistent, with around a half of most grades having just one arrangement (Table 8.1). However, women in senior and management positions were the least likely to rely on just one arrangement (33 per cent compared to 48 per cent for all employees).

We find that the most common change made as a result of care responsibilities was that employees are less prepared to work longer hours. This holds for male and female employees and full and part-timers although the share of female employees is higher (Table 8.2). Nearly half of male full-timers use flexitime more often as a direct result of their care responsibilities compared to around a fifth of women on atypical contracts. This lower share reflects the lack of access to flexitime in the occupations where female part-timers are concentrated. Not surprisingly it is women currently on part-time contracts that are the most likely to have moved to working shorter hours overall. Similarly around a fifth of part-timers finish work earlier. However, around a fifth of male full-timers also finish earlier or have adjusted their start and finish times. These care-related changes highlight the more substantial changes that one group of women workers have made in shifting to part-time work while full-time men and women have the opportunity to make changes at the edges of their working days. Furthermore where women work full-time we can see that they are more likely to rely on formal care arrangements than female part-timers.

The different coping strategies of higher-level workers can be seen in the increased use of flexitime by higher and management grades as a result of caring responsibilities (Table 8.2). This is particularly so for men, with more than half of men in these grades using flexitime more compared to a third in the medium grades and less than five men in the lowest grades. However, there was more consistency between the grades for employees being less prepared to work longer hours, with the exception of the lowest grades. The employees working shorter hours were once again mostly women, and proportions were similar across the grades with the exception of managers (Table 8.2). The

Table 8.2 Changes to work patterns as a result of care responsibilities by working-time status, gender and grade (per cent making the change)

	Less prepared to work longer hours	Use flexitime	Work shorter hours	Earlier finishes	More regular hours (same each day)	Start & finish work later	Travel/stay away less	Fewer/no weekends	Work at home (if possible)
Male									
Low	37	*	–	*	*	*	*	*	–
Medium	52	36	*	*	20	*	*	32	–
High	42	54	*	21	*	25	*	*	*
Mgt	39	57	12	28	10	20	28	*	10
Full-time	44	46	9	22	9	20	15	13	5
All	42	44	10	21	10	19	15	14	6
Female									
Low	40	24	44	20	22	10	10	16	6
Medium	52	36	39	16	13	13	10	6	7
High	64	24	36	24	26	14	24	12	12
Mgt	68	44	24	27	15	15	18	*	*
Full-time	51	41	12	15	22	12	14	9	10
Part-time	48	22	60	23	19	12	12	14	6
Other	48	18	52	27	11	11	11	11	*
All	49	29	39	20	20	12	13	12	8
Total	47	33	31	21	17	14	13	13	7

Note: see notes to Table 8.1.

shares of employees finishing earlier were also similar across the grades, although managers and higher-grade workers were around twice as likely to start and finish later than other grades. The different activities of jobs at the upper end of the hierarchy are shown by the greater proportions of managers and higher-grade workers working at home more and travelling less. Meanwhile non-management grades are more likely to reduce work at weekends, particularly men in the medium grades.

The results show that there are strong differences in the way that women and men in different positions within the organization balance their caring and working responsibilities. Women are more likely than men to make significant changes to their working patterns at all levels in both local authorities. However, employees with greater autonomy over their working time can take advantage of flexitime by adjusting their start and finish times. Those without access to flexitime or with limited control over their scheduling may have to make more drastic changes, such as permanently reducing their working hours or foregoing the opportunity to work paid overtime.

Diverging preferences

The study also explored the potential changes that employees would like to see to enable them to balance their working lives and home lives, and whether they thought these would be feasible. We included both types of 'family-friendly' arrangements categorized by Lewis (1997): (i) changes to working-time patterns involving the number and scheduling of working hours, which might benefit all employees, and (ii) the provision of facilities such as workplace nurseries which would enable carers to conform to the model of continuous, full-time employment.

As Brannen *et al.* (1994) point out, there are inherent dangers in asking workers about their working-time preferences. Societal hostility towards mothers with young children working full-time means that part-time hours are often stated as a preference because it is seen as more socially acceptable. Second, other constraints, such as the nature of the job, the availability of childcare, the domestic division of labour and the employment situation of a partner mean that some people may see only a limited range of options open to them. Finally, a preference for part-time work without an indication of the preferred number of hours can cover a wide range of possibilities since there is no exact definition of part-time work.

Bearing these problems in mind, our results reveal strong employee support for changes to working-time arrangements. More control over working time was one of the most important changes that employees wanted. Carers were the most likely to say that they would like more control over the scheduling and number of hours worked but, importantly, non-carers also stated a preference for greater control over this aspect of their work. While the advantages of flexible working arrangements are often discussed in the context of enabling carers to deal with family emergencies, they can help all employees deal with routine aspects of their lives.

One of the problems highlighted by the survey was that of fitting working time around school hours and care-related arrangements, and a greater degree of control, flexibility or changes to fixed working patterns would appear to be of benefit to large numbers of workers. For example, over one-third of the employees in the sample are currently able to exercise quite a lot, or a great deal of control over their working hours, with between one-quarter and a third also having control over the number of hours they work each week. However, the responses indicate that large numbers of employees, both carers and non-carers, would like more control over both the number and scheduling of their working hours, with over half of all respondents stating this as a preference. Employees who already have some degree of control over their working time are also the employees who want more control. We found the desire for more control over the scheduling of working hours positively and significantly correlated with current control over the number of hours ($r = 0.51$, $p < 0.00$) and with current control over the scheduling of hours ($r = 0.71$, $p < 0.00$). Similarly the correlation between the desired control over the number of hours worked was positively and significantly correlated with current control over the number of hours ($r = 0.63$, $p < 0.00$) and with current control over the scheduling of hours ($r = 0.54$, $p < 0.00$). It is possible that this indicates a desire to have control over unpaid overtime with those working the most unpaid overtime also having some control, in theory, over their current working hours.

Variable starting and finishing times would also help the majority of carers, especially women. If changes to fixed working hours were possible, earlier starts and finishes would be most popular among carers. However, a large proportion of carers would like to start and finish later, so it is apparent that not all carers would benefit from the same changes (Table 8.3). More flexibility, or working hours arranged to suit individual circumstances, are likely to be of most benefit. In both local

Table 8.3 Desired changes to working-time and care arrangements by grade and gender (per cent desiring change)

	Male employees					Female employees				
	Low	Med.	High	Mgt	All	Low	Med.	High	Mgt	All
Variable starts	56	50	77	75	68	65	77	85	86	73
Variable finishes	75	50	82	78	73	70	77	91	90	77
Later starts	*	*	*	57	45	41	42	58	58	46
Earlier starts	80	47	50	69	62	38	62	46	58	49
Later finishes	*	*	*	54	43	21	*	*	44	27
Earlier finishes	63	60	60	72	66	51	82	77	79	67
Longer hours	*	*	–	*	6	31	12	*	*	20
Shorter hours	*	52	24	53	41	15	27	26	43	22
More paid care	*	*	*	*	11	13	18	*	*	14
More cheaper care	37	28	33	26	29	22	30	26	21	25
More help form relatives	*	20	*	10	15	16	11	12	*	14
More help from friends	*	–	–	*	*	3	*	*	*	3
More help from partner	–	–	*	–	1	7	8	*	*	7
Longer nursery/school hours	*	20	*	10	13	11	19	12	15	14

Note: see notes to Table 8.1.

authorities it is those in management and the higher grades who are most likely to want changes such as variable starts and finishes, later or earlier starts and finishes, or a shorter working week. The only area where lower grades are more likely to want change is in the length of the working week which, again, may reflect the more widespread use of short part-time hours for jobs in these grades. Furthermore these results may reflect the fact that large numbers of part-timers in the lower grades may have deliberately chosen these jobs because the hours already fit in with their care arrangements and therefore do not wish to change them (McRae, 1989). This divergence may also arise because the higher grades are more likely to have desk-based jobs, where work can be started and finished more flexibly. Employees in some lower-grade jobs such as cleaning, catering and refuse collection may feel these activities can be carried out only at certain hours, or as part of a team working together.

Large proportions of carers and non-carers in the sample stated that they would like to work fewer hours each week overall. It is possible that this indicates a desire to have to do less unpaid overtime rather than reduce the number of contracted hours and, by inference, earnings. Over 60 per cent of those wanting shorter hours currently work longer than 36 hours per week, with approximately one-quarter working 41 or more hours per week. There is a significant positive correlation between the usual hours of employees wanting to work fewer hours and the number of hours less that they would like to work ($r = 0.78$, $p < 0.01$ for women and $r = 0.83$, $p < 0.01$ for men). However, although there may be support for shorter full-time hours, it is not clear whether employees would be prepared to reduce their earnings.

Predictably, the proportion of respondents indicating a preference for longer weekly working hours was smaller, at around 15 per cent, and the majority of these were women who currently work part-time, or who have other working-time arrangements, such as job-sharing. In fact, between one-quarter and one-third of all female part-timers wanted to increase their hours. There is a weaker relationship between the usual hours and the number of additional hours than we found for those employees wanting to work fewer hours ($r = -0.28$, $p < 0.05$ for women and no significant result for men). These results indicate, however, that some women with care responsibilities who currently work part-time would like the opportunity to work, if not full-time, at least more hours each week (and, by implication, increase their earnings). It appears they are unable to do so, either because this would not fit in with care arrangements, or because their employer does not make the option of working more hours available to them. This finding is consistent with other research on working time preferences, which indicates that many part-time employees would like to work longer hours, but not necessarily full-time hours (Fagan, 1996).

Not only does our evidence suggest strong support for changes to working patterns, the majority of local authority employees believe that, given the nature of the jobs they do and the services their department provides, it would be feasible to make these changes. For example, almost two-thirds of the total sample think it would be possible to work more variable finishes and almost three-quarters to start or finish at different times. There are some variations between grades and between departments, with those in lower-grade jobs and in departments such as cleaning and catering believing there is less scope for change.

Both local authorities currently provide some types of care-related assistance for their employees. Time off for family emergencies and the use of a work telephone for family reasons are the most widely available forms of help. Only small minorities in each authority have access to other forms of assistance, but a large proportion of carers would like their employer to provide more practical help (Table 8.4). For example around a third would like financial help with childcare, and a quarter would like workplace nurseries provided. Overall there is little difference between the preferences expressed by male and female carers, although women are more likely to want financial help with childcare and after-school or holiday childcare. However, again it is the higher grades in both local authorities that appear to want greater levels of support and more additional services than lower grades. Our survey also found that employees in higher grades made more use of any special provisions made available for carers. For example, in both local authorities higher-grade employees were more likely to use, and believe that they were entitled to use, special leave for a family emergency or around the birth of a child. Men were specifically asked how they would take time off around the time of a birth and lower-grade employees were more likely to use annual leave even though they were officially entitled to special paid or unpaid leave.

These desires for better provision may reflect a number of factors, including staff in higher grades having greater household income, and a greater ability to afford childcare services. Furthermore, higher-grade employees are more likely to continue to work full-time when they have children. This is one of the factors generating their greater household income, but it also contributes to households with higher-level workers being, in the often-used phrase, 'money-rich but time-poor'.

Table 8.4 Care provisions and desired care provisions from the employer by grade and gender (per cent with arrangement available (desiring))

	Male employees					Female employees				
	Low	Med.	High	Mgt	All	Low	Med.	High	Mgt	All
Time for family emergencies	32 (37)	24 (48)	43 (42)	37 (37)	34 (40)	39 (40)	49 (34)	36 (50)	38 (47)	41 (40)
After school/holiday childcare	*	* (*)	54 (−)	33 (*)	31 (*)	30 (*)	45 (*)	48 (*)	29 (*)	36 (4)
Financial help for childcare	*	* (*)	46 (−)	26 (*)	26 (*)	28 (*)	39 (*)	45 (*)	35 (*)	34 (3)
Workplace nursery	* (−)	24 (−)	46 (−)	24 (*)	26 (*)	20 (*)	35 (*)	29 (*)	21 (*)	25 (2)
Career breaks	*	− (−)	33 (*)	16 (*)	16 (*)	18 (6)	29 (12)	31 (12)	29 (*)	24 (9)
Nurseries supported by employer	*	* (−)	25 (−)	16 (*)	16 (*)	12 (*)	19 (12)	31 (−)	21 (−)	17.3 (*)
Help finding childcare	*	* (−)	29 (−)	10 (*)	13 (1)	11 (*)	21 (*)	14 (−)	21 (−)	15 (2)
Telephone for family reasons	*	*	*	*	9	6 (*)	13 (*)	19 (−)	* (−)	9
	(32)	(32)	(50)	(57)	(46)	(34)	(41)	(50)	(65)	(41)

Notes: figures in parentheses ( ) indicate the share that believe provision is already available.
options ranked by highest proportion.
Categories are not mutually exclusive.
* represents cells with fewer than five cases, − represents cells with no cases.

Conclusion

This chapter has highlighted the difficulties that carers face in balancing work and family life in the UK. Although local authority employees generally have shorter working hours than those in many private sector organizations, caring duties still have a major impact on their working lives. We have shown how employees use a wide range of caring strategies to cope with family responsibilities, often using a mix of care arrangements, both formal and informal, reflecting poor levels of public provision. As Brannen *et al.* (1994) report, the onset of family responsibilities is associated with a reduction in working hours for women, but appears to have little effect on the working hours of men. Many part-time jobs are low paid and so, for women, the move from full-time to part-time work often means moving to lower-status employment (Joshi and Davies, 1992). These trends are reflected in our study in which the vast majority of part-time workers are women who take a greater share of caring duties. These responsibilities have a greater impact on their working lives than is the case for other employees. However, not all part-time workers are happy with their jobs. Many part-timers expressed a desire to work longer hours, and some clearly felt that the transition to part-time work had damaged their career.

Our evidence suggests that many workers are unaware of entitlements which are already universally available, such as special leave for family emergencies and paternity or maternity support leave. Some employees may not feel entitled to special treatment, either because of their gender (in the case of job-sharing or career breaks for men, for example) or job grade. On the other hand it does appear that there is a group of employees higher up the occupational hierarchy who are able to make greater use of formal support structures both inside and outside the organization. These workers not only have the income to enable them to pay for care services provided by the market, but they also have access to forms of working-time flexibility which help with care responsibilities. Those employees in higher or managerial grades in both councils were more likely to express a preference for financial help with childcare, including workplace crèches, possibly because they saw these forms of provision as more realistic options given their work patterns and income. Their greater use of paid care and longer working hours may also mean that they have stronger opinions about how to improve both their working arrangements and care options. On the other hand in the lower grades there may be a lack of a 'sense of entitlement' to the provision of 'family-friendly' arrangements, with employees regarding these provisions as perks rather than basic rights (Lewis, 1997, p. 15).

Finally the survey also provides evidence that both carers and non-carers would like more control over their working lives. This fits with the shift from 'family-friendly' to 'work-life' terminology at the policy level and moves away from focusing on women and children. The harmonization of working conditions under the Single Status Agreement in local government provides an opportunity to implement working practices that can help employees balance work and domestic life. The inclusion of carers and non-carers in changes not only alters the emphasis on women's responsibility for care but also reduces the threat of a potential 'non-carer backlash' against changes. On the one hand developments such as the enactment of EU directives on working time and parental leave mean that the issues are now being widely debated. However, on the other hand there remain a number of barriers to the effective balance of work and family life in the UK, including the long hours worked by employees and the attitude that the care of dependants is largely the responsibility of the individual or family. The participation of women in the labour market on a more continuous and permanent basis creates the need for new patterns of support in the workplace, in the home and in the community. Some employers are seeing the need to adopt 'family-friendly' employment policies in order to attract and retain staff. These can benefit both men and women and have the potential to facilitate a redistribution of care responsibilities. However, whilst they are regarded as 'women's issues', women will still take a greater share of the care responsibilities for children and dependent relatives.

Acknowledgements

This research was supported by Fair Play North West and two local authorities in the North West of England.

9
Making Time for Management: The Careers and Lives of Manager-Academics in UK Universities

Rosemary Deem and Sam Hillyard

Introduction

Academics who take on management roles in universities, whether reluctantly or enthusiastically, face many personal and institutional dilemmas connected with time. Examining these dilemmas sheds light on how current ideas about public service management and organizational practices are affecting academic careers and the academic labour process. This chapter draws on 79 recent interviews with male and female Pro-Vice Chancellors (PVCs), Deans, and Heads of Departments (HoDs) in UK universities. Time dilemmas encountered by manager-academics[1] include the question of when in an academic career to take on management roles, the impact of management responsibilities on research and teaching, and the apportionment of time between work and non-work. For manager-academics, work time is often given a high priority in their lives: 'The social world that draws a person's allegiance also imparts a pattern to time. The more attached we are to the world of work, the more its deadlines, its cycles, its pauses and interruptions shape our lives' (Hochschild, 1997, p. 45).

The importance of time to manager-academic roles is closely connected to other substantive themes in an ESRC-funded research project on new managerialism in UK universities[2] from which the interview data utilized here are drawn. The project's starting-point was to examine the extent to which theories about new managerialism in public service organizations (Clarke and Newman, 1997; Exworthy and Halford, 1999; Ferlie *et al.*, 1996) are applicable to higher education. This involved exploring the extent to which management practices such as team-work, flexible use of labour, devolution of budgets, emphasis on entrepreneurial activities and the overt monitoring of academic work are present in UK universities. Methods used included focus groups with members of learned societies, interviews with manager-academics and senior administrators in 16 universities, and case studies comparing the views of manager-academics with those of 'managed' staff and students.

The control and use of work time is an important but scarcely new aspect of managing organizations. New managerialism, though, may place different emphases on time usage and be more concerned to regulate and account for its use by professionals previously allowed considerable autonomy. Indeed, the Transparency Exercise carried out by the Higher Education Funding Council for England in 2000 asked academics to say, on a monthly and termly basis, what percentage of time they spent on research, teaching and administration.

Though there is evidence in the UK universities we studied of the merging of old and new forms of management practice, just as Ferlie *et al.* (1996) found in the National Health Service, there is also some indication of resistance to and ambivalence about managerialism amongst academics. This shows itself as a scepticism about performance games such as the Research Assessment Exercise (RAE), a concern to maintain democratic academic self-governance in the face of moves to professionalize administration and management, and a protection of the right to work autonomously and using discretion. There was also ambivalence about whether what HoDs and Deans do is actually management rather than leadership. It is in the context of such ambivalence about forms of managerialism, old and new, that this analysis of manager-academic careers and working lives is set.

Time and the work of manager-academics

Time and work have been recognized as intertwined from the onset of industrialization (Burns, 1973; Thompson, 1991). In contemporary work organizations, the use of time, including linear and cyclical processes, remains important. For educational institutions and educators, time is a key element of educational practices (Hoeg, 1995; Morrison, 1992, 1995; Watkins, 1993). Time is highly relevant for manager-academics in universities. The nature and shape of academic careers, the timing of moves into and out of management, the way management tasks must be balanced against research and teaching, and the extent to which management eats into out-of-work and household time (where competing time horizons of others are often relevant too) all implicate time. Linear time (getting older, progressing in a career), cyclical time (the academic year restarting or ending) and the social, cultural and economic significance of time as a resource, cost, challenge and constraint, are also significant for manager-academics.

Unlike those with set hours of employment, academics seldom have 'regular hours' for their work (although sometimes the opening hours of buildings at their university may assume otherwise) and hence may find it more difficult to make use of the classic notion of 'produced' free time, that is, time left over once paid work and other commitments have been completed (Deem, 1995, 1996a). Indeed, new technologies, particularly e-mail and mobile phones, allow work to be done or work-related contacts to occur, in places and also at times and at faster speeds than previously possible. 'The permeability of the time boundary between present and future is increased by technologies which facilitate temporal uncoupling and decentralization' (Nowotny, 1994, p. 11). As Adam notes, 'my time', 'our time' and 'other time' are amongst the many implicit coexistences of time in contemporary societies (Adam, 1995). These are all problems for manager-academics as they attempt to prioritize different tasks, routines and cycles of their staff and students. This pressure is not necessarily experienced evenly by all manager-academics. With some 35 per cent of the UK higher education academic labour force now female (Bett Report, 1999) and 68 per cent of all women of working age in employment (Equal Opportunities Commission, 1999), gender processes have become increasingly relevant to the timing of lives both inside and outside work. Many of the households from which academics come may be time-poor, even if otherwise relatively culturally and socially advantaged. Academic work, with its propensity to spill over into all aspects of people's lives, is particularly demanding of household and out-of-office time, and for parents (especially mothers). In what follows, we examine some of our interviewees' responses to time and time dilemmas in their career trajectories, daily practices and work and home lives.

Time and manager-academic careers

The careers of manager-academics are often quite serendipitous (Deem, 1996b). Evetts's work on senior post-holders in schools suggested that women saw their careers as unintentional and unplanned, whilst men claimed theirs were planned (Evetts, 1990, 1994). Our data suggest that over half our interviewees, both women and men, found themselves taking a management route they had not planned at an earlier stage of their academic careers. We also found that the presentation of accounts of careers and self varied considerably. Why is this? Women and men may experience the same organizations differently (Halford *et al.*, 1997; Wajcman, 1998), and are differentially rewarded for doing the same job at the same level (Bett Report, 1999). Age also affects the careers of manager-academics; many but not all achieve management positions in late career. The academic discipline of would-be manager-academics could also be important in shaping careers. Are scientists more likely than non-scientists to enter management because of the greater likelihood of prior industrial experience and because of the tailing off of scientific research in late career? Between 1960 and 1980 many Vice-Chancellors (VCs) were scientists (Bargh *et al.*, 2000; Farnham and Jones, 1998) for such reasons. Our own data show little specific connection between management careers and disciplinary background.

The type of university may also affect accounts of careers. The point at which manager-academics step into management roles differed between pre- and post-1992 institutions,[3] with both women and men in the latter tending to reach HoD posts and deanships somewhat earlier in their academic careers. Most PVC interviewees and a number of Deans from the pre-1992 sector reached that level relatively late in their academic careers. Some middle managers who aspired to reach top-level management did not expect to do so:

Interviewer: Would you like to be more senior, are you ambivalent about that?

Respondent: I'm too old ... I applied for pro vice-chancellorship at my previous university moving on from a head of department, and didn't get it ... in any case now um, I'm 56, I've got at best another nine years um, and I'm not absolutely certain that I shall stay until I'm 65. I haven't got time really, by the time I give up doing this ... job, um, I shall be 60, that's too old to start anything new. (Female Dean of Humanities, pre-1992)

The kind of role also affected the accounts provided. Thus we found a number who had only reluctantly become HoDs:

I got a letter from the VC in December asking me if I would be head of department, which I did not want to do, I felt completely trapped, and ... if you have a full-time post at the university and accept promotion, then I don't think it's fair to refuse to do that task, nobody wants to do it as far as I can see. And um, so I said I would with great misgivings because it's had a terrible effect on my research output (HoD Arts, pre-1992)

For Dean positions, there was evidence of a more deliberate choice, with people wanting to protect and nurture their discipline or feeling that they would prefer to do the job rather than see it go to a colleague:

I also felt that ... Social Sciences at the university was undervalued and I felt that one could get involved with Senate discussions and hopefully protect and advance the Social Sciences. (Dean, Social Science, post-1992)

I arrived at a stage in my career when I couldn't bear the thought of anybody else managing me, particularly I suppose one scans one's um, colleagues, ... And er, so that persuaded me that I'd better do it rather than have anybody else do it. (Dean, Business, post-1992)

The notion of the challenge and the novel was an important influence cited by many manager-academics. In terms of the structuring of a career as a whole, the longer-term view also structured some academics' decisions to progress:

You suddenly realize that you've got that job for 34 years and in order to handle the fact that you've got a job for life and do much the same for 34 years, I then split my life into sort of three-year chunks. So I decided to do something, some sort of focus for three years and then move on and do something else. (Dean, Health, pre-1992)

The move into a senior role necessitates a wider view, but with that shift away from motivated self-interest, new benefits and rewards appear. For example, in comparison with the time-scale in which an individual can make an impact upon their discipline or department, 'management' roles offer a quicker fix:

One of the big ideas in my thesis, which was published in 1981, went mainstream about five years ago and is popping up in all the publications. Fifteen years to have people say whether you're right or wrong is quite a long time. (Dean, Arts, pre-1992)

The new 'audit culture', with external research assessment and subject teaching review, as well as internal reviews and emphasis on performativity (Cowen, 1996), presents a cyclical turn-round time for HoDs in terms of the way they manage their staff:

> Somebody can't, as far as I'm concerned, somebody can't say 'Well I'm going to write the best book that's ever been written on Goethe and it's going to take me 10 years to do the research' if RAE is next year. (HoD, Languages, pre-1992)

This sense of needing to do things quickly is exacerbated by those who hold management posts only temporarily (most common in the pre-1992 universities):

> There are one or two experienced Heads of Departments and many others are in a situation like me, two or three years into the job. (HoD, Social Sciences, pre-1992)

In summary, a number of factors, including gender, age, boredom, seeking new challenges, wanting to protect their subject, feeling there is no one better to do it and institutional type, all feed into academics' decisions to move into management roles. However, once in a management role, there is also a question about subsequent career options, since research is often curtailed by moving into management:

> I still do research, I still have research grants, it's hard and you're constantly in tension between the two activities and I think that the pressures on people like myself are greater than they would be on the full-time researcher or the full-time manager, you're trying to do both. (HoD, Built Environment, post-1992)

The subject or disciplinary commitment, which may have provided an initial attraction, when placed alongside the decisions required of an HoD or Dean in 'stormy times', may leave the future uncertain in other ways too:

> As Head of Department you have no friends whatsoever. The only friends I have are outside the institution because it's a managerial type job. You can't really have any reasonable relationships with other Heads of Departments. You have acquaintances, but you don't have any real friendships … Career-wise there's nowhere to go at

this university, because I've got the mark of Cain. (HoD, Applied Science, post-1992)

Deans and PVCs in particular, especially those in the pre-1992 sector where such jobs are more likely to be temporary, face the question not only 'what next?' but also 'what is still an option?' Age is crucial here, particularly for late entrants to academe and women who have taken career breaks. Many Deans and PVCs described how, once involved in strategic planning and institution-level decisions, it becomes more difficult to return to 'the back benches', even if this was once their intention. Returning to a conventional academic role of research and teaching, following several years as a manager, is not 'an easy road back' (PVC, pre-1992). Senior manager-academics' careers now require considerable self-management of their own career pathways in a way perhaps not anticipated when entering academe; interestingly, advice on this is now beginning to appear (Blaxter *et al.*, 1998). The timing of moving into management posts for academics and the way in which it relates to their career pathways reveals the extent to which there is a further dimension to what it 'means' to be an academic, adding to the debate about who academics are and where they are going (Fulton, 1996, 1997; Halsey, 1992; Halsey and Trow, 1971). Whether this constitutes a fundamental redefinition of what it means to be an academic and whether the move to a greater emphasis on management has redefined the academic professional remains to be seen. Though some recent work with UK academics suggests much continuity remains in academic identities (Henkel, 2000), many of our interviewees did not convey this impression. It may be that academics with traditional ideas about academic work do their best to avoid management roles.

Finding time for management

The issue of balancing and prioritizing their management responsibilities in relation to the rest of an academic-manager's workload, including teaching and research, is a continual problem. For some becoming a manager-academic, albeit temporarily, takes away some of the academic pressure to which they might otherwise find themselves subjected:

I'm planning to do very well in my research [after stopping being HoD]. Of course I don't know if I can. It's quite convenient to have an excuse not to be doing more ... You know, I've kept my head up in research, it's just that I didn't do brilliantly, so now I'm supposed to be doing brilliantly. (HoD, Social Science, pre-1992)

The more senior the manager-academic's position, the more difficult it becomes to carry on research:

> I try to maintain some of my own research which is proving very difficult. It was sold to me that I spend hopefully 10 per cent of my time on research, I'm trying to do that, but ... it's something that happens over the weekends and nights, it's very difficult with the wall-to-wall meetings, day in and day out. (PVC, post-1992)

If maintaining research is difficult, teaching is something that is even more challenging to maintain. Nevertheless some senior managers do maintain their teaching because of a love of the subject and maintaining contact with students:

> I still, although the position essentially says that ... it's appropriate for an academic involved in the Senior Pro-Vice-Chancellor's role to drop teaching activities, I still teach the two modules that I love so much. (PVC, pre-1992)

> My commitment to my department at the moment is that each year I do two five-week level-one courses of lecturing ... the yellowing notes are there and don't really need updating ... I still give my honours course which is ten lectures every two years. (Dean of Arts, pre-1992)

At the next level down, for HoDs, teaching may be made difficult by the demands of central administration and management, which suggests some tricky time-politics issues:

> It's quite difficult to allocate a slot on a weekly basis to class teaching at undergraduate level, it's impossible, because you can't control all the events and meetings that come into your diary. You know, those are often imposed from other parts of the university. (HoD, Humanities, post-1992)

Some senior roles, especially those focusing on relationships with industry and the community, or national and international representation, require the incumbent to spend considerable time out of the university. Where this happens often, someone frequently has to cover their work at the university:

I find it a very heavy workload ... you do end up with an awful lot of jobs ... the dean this week has been away, he's away today and has been away on the two previous days so that means you do two jobs because you have to pick up all the people who are coming to see him, who need to see him urgently, things like that. So it is an unreasonable load. (Associate Dean, Humanities/Social Sciences, post-1992)

Managing generally consumes a lot of time. Many respondents at senior and middle levels saw long hours and a heavy workload as part of the job, though not always one of which they approved:

You have to apologize, I think, for not working at least a ten-, eleven-hour day and you are expected to work at weekends and that's endemic throughout, at all levels, throughout the organization. So as a matter of routine we expect our academic staff to mark at weekends. (Dean of Engineering, post-1992)

HoDs often tried to protect the time of those for whom they were responsible:

because I'm stuck with the situation of sort of low staffing levels we've got and I'm mindful that other people, even more so than me need to maintain their research career and they need to teach and to have time with students. And if I, just because I want rid of some of the paperwork, impinge upon their valuable time, then that's not necessarily the thing for me to do. (HoD, Nursing, pre-1992)

So far as own work time is concerned, inevitably much of manager-academics' time is spent in a variety of meetings, whether formal or informal:

What's most time-consuming would certainly be meetings, both informal and formal, talking to people definitely. (Head of School Management, pre-992)

I would guess that about a quarter of my life is spent on university committees and servicing that ... a quarter of it is spent on departmental meetings ... and I guess a quarter of it is really spent on managing the office area ... and organising other things like the School Recruitment fair ... and I guess a quarter of it is really ... we operate an open door policy, my office door is open and students, staff, the whole works come in. (Dean, post-1992)

If the nature of the academic labour process is increasingly time-consuming for ordinary academics as loads increase and resources decrease (Cuthbert, 1996; Slaughter and Leslie, 1997; Trowler, 1998), it is more so for manager-academics. A number said that keeping day-time free to read correspondence, write reports, telephone people or just do some thinking, was much harder:

Interviewer: How much time do you actually get to spend on your own?

Interviewee: During the day very little, because if I'm not actually talking to people, I'm individually trying to get them on the 'phone. I mean one of the problems I have is to actually keep enough time in the diary free in order to actually deal with correspondence ... to think and to 'phone. I would think I do most of my thinking and a lot of the more detailed reading and preparation for the meetings in the evening actually. (Dean of Medicine, pre-1992)

One or two respondents felt that there was a gender dimension to this, with men more prepared to be more single-minded than women in deciding which tasks to do and which not to do:

I have seen more men be more ruthless in cutting down the time they spend on personal tutoring, on follow-up work with students, supervision of their dissertations, who have been more willing to say, 'No, what matters is this. I will give that much time to that. I'll measure it and I'll give no more'. (Female HoD, Languages, pre-1992)

This view accords with research on women teacher-educators who felt they were the good citizens of the department, whilst men preferred to get on with their research (Acker, 1997; Acker and Feuerverger, 1996), and a study in an Australian university, where women staff felt that men got on better because they refused to do activities which were mundane (Harris *et al.*, 1998).

Though some manager-academics felt that technological changes such as e-mail simplified their job, not all our respondents agreed – e-mail was quite widely regarded as adding more time to the working day and as presenting a particular burden when added to the paper-work mountain:

> At one time you could write a memo and send it and OK, somebody might telephone you about it, but you may wait for a week for it to come back. Now, it's becoming a tremendous number of e-mails coming through. (HoD, Design and Technology, post-1992)

Whilst some senior respondents discussed the extent to which they did strategic work in their work time and planned well ahead, others were clear that they had much shorter time horizons;

> *Interviewer:* Do you set yourself certain goals and objectives that you want to try and achieve?
> *Respondent:* No, no, it's much more intuitive. I don't have five-year plans or one-year plans, I don't know really if I analysed it, how I do think about. (Dean of Science, pre-1992)

This response has similarities with Bargh *et al.*'s (2000) findings from their research on UK Vice Chancellors. They found that whilst VCs talked a great deal about their involvement in strategic activities when interviewed, in practice work-shadowing revealed that much more of their work was reactive and driven by current events and crises. At the other end of the management continuum, HoDs often complained that their time-scales were set by others at more senior levels or outside the university:

> There's something wrong with the system where it says 'I need this, this afternoon' OK? Because it's management on the hoof, it's not management with thought and preparation. (HoD, Maths, pre-1992)

Where people work may have an impact on how much time they spend in their place of employment. Both in our observational fieldwork and in respondents' comments, we noticed the differences between working in an inner urban site (where some academics may be commuting long distances daily), a campus-based institution (where weekly commuting may be more common), and those institutions where many live locally. One respondent who had previously worked in a city location where long-distance daily commuting was common and then moved to a university where this was less usual, had this to say:

Working in X is slightly odd because there is this tendency, you know, you go in on the days when you have commitments and you teach and you work at home and from a practical point of view I actually think that that's quite sensible. I mean from a social point of view it's not so good because you don't see students and you don't see colleagues, but you get, don't half get a lot done. (PVC, pre-1992)

A weekly commuter in a campus-based university reflects on how her week divides up:

I do this as a weekly commute, so that brings in, I suppose the pressure that I have a tendency to fester over what's happening at the university during the evenings because I'm not being bombarded with teenage problems. (Dean of Health Studies, pre-1992).

The sense of time moving on rapidly, in a linear way, as well as the frequent return of cycles and seasons, was conveyed by many of our interviewees. Though some of them tried hard to control what has been called the politics of time (Nowotny, 1994), the competing demands of other time cycles and events and others priorities and power-plays made it very difficult to achieve. Middle-level manager-academics like HoDs have little or no control over much of what they do and also often feel an obligation to their colleagues to relieve them of time-consuming administration. At more senior levels, manager-academics may exercise more direct control over their workloads and have the capacity to delegate work to others, but their research, which requires more personal 'me' time, becomes difficult to sustain yet is essential if a management career is ultimately rejected or not forthcoming. Teaching may also be retained in the face of many competing time demands, for similar reasons but more often just for its own sake. University management roles are demanding, with little or no downtime. In the next section we examine how this affects manager-academics' lives outside of their formal employment commitments.

Work time and home time

Finally, we explore the relationship between the time manager-academics spend on their working lives and the time they spend not doing academic work. Universities are 'greedy institutions' (Coser, 1974) which eat up time and energy. For academics in general, the division between home and work is a particularly problematic one, since their involvement in research and teaching often means working at home and at unsocial hours. New technology is often offered by policy makers and even some academics as a way in which universities can cut costs and modernize their work (Ford *et al.*, 1996; National Committee of Inquiry into Higher Education, 1997). New technologies do enable academics to do more of their work at places geographically distant from their place of employment or to do work such as PhD supervision in new ways, but they also make escape from work more difficult. Some of our female interviewees voiced the view that women in a paid work context might be better at multi-tasking than men:

> One thing that I think is a real gender difference is the incapacity of some academic male colleagues to be able to do more than one thing at a time [laugh]. You know, they have to be focused and do one thing and then they can go on to another, whereas it's always seemed to me that probably women get more practice of keeping several balls in the air. (Associate Dean, Social Science/Humanities, post-1992)

If this difference does exist, and if in part it derives from the experience of motherhood and/or running a household, it becomes even more crucial when we look at balancing home and work. The different demands of household and paid-work time, partners and dual-career households, care of children and other dependants, all raise dilemmas about how scarce time resources are deployed, by whom and for whom. In this respect, the notion of gendered time (Nowotny, 1994) was highly visible in the descriptions of home and work provided by our respondents. Many male respondents talked at length about how their partners had sacrificed personal careers in order to bolster their own and taken on most household duties in order to provide them with the ability to concentrate on work time and 'my time' rather than 'family time'.

The issue of mothers and academic work has already been raised by other researchers (Leonard and Malina, 1994). Many of our female respondents who were mothers, particularly those with young children, discussed how difficult they found it to combine university work with childcare, especially if they wished to climb the promotion ladder. The juggling of job, household time and household responsibilities was often felt to be arduous:

In the career as a whole there is no doubt that in the university sector at the moment it is very difficult to combine family responsibilities and the level of hard work that is needed to get you to the stage which will give you the status to enable you to go into a senior position ... you're not going to get appointed a professor unless you had a good track record in research ... Now you try combining a 65-hour working week with any kind of family responsibilities and you're going to have problems. (Female Dean of Humanities, pre-1992)

Though young children pose particularly demanding schedules on mothers (and some fathers), the problem does not necessarily end when children turn into teenagers. The demands on parents may just be of a different order:

Nobody tells you that actually children in their teens are a lot more demanding than babies ... they don't want you to arrange alternative care and they can look after themselves but it's you they want the argument with. (Female Head of School, Social Sciences, pre-1992)

For almost all our respondents, the problems of coping with work which spills over into home life are considerable. A few respondents dealt with this by getting up very early, or by avoiding housework altogether:

My wife works, yeah, and so we lead a very busy life ... My wife stopped work when she had children and then came back gradually. We were rather fortunate in that the right job and so on came up at the right time for her ... Um, even so we both work very hard, we both work extremely hard now, because in a sense she runs the house, does a full-time job and runs the house. And I do a full-time job and then, well I work roughly double a sort of minimum working week. I work at least 60 and more like 70 hours a week. And that's fine. (Male PVC, pre-1992)

Only a minority of men in heterosexual-couple relationships were at pains to point out that they did their share of housework:

I do all the teaching and the washing and part of the housework ... No, they don't have much cooked food if I'm away. (Male HoD, Humanities, pre-1992)

Many male interviewees, and some women, found that their work permeated all their activities and that it was difficult to switch off and

keep time free for non-work activities, be they household, other obligations, or leisure. None the less, some respondents, of both sexes,
claimed to achieve it at weekends, if not on weekday evenings:

> My situation at the moment is that the university has me a hundred
> per cent lock, stock and barrel from five fifteen on Monday morning
> to about half past eight on Friday night ... I don't work at weekends.
> I take every day of holiday that's due to me ... on holiday I switch
> off and don't think about the place. (Female PVC, post-1992)

> I've got seven children ... they range from 28 to 10 and I've never
> worked on a Saturday as a matter of principle and also as my princi-
> ple I only work on Sundays if I have to ... no I won't let it impinge
> on home life because I think it's too important and I'm quite con-
> vinced anyway that people work better if they work in intense
> bursts rather than never getting a break from it. So I don't do that.
> (Male Dean of Social Sciences, pre-1992)

A few respondents talked about coping with their managerial and academic work in a relatively flexible manner, though it still seems to be at
some cost to themselves, not least because the work still has to be done:

> I do in fact take one day a week when I work at home on my
> research, but I come into the office all day on a Saturday to compen-
> sate for that, when I get no interruptions or 'phone calls or staff or
> students ... I do take work home with me. (Female HoD, Business,
> post-1992)

The issue of whether manager-academics 'choose' to work long hours is
not a straightforward one. Many of our respondents claimed to be
working for upwards of 60 hours per week:

> In here for half seven and I suppose gone by seven in the evening.
> So, I typically put in eleven and a half, twelve-hour days. I find that
> my, if I put in more than a fourteen hour day, fourteen and a half
> hours, if I put two or three of those in on the trot, I'm totally
> washed out, right, but there is a level of stamina, you know, that's
> needed day on day. (PVC, post-1992)

Our data suggest that many manager-academics find it hard to confine
their work to their workplace and daytimes only. Their work

substantially permeates all of their life. Though this may be no different from other managerial jobs, outside the public services pay rates
and fringe benefits are likely to be much higher and may compensate
for lack of time by providing more money and consumption opportunities. Schor found in her research on work and leisure in the USA that
few private sector workers would choose shorter working hours in
return for less money and more leisure time (Schor, 1991). Hochschild
(1997) suggests that many people use work as an escape from the more
difficult challenges of family life. Indeed, a considerable number of our
male respondents, including fathers, did not see their work hours as a
matter of concern; rather, it tended to be mothers who saw long hours
as a problem. Some argue that the gendered division of labour in
households is lessening or makes use of paid help (Gershuny, 1992;
Goodnow and Bowes, 1994; Gregson and Lowe, 1994). Nevertheless,
gendered differences persist (Office for National Statistics, 1998) even
in middle-class households, though research on same-sex couples indicates that divisions of labour in households tend to be on a different
basis from that in heterosexual couples (Heaphy *et al.*, 1999). The pri-
oritization of men's employment was most marked for men from the
fifties and sixties age group, so this may also relate to generational
factors. Three decades ago, the percentage of employed mothers of
young children was much lower and so older male manager-academics
may have experiences which are distinct from those of their younger
colleagues.

The impression we gleaned from many manager-academics was that
work and time pressures have increased in universities in the last
decade, perhaps as a consequence of some of the new managerial techniques and ideas discussed at the beginning of our chapter, as well as
being related to increased undergraduate intakes. This in turn has
meant that evenings and weekends are spent not, as in the past, on
research but on teaching preparation and administration, and that
further inroads are being made into life outside work. The question of
how much harder manager-academics can work, however, is undoubtedly an important one and one to which the answer must surely shape
the future of the sector.

Conclusion

The use and deployment of many different kinds of personal, departmental, activity-specific, institutional, extra-institutional and

home/personal time horizons, cycles and priorities is a major feature of the careers, management practices and work/home relationships of many of the manager-academics we have interviewed. Though individuals respond differently to the pressures they experience, some common patterns were visible, including those based on gender processes, parenthood (especially motherhood), the employ-ment situation of partners, continued involvement in research, and generational values and practices. To what extent the long working hours and spilling over of work time into home time is a product of personal choice and the 'traditional' academic way of life, and to what extent it is brought about by new forms of managerialism, is something which will need to await further analysis of our data. However, it does seem that some of the external pressures (research assessment, subject teaching review, declining unit of resource, widening participation for students) which government and higher education funding agencies have introduced to UK universities may have increased workloads and raised the expectations others have of academics, and those who manage them. Academics with a passion for research have probably, like others with an obsessional interest in their occupation, worked long hours in the evenings and at week-ends for decades. However, it seems unlikely, until recently, that those in manager-academic posts worked such unsocial hours on administration. It is certainly a time *of* management in higher edu-cation and perhaps too a time ripe *for* management, but finding the time for that managing seems to be proving ever more challenging.

Acknowledgements

Thanks to the rest of the project team for many discussions on the careers and institutional context of manager-academics. Many thanks also to our many willing interviewees, to Rachel who collected much of the interview data used here, and Heidi Edmundson and Cheryl Scott for their tape transcriptions.

Notes

1. Manager-academics is a term used to refer to academics who have taken on management roles. It is preferred to the term academic manager, which could equally refer to a professional manager or administrator who has responsibility for some aspect of the work of academics.

2. The project was funded by the ESRC, grant number R00237761, between 1/10/98 and 30/9/00. The research team consisted of the authors plus Oliver Fulton, Rachel Johnson, Mike Reed and Stephen Watson, all based at Lancaster University at the time of the study.
3. The post-1992 universities are former polytechnics, which were once run by local government and were more hierarchical and bureaucratic than the pre-1992 universities.

10
'Big Brother is Watching You!': Call Centre Surveillance and the Time-Disciplined Subject

David Knights and Pamela Odih

Introduction

The growth of call centres in the UK has been rapid and extensive. Approximately 250,000 people work in call centres – more than 1 per cent of the working population (Datamonitor, 2000). Female part-time and full-time workers constitute 70 per cent of all call centre staff (Belt, 1999). But the industry has been beset by attrition rates averaging between 45 and 70 per cent and absenteeism at 4.7–6.1 per cent per month (Datamonitor, 2000). Part of the problem relates to 'work intensification' and an endemic 'culture of surveillance'. Within academic circles and in the media, call centres have often been described in distinctly Orwellian terms. In these 'white-collar factories' hundreds of employees are arranged in serried ranks to handle a seemingly endless flow of customer telephone inquiries. The new generation of monitoring technology is extremely powerful. It can analyse 'keystrokes' on terminals to determine whether employees are making efficient use of their time between telephone conversations. Employers can tap phones, read e-mails and monitor computer screens. The possibility, and in some cases the coercive use, of surveillance techniques for call centre personnel is dramatic, intense and secretive. This surveillance can involve not only a constant measurement of performance but also other pressures associated with an intensification of work.

As a result of these processes, there has been a tendency to see call centres as a contemporary version of the nineteenth century sweatshop or those 'dark Satanic mills'. Theoretical supports for the 'sweatshop' view of call centres and similar IT-intensive workplaces has, in part, come from an increasing use of a deterministic Foucauldian perspective on discipline at work (Arkin, 1997; Fernie and Metcalf, 1997; Sewell and Wilkinson, 1992). Incessant dedication to electronic performance monitoring and ubiquitous accumulation of coded information are described as typifying disciplinary modes of regulating activities in time-space. But there is a tendency in these accounts to read Foucault's conception of subjectivity 'as a product of controlling and dominating social bonds ... of the person as simply responding to disciplinary power' (Ezzy, 1997, p. 428). In short, this use of Foucault fails to recognize the distinction between subjects being constituted *through* rather than *by* a variety of disciplinary technologies that reinforce and reproduce existing inequalities at work and within wider society more broadly (Knights and McCabe, 1998a). Conversely, our research has been more sanguine concerning the realistic, as opposed to the theoretical, potential of using technology to control employees in this fashion. Employers' dependence on emotional labour (Hochschild, 1983) and the social skills of their call centre staff to ensure high levels of customer service mean that the employee relationship has to be managed extremely carefully (see also Frenkel *et al.*, 1998; Taylor and Bain, 1998).

The ethnographic research presented in this chapter was conducted in a UK financial services call centre that historically had seemed to switch back and forth between 'hard' performance-driven, and 'soft' service-quality-based, management strategies. When the research began in February 1997, management stressed the quality of service encounters and thereby within that framework allowed staff considerable time and space to perform their jobs as they thought fit. This 'process' style of management had been in existence for five or six years, having partially replaced earlier quantitative 'task'-oriented concerns with productivity. By the end of the research in October 1998, a rekindling of the anxiety about productivity levels resulted in a demand for a stricter timing of calls and performance measurement. As we shall see, this created tensions not least because it conflicted with recently introduced quality management initiatives but, more importantly, it violated the levels of service quality with which staff had begun to identify. Consequently, the performance programmes, which seek to increase productivity through reducing call handling and abandonment rates, were met with a mixed reception, ranging from resistance to reluctant accommodation. The close attachment to service quality had arisen, partly despite management, largely because of an identification with customers that could be seen as a response of staff to a situation that otherwise might have little to offer except a monotonous routine and increasing levels of work intensification.

But staff had another weapon in their armoury to resist too coercive or heavy-handed a system of management control: the company brand. If calls had constantly to be terminated abruptly because of standard times, what might this do for the brand reputation that had taken years to establish? There was not militant resistance to the intensification of time discipline because, like all call centre staff, they were used to the pressure to keep down call waiting times and the electronic call boards were a constant reminder of this obligation both to customers and colleagues. Also, given the importance of meaningful projects to the securing of a solid sense of identity, it is not surprising to find self-disciplined individuals transforming themselves into time-disciplined corporate subjects. What is surprising is the failure of some academic literatures to recognize this aspect of Foucault's (1979) analysis of disciplinary technology and, perhaps more importantly, the subtle forms of resistance that often ensue.

This chapter is structured as follows. The first section provides a brief overview of the literature on call centres in so far as this has implications for work intensification and time/space discipline in the labour process. Second, the ethnography of the call centre and several key analytic themes emergent from the ethnography are defined and discussed in relation to concepts, issues and topics in the literature. Finally some concluding reflections are offered on how the chapter contributes to the development of workplace analyses of call centres.

Time discipline at work

Recently, several literatures have challenged the prevalence of linear discourses of time in organizational analysis. Hassard (1990) and Clark (1985), for example, have drawn attention to the limitations of treating time as exclusively homogeneous and quantitative and to the plural temporality of organizational life. As Clark (1985, p. 6) expresses it, 'the central time problem' for organizational sociology is to penetrate behind the metaphor of clock time, upon which existing approaches to the 'time dimension' rely. Whipp (1994) describes the way in which Clark shows 'how contrasting industries lead organisations to develop "repertoires" of rules, structures and forms of action to meet the varying rhythms of demand, competition and regulation' (p. 103). Such rules rely upon everyday common-sense knowledge (Schutz, 1967) but, none the less, are vital means of accounting for and coping with the negotiated timetables of organizational life. Whipp

(1994, p. 103) draws upon the notion of temporal repertoires in his work on time and management stating that "the notion of structural and temporal repertoires is based on the recursiveness of the irregular, sometimes cyclical, event-based trajectories of the firm". This reading of temporality recognizes the extent to which subjectivity is a reflexive, fluid and often precarious process instantiated through the time-space events, which it also serves to constitute (Mouffe, 1992). In this sense,

> governable spaces are not fabricated counter to experience; they make new kinds of experience possible, produce new modes of perception, invest percepts with affects, with dangers and opportunities, with saliences and attractions. (Rose, 1999, p. 32)

Our work extends this Foucauldian-inspired proposition by identifying how our call centre staff secure a sense of their own subjectivity and identity through the incessant codification and material organization of conduct in time and space.

The ethnography of the BNFS call centre

The ethnographic case study took place in the call centre of a major retail financial services company whose brand name and reputation were well established: the pseudonymous Brand Name Financial Services. The research focused on the telephone service encounter although various departments were investigated on a systematic basis. The main departments were customer service, including resource and support, credit services, new business and life and pensions/savings and investment. The research involved intensive fieldwork and feedback meetings with the company's management and staff (see Knights et al., 1998; 1999). The methodology adopted combines 'critical ethnography' (Wainwright, 1997) with 'organisational ethnography' (Bate, 1997), thus synthesizing a focus on the meanings and definitions of organizational members with a critical examination of the historical and organizational context of their production and reproduction.

Our research methods comprised conversational analysis of tape-recorded service encounter interactions, observational techniques, discourse analysis of organizational documents and unstructured interviews. Telephone customer advisers in BNFS work in teams of eight with a senior adviser and a team manager. Typically an adviser will simultaneously be doing screen work and scripted call work with the customer while at the desk on a set of headphones. The average numbers of calls per hour is 26 and time spent on the telephone is 80 per cent of the working day. The abandonment rate (i.e. calls not taken to a successful conclusion), the reduction of which is highly prioritized, is 7 per cent. The centre is open 8am until 8pm with a mix of full-and part-time staff doing various eight-hour shifts. To borrow a phrase, it is 'all day, every day' (Westwood, 1984).

Analytic themes, data and discussion

The shift away from a 'task'-oriented focus on productivity towards a more 'process' concern with the quality of service encounters had occurred just before our arrival as researchers at BNFS. Characteristic of the 'hard' aspects of quality management (Hill, 1991), the previous 'task'-oriented culture was predominantly concerned with statistical monitoring and performance measurement standards. Recognizing that statistical measurements take place within a social context, where their human interpretation remains paramount, the process approach seeks to complement quantitative calculations of performance with qualitative support for staff to improve customer service.

A series of structural changes (the emergence of team managers, for example), initiatives and strategies (such as tape reviews, team talks and Quality Assurance) dedicated to quality resulted from the development of a more 'process'-oriented culture. The following transcript excerpt provides an insight into the impact of this approach on the service encounter:

> Those techniques are actually trained to actually help the adviser deal with the calls. Not, that is, not necessarily trained in terms of high call volume, it is overall in terms of telephone techniques in order to help the adviser. When the calls are queuing we don't say you better hurry up, because that is not what we are about, we are about customer service and how ever much that customer requires our attention we hope that we can give it. The call control training just helps them ... but by no means is it associated with when 23 calls are queuing then you use the speed up process, that's not what it is about at all. (Trainer)

Partly as a result of this training but perhaps also because of the relational conceptions of time held by the staff, customer service was a deeply embedded value that strongly defined the meanings, reality and sense of self-identity of customer advisers. Characteristic of the 'soft' aspects of quality management (Hill, 1991), this 'process' orientation has, as its main concern, the gearing of every activity and member of the organization towards serving the final customer. Activities performed within the organization are reconstituted into interlinking segments of a 'quality chain'. Through quality initiatives, every level of the organization reflects and reinforces the corporate desire for excellent quality service. The levels of commitment and quality performance needed to sustain the desire for excellence are achieved through a process-centred training programme.

Process time and 'emotional labour'

It is significant that the call centre is staffed predominantly by young women, although BNFS has begun to see the benefit of recruiting more mature women, especially because of their potential to assume informal leadership roles in team-working (Kerfoot and Knights, 1994). This gender division of labour conforms to a well-established tradition of service industry employment. However, it could be argued that women's experience of surviving in a male-dominated and often macho culture has meant that they have acquired social skills that prove highly effective in service and sales encounters (Hochschild, 1983). One particular skill that was heavily emphasized by training and personnel managers was 'empathy', eloquently expressed in the following excerpt:

> [Empathy] which is all about looking at you and the customer's relationship, [and asking] what else can we do for the customer. So it is going beyond APTUS [Consultant techniques of how to handle the customer, how to control, how to keep the customer informed]. It was looking at OK you have got the customer on the line. You have got your techniques your telephone procedures but what else can we do to exceed their expectation with BNFS so that they will always remember us with yes BNFS have always provided me with an excellent customer service. (Trainer)

'Emotional labour' is an integral feature of achieving empathy. Following Hochschild (1983, p. 7), we define emotional labour to mean 'the management of feeling to create a publicly observable facial and bodily display'. It is our contention that empathy's emotional labour encourages a 'process orientation', where time is enmeshed in social relations. Several processes may intertwine simultaneously and the fabric of life is patterned by the multiple criss-crossing chains of processes. In some cases, schedules and clock time may have structured the activity originally but unexpected exigencies frequently call for the abandonment of a clock-time relationship and bring process time to the fore instead. (Davies, 1994, p. 280)

This involves a more flexible relation to time, where 'the task itself defines the amount of time to be consumed, rather than a time limit or temporal demarcation being placed on the task' (Davies, 1990, p. 37). These literatures provide for highly insightful attempts to deconstruct dominant understandings of time (see especially Davies, 1990 and Leccardi, 1996) through, for example, drawing our attention to 'women's time' as embodied in daily life (Davies, 1990). Whilst feminist suggestions of distinct 'male/linear' and 'female/process' times draw our attention to the significance of gender in the discursive constitution of time, their insufficient theorization of power and subjectivity has the unintended consequence of reproducing the very phallocentric discourse (Irigaray, 1980) that feminism seeks to challenge. Conversely, primarily informed by the writings of Foucault, the discourse of gendered time expressed here has as its premise a conceptualization of power and subjectivity as grounded in the exercise of power through social practices in which subjects are embedded. Subjectivity is constituted through the exercise of power within which conceptions of personal identity come to be generated:

Where subjectivity is constituted in and through discourse, the gender identity of men and women as masculine and feminine subjects is socially constituted in and through certain sites, behaviours and practices at any one time. (Kerfoot and Knights, 1994, p. 70)

Gender identities are, in this sense, historically contingent, unstable and potentially multiple. This notion of the discursive production of gendered subjects within and between power relations provides a means of reconciling the 'women's time'/linear time dualism inherent in feminist discourses of gendered time (Odih, 1999, p. 11). Instead of polarizing the masculine and feminine conceptions of time along the lines of biological/social gender, we conceptualize 'feminine' time as discursively constituted as 'feminine' through particular identities but not in such a way as to be exclusive to, or exhaustive of, the lives of women. The dualistic opposition between an essential 'female time' and equally essential 'male/linear time', evident in feminist discourses of gendered time, is dissolved by a recognition of the discursive constitution of gender identities and their potential multiplicity. However, the materialism of modern existence and the social practices that flow from it reflect and reinforce expressions of time grounded in the hegemony of commodified, economically valued, individualistic, linear time (Knights and Odih, 1995; Odih, 1998). Game (1991, p. 26) describes how 'a conception of time as homogeneous and empty, or abstract is associated with a desire for identity and a whole, a desire to know what the social is in its totality'. For it is only when time is conceived of as homogeneous that it can be held still in order that the 'whole' can be revealed to the 'objective' observer.

Linear discourses of time, therefore, reflect and reproduce conceptualizations of the social world which seek to represent the world as an intelligible whole, rendering it readily manipulable for instrumental purposes. Clear parallels exist between this instrumental manner of relating to the world and 'masculine' ways of being. Writers have variously identified contemporary discourses of masculinity as discursively bound up with an estrangement and disembodiment from the particularity of human existence (Seidler, 1989). Kerfoot and Knights (1994, p. 86) describe this form of masculinity as 'abstract and highly instrumental with respect to controlling its objects, thus sustaining a mode of relating to externalities that is self-estranged and wholly disembodied'. Linear time by definition involves a kind of transcendence that trivializes the specificity of the finite moment. It requires a kind of estrangement from the present that entails dematerialization, abstraction and disembodiment (Ermarth, 1992). In the writings of Foucault (1979, 1982) we come to recognize the inextricable links between subjectification and linear conceptions of time. *Discipline and Punish* (1979) is replete with references to subjectification as necessitating the 'control' of time/space in strategies such as the separation of individuals, the homogenization of physical being, activity and the installation of permanent and intensive forms of surveillance.

Returning to our case study, masculine preoccupations with control and conquest are routinely reproduced by task-oriented demands for quantitative results in improved performance, productivity and profitability. An incessant dedication to electronic performance monitoring and ubiquitous accumulation of coded information typifies masculine preoccupations with transforming everything and everyone into an object of control and conquest (Kerfoot and Knights, 1994). The introduction of processual working practices implied a challenge, discontinuity and/or disruption of the hegemonic linear rationalities associated with task-oriented production. Process time is both a condition and consequence of specific management practices, geared towards the achievement of 'empathy' with consumers. Accountability and self-discipline are central to the production of 'empathy'. But the demand for empathy means that adviser–customer relations and interactions rather than productivity performance measures are more likely to condition the time that is spent in service or sales encounters. This generates some tensions, if not contradictions, in the management of call centre staff.

Task and process tensions

The organization's task and process orientations are productive of two specific modes of relating to call duration. The task orientation assumes that the call occurs within a predefined amount of time (i.e. a 200-second average handling time). Call duration in this sense is a specified quantity, an abstract singular unit, homogeneous though divisible into discrete elements (i.e. 200-seconds). According to this task orientation, the duration of the call translates directly into money; it is a commodity – a resource that can be used to coordinate activities. But this task-oriented perception of the call duration is deployed without reference to content or context. It is unable to recognize that empathy is a relational quality and not a numeric quantity.

By contrast, the process orientation has no predefined perception of call duration. The service encounter/call itself defines the amount of time to be consumed rather than a time limit being placed on it. For customer advisers, a process orientation to the service encounter facilitates a holistic comprehension of their role and its significance to the organization as a whole. Furthermore, a process orientation can ameliorate some of the repetitive monotony of telephone work, the separation of employees from one another, and the routinized processing of abstract or depersonalized pieces of data or information. The benefits and advantages of a process orientation to the service encounter are expressed in the following transcript:

> I think that the only way that I can get overall satisfaction is to really know that I have done the job properly. In a way you become a robot. You do generally, I'm not saying that I achieve it every time. You do have to feel that you have done that right and that

you have done everything that you possibly can. It is the only way that you get satisfaction. Otherwise it does get very, very repetitive. And even sorting out queries you know if there is an ongoing thing. To sort of trace it up. I quite like doing that. Usually it is quite nice to have to see where it leads. To come in on Monday morning it is quite nice to start that off ... (Customer Adviser)

Whilst customer advisers are trained to be processual in relation to the service encounter and prioritize the needs of the customer, this often runs up against the task-related pressures of call volume. As the following excerpt demonstrates, the conflict between call volume and quality of service presents a continuous dilemma:

there is in the fact that if they do follow something through and it is something which is a little bit unusual then we say keep a note of it so when you go for your review to the team manager they are aware that you are taking customer service a step further ... But time wise, call volume wise doesn't allow them to. But again if you have a customer that is really upset and you take it upon yourself to sort it out it is going to make your job more interesting, isn't it? (Trainer)

Towards the end of our research it was noted that the re-adoption of a task-oriented approach (evidenced by productivity measures) was encouraging a rigid time perception of call duration, which contradicted the processual time perceptions promoted during training. A sophisticated management control system, including monitoring technology, forms part of the disciplinary apparatus for staff. The call centre is clearly an environment where staff are under pressure to perform, in terms of both quality and quantity of output. In terms of quantitative measurement, staff operate under a timed pressure system where everything is routinely measured and monitored. The number of calls queuing (NCQ), average delay in queuing (ADQ), average speed of answer (ASA), number of agents signed in (NAGNT) are calculated instantly and visually displayed on electronic call boards in the centre for all the teams to see. A range of productivity statistics is then produced relating to individual and team performance on a daily, weekly and monthly basis. Although there are no formal statements, an informal understanding of around twenty calls handled per hour has emerged as the norm. This ultimately serves to discipline the staff in a competitive way since they attempt to reach the norm and, indeed, feel guilty if they fall below it with any regularity. Equally, to miss a queuing call is frowned upon by the staff themselves as not only underperforming but, more importantly, 'letting the customer down'. Here we can see a collective commitment to customers that operates to discipline performance, yet requires no explicit sanctions from management. Telephone performance thus becomes individualized and competitive even though there is no formal system of reward such as commission-based salaries to support it. In terms of the quality of performance, service encounters are taped regularly for purposes of appraisal monitoring and quality audits. Within such tape reviews ordinarily between the adviser and her supervisor (see also Frenkel *et al.*, 1998), staff are marked according to scripted responses and techniques such as politeness, conversational control, clarity of information, addressing service opportunities and standard opening and closings. Throughout the exchange, staff are expected to adhere consistently to the mission messages of 'quality, value and service'.

Temporal clashes, resistances and attrition

Motivation and staff training have become big issues within the call centre industry although, according to Frenkel *et al.* (1998, p. 965), companies typically spend only 5 per cent of their business unit budgets on training. Recruitment consultants Austin Knight (1997) conducted a study into call centre management and staff motivation. The survey of 1,000 call centre employees revealed that more than half felt morale was low. While some companies have labour turnover rates as low as 4 per cent a year, in others it is above 30 per cent. Burnout varies depending on the company and the product but, on average, call centre operators last 18 months before moving on to another job, albeit in exactly the same line of business. Whilst presently experiencing lower than average attrition levels, BNFS's customer service employees spoke of low morale and significant levels of stress and frustration. Our findings suggest these emotions to be in part the consequence of temporal clashes between task and process orientations to the service encounter. This conclusion is further confirmed by the following reports of dissatisfaction as regards the role of Senior Customer Advisers.

The role of Senior Customer Advisers (SCAs) is critical in call centre culture. They act as a buffer between advisers and management. Half of their time is spent on calls and half on escalated problem calls and project management. They are encouraged to become multi-skilled across various functions to increase their flexibility and ensure service quality. A central objective of quality management is that of involving every member of the organization in the corporate pursuit of excellent service quality. But when the metaphorical 'quality chain' is directly competing with call volume, then task becomes paramount. SCAs are currently being encouraged to subordinate their quality exercises to more task-oriented activities during periods of high call volume.

> Well at the moment I think that it is almost to do with the TCS and the monitoring of the seniors' roles. I can understand that I ought to get on the 'phones, on the other hand I think that they ought to take us out of the 'phone equation and anytime we can get on to the 'phone it is a bonus. Rather than try and sort of say that you have got to be on the 'phones for 25–60 per cent of the time. Because I think my prime part of the job is helping the other people not just in my team but throughout the whole company. (Senior Customer Adviser)

This process versus task clash is even more evident when one enquires into the SCAs' role in Quality Assurance (QA), the period immediately after training in which the newly qualified Customer Advisers (CAs) are quality checked to ensure that their work meets the necessary standards. According to their original role description, SCAs are responsible for Quality Assurance, yet they are not being allocated sufficient time to provide the QA coaching prescribed by their role. Moreover, it is quite often the case that, in the absence of SCAs, other less experienced members of the team are providing the quality assurance for new starters. This situation, and the resulting tensions, would appear to be a consequence of a growing conflict between output/performance and quality/service cultures within the organization. But what is particularly interesting here is how employees negotiate the conflicting temporal and other demands of a re-emerging task-oriented organizational culture. This is evidenced in the following excerpt where the respondent discusses her forthcoming performance tape-review:

> You do have choice on whether they tell you or not. Sometimes you prefer not to be told about it. It is good to get appraised because it confirms that you are doing the right things once it's pointed out to you. (Customer Adviser)

Significantly, by opting not to be told when her performance manager would be listening to her transactions to assess their quality, this individual had inadvertently extended the realms of her regulation to any time during the performance review. Our point is that, through identifying with an idea of quality inscribed in organization culture, ideology and practice, employees contribute to the intense forms of surveillance that serve to regulate their conduct. Integral to these conditions of subjectification is the articulation of what staff commonly refer to as 'the company way': a combination of commitment to exemplary standards of customer service quality and ongoing customer focus. Although partly organizational mythology, the 'company way' is simultaneously a descriptive category used by many staff to reconcile the tempo-spatially conflicting shifts, transformations and contradictions in organizational dictates and procedures.

Discussion

For a generation of sociologists, advances in information technology provide a near-perfect analogy of the principle of discipline. The incessant dedication to electronic performance monitoring and ubiquitous accumulation of coded information evident in call centre operations are often cited as typifying disciplinary modes of regulating activities in time-space (e.g. Sewell and Wilkinson, 1992). But there is a tendency here to interpret Foucault's account of disciplinary technologies as hyper-rational tempo-spatial systems capable of 'electronically tagging' (*ibid.*), tracing and regulating passive bodies within insidiously coercive 'information panopticons'. Axiomatic to this techno-determinist reading of Foucault (1979) is an absolutist conception of linear time/space as well as a heavily circumscribed, if not deterministic, conception of subjectivity. But this limited reading fundamentally fails to recognize Foucault's *Discipline and Punish* as detailing technologies and techniques constituted through the cooperation of linear and social times. As he expresses it:

> The disciplinary methods reveal a linear time whose moments are integrated, one upon another, and which is orientated towards a terminal, stable point; in short, an 'evolutive time'. But it must be recalled that, at the same moment, the administrative and economic techniques of control reveal a social time of a serial, orientated cumulative type; the discovery of an evolution in terms of 'progress' ... (Foucault, 1979, p. 160)

Foucault's account of discipline is clearly not limited to the quantitative dimensions of linear time. Rather, social times involve a 'discovery of an evolution in terms of genesis ... of individual', whilst linear time makes possible the 'serration of activities ... in each moment of time', the 'possibility of accumulating time and activity, of rediscovering them, totalized and usable in a final result ... ' (p. 160). Social times enable the subjectification of subjects, whereby 'the small temporal continuum of individuality-genesis certainly seems to be, like the individuality-cell or the individuality organism, an effect and an object of discipline' (p. 161). The co-presence of objectifying linear and subjectifying social times induces 'a macro- and a micro-physics of power', a 'temporal unitary, continuous, cumulative dimension in the exercise of controls and practices of domination' (p. 160). It is at this interface that 'power is articulated directly into time', assuring its control and guaranteeing its use.

To varying degrees our case study illustrates subjectification as concerning the establishment of forms of relations of self with self through disciplinary practices and the incessant codification and material organization of conduct in time and space. It illustrates how subjectivity is constituted in and through the embedded temporalities of management practices in general and quality processes in particular. Consistent concerns with achieving 'empathy', through person-centred service delivery encouraged a 'processual' orientation to both the content and duration of the service encounter. Reconstituted as a care-centred activity, the service encounter is neither linear, continuous nor entirely measurable, rather it is part of several different ongoing, non-abstract processes, whereby, 'the task itself defines the amount of time to be consumed, rather than a time limit or temporal demarcation being placed on the task' (Davies, 1990, p. 37). The language and timing of empathy enabled employees to secure a sense of meaning and identity by acting in accordance with the norms and values that the quality programme conveyed.

But this process of identification also served to reproduce the employee's conditions of regulation and subjugation. For empathy as a form of emotional labour demands an engagement with self whereby 'she [sic] offers *personal*ized service, but she herself becomes identified with the -*ized* part of it' (Hochschild, 1983, p. 187; emphasis in original). Constructed and reconstructed through the qualitative embodied times of process, the subject becomes self-disciplined to securing work conditions which on the one hand offer a means of ameliorating the stultifying monotony of call centre work whilst on the other subject the employee to increased performance regulation. For empathy to be productive is has to be standardized. Or as one team manager expressed it, 'efficiency linked with quality ... at the end of the day, with the nicest will in the world it is still a business. It still has to make money.' Consequently, there is no question of quality programmes resulting in the abandonment of performance as a control in our case study. Indeed, our work further confirms that the distinctively social character of call centre work demands a greater reliance on managing through identity and this is often a process dependent on comparative performance. The team manager quoted earlier described at length how customer advisers had increasingly sought quantitative measures by which to compare their progress; as he expresses it:

> Conversations I have had, it becomes apparent to me that people want to measure themselves against something. They feel starved of some kind of, I don't whether it is efficiency measure but they feel starved of some kind of target. They want something to work towards. (Team manager)

Munro (1998, p. 53) describes how in the post-bureaucratic organization 'what counts is both singing from the same hymn sheet as your superiors and delivery of the auditable numbers for which you have agreed to be responsible'. Dividing practices (Foucault, 1982) then separate the good performers from the bad, with extra training from the former often being given to the latter in case the identity of performance delivery has not 'caught on'. It is necessary to recognize that, despite considerable tension and some conflict surrounding working intensification demands, resistance to new productivity and performance measures is comparatively constrained. Rather employees willingly engage in training programmes geared at producing normative standards of delivery. But here resides a paradox. If the social times of quality management have effectively transformed individuals into self-disciplined subjects who are involved in their work body and soul, why is the call centre industry currently beset by high rates of attrition?

Knights and McCabe (1998b, p. 192) identify quality innovations as frequently failing to reconcile 'an internal drive for control over processes and people' with 'the trust, teamworking and creative processes that are also asserted to be a condition of quality management'. Consequently the conditions of quality innovation are simultaneously contradicted by management's preoccupation with control translated as the standardization of quality service delivery. Whilst alleviating the repetitive and routinized conditions of call centre work, the embodied qualitative times of process provide little protection against the quantitative disembodied times of 'speed-up'. Variations undoubtedly exist with regard to employees' means of reconciling the conflicting temporal demands of quality and increasing levels of performance measurement. But for those employees seduced by the promise of a secure sense of self, the choices are limited. If they persevere with trying to meet the performance targets until the self is depleted and no longer able to achieve empathy, the quality of their work will suffer irretrievable deterioration. But if they try to preserve the quality of service encounters, it is likely they will miss their volume or performance targets and be subject to management discipline or dismissal. Either they reject the meaningful embodied social relations of quality or risk losing their jobs.

The management of the call centre labour process is therefore caught on the horns of a dilemma. On the one hand, managers are attracted to an intensification of work through IT-supported performance measures and techniques of surveillance. On the other hand, however, call centre employment is characterized by a uniquely social mode of work where staff performance is dependent on socially sensitive communication and involves the whole person and not just the employee's physical participation. Meeting call volume performance targets, for example, may totally contradict the demands for quality and customer service.

Summary and conclusion

This chapter has examined the conduct of call centre staff in one case study and has questioned the labelling of these new, admittedly work-intensive developments in workplace organization as a modern equivalent of the nineteenth-century sweatshop. Part of the analysis is focused on developing our understanding of the self-disciplined subject and call centre workplace subjectivity. Some recent research on call centres has recognized subjectivity as both the medium and outcome of time/space events (Baldry, 1998; Taylor and Bain, 1998). Of particular interest to our work, Collinson and Collinson (1997) examine the processes of negotiation and resistance through which global processes of time/space come to be translated, within particular workplaces, into surveillance practices that have significant gender effects. Cognizant of a tendency for gendered discourses of time to 'romanticize' and 'essentialize' women's differences, Collinson and Collinson (1997) avoid conceptualizing 'gendered time/space'. Consequently, gendered time struggles to avoid an association with essentialized gender difference. Conversely, gendered time has been conceptualized in this chapter as discursively constituted through socially contingent gendered power/knowledge relations. Process time is both a condition and consequence of specific management practices, geared towards the achievement of 'empathy' with consumers.

Gendered time enabled an understanding of the social process whereby BNFS staff willingly turned themselves into self-disciplined subjects who put in performances without management having to use up resources in distributing rewards and sanctions. It was argued that the principle and practice of achieving empathy encouraged a processual relation to the service encounter. Integral to this orientation is an engagement with self and the exercise of emotional labour. These features enabled employees to attribute meaning and value to their work, and to limit the negative effects of the participation in routinized and repetitive tasks. But the capture of self in a culture of identifying with the customer and the emotional labour that this involves was also highly vulnerable to burnout frustration and even resistance. So, for example, there was muted if not open resistance to the 'speed-up' or accelerated work processes that were consequent on the re-emergence of a task-oriented culture. Part of this 'muted resistance' and/or resigned accommodation appears to be the consequence of subjective identification with BNFS's organizational commitment to quality, customer service and the brand. One might argue that inherent conflicts between the company's process and task orientation were reconciled by a renewed identification with and commitment to achieving the company's desire for quality customer service. This was evidenced by the desire amongst some employees for the re-introduction of quantitative measures to enable comparative assessments of their progress.

Our case study at BNFS may be seen as unique because of the distinctive role of the brand, the discretion, and the ease with which the company achieves its competitive success but the arguments arising from the case could have analytical purchase elsewhere. By understanding call centre workplace subjectivities in terms of their embeddedness in organizational imagery, branding, service ideology and work, we can begin to unravel the conditions and consequences of staff members' self-subjugation. If nothing else, the study encourages the analysis of call centres to move beyond the abject pessimism of research that sees call centres only in terms of the technologies of surveillance, on the one hand, and the uncalled-for optimism of the quality and virtual reality gurus, on the other. While not necessarily endorsing Frenkel *et al.*'s (1998) thesis regarding call centres being a hybrid form of organization that they call 'mass customised bureaucracy', we certainly share their view that current representations of call centre practices are far from satisfactory.

Part III
Time in Everyday Life

11

Are Long or Unsocial Hours of Work Bad for Leisure?

Ken Roberts

Working time – once again an issue?

Working time has resurfaced as a political issue in the UK partly as a consequence of European integration. We have been alerted to the fact that in Britain we work longer than our counterparts in all other European Union (EU) countries (Fagan, Chapter 6 in this volume; Fajertag, 1996; Noon and Blyton, 1997). Maybe we in Britain are less aware than our continental counterparts that European working hours are slightly shorter than in North America and in the Far East 'tiger economies'. The character of this issue varies considerably between what are otherwise very similar societies.

Another trend that has revived working time as an issue is the post-1970s lengthening of full-time employees' average hours of work. This trend first attracted comment in North America (see Schor, 1991), but it appears to be common to all the older, now mature, industrial countries. The spread of part-time jobs has concealed this trend. When part-time employees are excluded from the calculations, the same upward trend in full-time employees' typical working hours becomes evident in Britain and other EU countries (see Tyrell, 1995; Zuzanek *et al*, 1998). No one is certain as to the reasons for the recent reversal of the earlier, long-term decline in weekly working time. The 'greedy economy', fuelled by globalization and pressures on businesses to make themselves competitive and flexible, is a favoured, but not necessarily the correct, explanation. We know that in Britain it is managers and professional-grade employees, plus the self-employed, who have been responsible for the new trend (Holliday, 1996).

Two sets of reasons have been given for restoring downward pressure on working time in Europe and North America through collective bargaining and/or state intervention.

Redistributing work

Across continental Europe (unlike in Britain) it is widely believed that current levels of unemployment will be hauled down only by redistributing work from those already in paid jobs (see Blyton and Trinczek, 1996). A type of redistribution that has even wider support is from the current working population to the (early) retired. In the advanced industrial countries the long-term trend towards paid work accounting for a declining proportion of lifetime is in fact continuing, but in recent years nearly all of the extra free time has been accounted for by people retiring earlier and then living longer (see Robinson and Godbey, 1999).

The European Commission (1998, 1999) sees economic growth and the resultant job creation as the answer to Europe's current unemployment. The Commission points out that the number of people in employment in Europe is now at a historical high, and expects demand for labour to continue to grow steadily, and, it is hoped, even more strongly than in the recent past. Labour shortages, and acute skill shortages in key occupations, mainly connected with information technology, are now being predicted, prompting proposals to liberalize immigration policies. Other commentators dispute whether there really is more paid, or useful, work around than ever before. Some draw attention to the increase in the proportion of jobs that are part-time, and others to the spread of 'unproductive' work (see Bowring, 1999). Even the European Commission is persuaded of a need to redistribute paid work in favour of older (early retired) age groups, partly in order to prevent labour shortages spreading, but also to reduce the dependency ratio, which, it is feared, could impose intolerable burdens on social security systems.

The quality of life

The case for redistributing paid work can also be argued on quality-of-life grounds. Redistribution from those alleged to be overworked to the underworked – the unemployed and the (early) retired – is expected to lead to all-round improvements in the quality of life (see Martin and Mason, 1998; Robinson and Godbey, 1999).

Paid work is generally good for people. Having no paid work is damaging. The main exceptions are the principal carers of young children, people who are able to retire on adequate pensions and with interests around which to organize their time, and those whose jobs are physically or psychologically damaging (Haworth, 1997; Jackson and Taylor, 1994; McGoldrick, 1983; Warr, 1983). All these cases are exceptions to the general 'rule' that work is beneficial (for mental well-being), and that this usually still applies even when people do not like their particular jobs (Haworth, 1997). But it may be possible to have too much of what is basically a good thing. Critics of current trends argue that full-time employees are now becoming the kind of harried leisure class that Staffan Linder predicted in 1970. Complaints of time pressure are now common, particularly among women, and most especially among women with young children, but the complaints are more widespread. There is a widespread perception that life has speeded up, and that time has become more congested, thereby making life as a whole less leisurely than formerly (Garhammer, 1998; Robinson and Godbey, 1999; Zuzanek and Mannell, 1998). According to Mulgan and Wilkinson (1997), this will elevate time into a major political issue of this new century.

Long hours of work are believed to impair the quality of family life. Fathers in particular are said to be denied the opportunity to spend quality time with their children (Ferri and Smith, 1996). Moreover, the long-hours culture is alleged to be incompatible with sex equality: the demands on employees are said to be impossible unless the employees are either childless or have someone else (usually a wife) to act as principal child carer. Sex equality is seen as requiring moderate hours of work for all. Hence the case for seeking new strategies and alternatives to the long-hours, work-and-spend culture (Martin and Mason, 1998; Schor, 1998).

The spread of paid work into 'odd hours' can be seen as exacerbating any damaging effects of long hours on workers' quality of life. Shifts and unsocial hours are not new, but the amount of work scheduled outside the conventional working (week)day has increased due to the growth of spending on, and hence employment in, consumer services. It is likely that any damaging effects of shiftwork on people's social and domestic lives are becoming more and more widespread (see Roberts, 1999).

Methods

This chapter does not attempt to engage in, let alone to resolve, all these arguments. Its concern is limited to the relationships between hours of work (length and scheduling) and uses of leisure. The evidence is from a 1999 interview survey of a nationally representative English sample of 522, all aged 16 and over. The fieldwork was conducted by MORI, and the sample was selected from 58 sample points with quotas, based on 1991 census data, set for age, gender and working status.

The main purpose of this investigation was to develop and test measurements covering all aspects of the respondents' leisure, but here we focus on out-of-home leisure. In-home leisure is dominated by television viewing, and is known to expand or contract depending on whether or not people have other commitments or other things to do with their uncommitted time (see below). Checklist prompts were used to measure the total number of occasions on which respondents had taken part in out-of-home leisure activities during the previous four weeks, the total time devoted to these activities, the total money cost, and the number of different types of out-of-home leisure in which they had engaged during the previous year. These types (eight in total) were: participant and spectator sports and arts; entertainment; day visits and holidays; visits to libraries, art galleries and museums; and other local recreation. Questionnaires covering so many types of leisure are necessarily long and complex, but most items do not apply to most respondents because they never take part in the type of leisure in question. In order to assist its administration, the questionnaire used in this survey was programmed for computer-assisted interviewing (CAPI) using the In2itive suite of software. The questionnaire was adminstered in home-based face-to-face interviews. Answers were recorded on pen-operated tablet computers, and returned for analysis by modem link. In addition to the questions on leisure, respondents were also asked about their normal hours of work – the total per week, and whether they regularly, occasionally or never worked in the evenings, on Saturdays, and on Sundays. We know that people tend to exaggerate their hours of work when asked to estimate (compared with evidence from official statistics and time budgets), and we also know that, in the USA at any rate, this propensity to exaggerate has been increasing since the 1960s (Robinson and Godbey, 1999). Assessments of the extent to which people are now working longer have sometimes been inflated, but the apparent trend is not wholly accounted for by this rising propensity to exaggerate, though the fact that people tend to exaggerate is probably at least partly responsible for the widespread perception of life having become more hectic.

The analysis that follows (as opposed to the raw figures) is unlikely to be affected by any propensity to exaggerate. We compare groups with different self-reported hours of work (the propensity to exaggerate is not known to vary alongside hours actually worked). Moreover, the inequalities in self-reported working time are so great that it is inconceivable that they do not reflect real differences. Our analysis compares groups who said that they normally worked up to 29, 30–39, 40–48, and 49 and more hours per week, and those who reported that they regularly worked in the evenings and/or at weekends, those who did so occasionally, and those who never did so. The sample contained plenty of self-reported long hours of work: 24 per cent of the men and 7 per cent of the women with paid jobs said that they normally worked for more than 48 hours a per week. Working at 'odd hours' was even more common: 51 per cent of the men and 46 per cent of the women with paid jobs reported that they did so regularly.

The interviews also gathered information about each respondent's age and sex, household composition and income, and other standard demographic data. The total sample size, 522, is adequate for establishing aggregate norms and tendencies. In contrast, the numbers become small when the sample is split by age, sex and social class, and the findings in respect of particular socio-demographic groups should be treated cautiously.

Age, class and gender

It seems sensible to preface everything else by reporting that age and social class were by far the best predictors of the sample's overall levels of out-of-home leisure activity (see Table 11.1). The youngest age group (18–34) did the most, however 'most' was measured: the number of different occasions when they had participated in out-of-home leisure, the range, and the total time and money spent. People in mid-adult life (35–54) did and spent less, and the oldest age group (55 plus) did and spent less still.

The relationship between leisure and social class was similar. The middle class (ABCi) was more active than the working class (CiiDE) in every respect – total number of activities, range, time and money. These relationships were strong, linear, and present within all gender and class groups, and gender and age groups, respectively.

The relationship between leisure and gender was rather more complicated. Overall the women were participating in more separate out-of-home leisure occasions, and devoting more time overall to out-of-home leisure than men, but the men were spending more money. All these differences are fully in line with the findings from previous, comparable research (see Roberts, 1999).

Table 11.1   Sex, class, age and leisure

	Sex		Class		Age		
	Male	Female	ABCi	CiiDE	18–34	35–54	55+
Last 12 months							
Types of leisure (no.)	4.7	4.6	5.3	4.4	5.1	4.9	3.9
Last 4 weeks							
No. of occasions	38	45	57	32	51	47	26
Total cost (£)	317	278	337	276	351	280	230
Total time (hours)	79	94	103	77	115	80	65
N=	249	273	186	239	166	167	172

Source: National Leisure Survey pilot, 1999.

Relationships between leisure and all job characteristics (except social class) were weaker, often non-linear, and varied between socio-demographic groups. So although length of working time and whether or not people worked at 'odd hours' appeared to be making some difference to some groups' uses of leisure, these differences were neither as wide nor as consistent as those associated with age and social class.

Income

Following the variables subsumed under social class, the job-related factor exerting the strongest and most consistent effects on leisure was income. Income was unrelated to range (number of different types) of leisure activities. Otherwise, it appears from this evidence, as far as leisure is concerned, the higher the income the better. The highest income groups recorded the most leisure activities, and were spending the most time and (unsurprisingly) the most money on their out-of-home leisure (see Table 11.2). This applied throughout the sample overall, among men, among women, within all age groups, and within both social classes, though the income effect on leisure was somewhat more pronounced within the working class than within the middle class.

However, in all the socio-demographic groups it was only at the higher household income levels, above £500 per week in the cases of total time and occasions, and above £700 in the case of leisure spending, that income effects on leisure were consistent and pronounced (see Table 11.2). At lower levels, increases in household income may sometimes have boosted leisure activity and spending, but, in general,

Table 11.2 Income and leisure: weekly household income

	Under £100	£100–199	£200–299	£300–499	£500–699	Over £700
Last 12 months						
Types of leisure (no.)	2.2	2.6	3.0	2.6	3.2	2.4
Last 4 weeks						
No. of occasions	34	40	37	45	61	52
Total cost (£)	265	250	274	348	257	571
Total time (hours)	94	77	73	77	105	115
N=	75	69	66	67	52	31

Source: National Leisure Survey pilot, 1999.

it appeared that households with different below-average income levels must have been spending and saving the differences on general living costs rather than leisure activities. Leisure was really boosted only at above-average levels of income.

One qualification to this otherwise reasonably clear picture is that time devoted to leisure activities was in fact lowest in the middle-income groups. It was higher within the lowest-income groups, where many respondents were not employed (pensioners were well-represented) and therefore had plenty of spare time. However, the highest peak in time spent on out-of-home leisure activities was in the very highest income groups (where the main source of income was employment). Even in this specific (time-spent) respect, income was proving a more powerful booster of out-of-home leisure than time available: vivid confirmation of the power of money.

Length of working time

The relationships between working time and leisure were less clear cut. Length of working week was completely unrelated to levels of leisure spending, but positively related to the range of the sample's out-of-home leisure activities (those working the longest hours had the widest range) (see Table 11.3). Total time spent on out-of-home leisure and the number of separate occasions when people participated were highest in the groups with the shortest and longest working weeks. Part-time hours (29 or fewer per week) were boosting the amounts of time that respondents were spending on out-of-home leisure, and the number of occasions, but very long weekly working hours (over 48) were associated with even higher scores on leisure occasions, albeit

Table 11.3   Total hours worked and leisure

	Up to 29 hours	30–39 hours	40–48 hours	Longer
Last 12 months				
Types of leisure (no.)	2.8	2.5	3.0	3.3
Last 4 weeks				
No. of occasions	51	36	37	58
Total cost (£s)	361	338	376	333
Total time (hours)	116	66	81	91
N=	51	89	58	39

Source: National Leisure Survey pilot, 1999.

accounting for less time in total than the part-time workers' lesser number of leisure occasions.

This evidence suggests that hours of work need to be very short (officially part-time) before there is any leisure boost. Moreover, within our sample these advantages were confined to men (see Table 11.4). It was men's leisure (and not women's) that was benefiting (in terms of time spent and the number of separate out-of-home leisure occasions) when they worked less than 30 hours per week. In contrast, women on part-time schedules appeared to be deriving no leisure benefits whatsoever vis-à-vis women with longer work weeks. In fact it was the women who were working over 39 hours per week whose out-of-home leisure was the most buoyant.

The implication of this evidence is that hours of work need to be very short (officially part-time) before there is any leisure boost, and that this boost is distributed in a highly selective manner. In fact the

Table 11.4   Gender, hours worked and leisure: weekly working time (in hours)

(a) Men

	Up to 29 hours	*30–39 hours*	*40–48 hours*	*49+ hours*
Last 12 months				
Types of leisure (no.)	2.6	2.7	3.2	3.4
Last 4 weeks				
No. of occasions	66	31	36	45
Total cost (£s)	155	59	79	77
Total time (hours)	544	382	371	349
N=	17	41	39	31

(b) Women

	Up to 29 hours	*30–39 hours*	*40+ hours*
Last 12 months			
Types of leisure (no.)	2.9	2.4	2.9
Last 4 weeks			
No. of occasions	43	40	58
Total cost (£s)	98	72	105
Total time (hours)	281	299	345
N=	35	49	27

Source: National Leisure Survey pilot, 1999.

boost appears to be confined to the sections of the population with relatively light domestic obligations, typically men rather than women.

Odd hours

The evidence from this inquiry does not corroborate the view that odd hours of work damage people's leisure. Respondents who never worked at odd hours were spending the most money on out-of-home leisure, but only slightly more than those who worked odd hours regularly, and the latter had the highest scores on leisure occasions (see Table 11.5).

Time and money

Could the scarcity, indeed the almost complete absence, of strong and consistent relationships between hours of work and the leisure variables have been due to the countervailing influence of money? People who worked long and/or unsocial hours could have been over-represented among the higher earners. In reality money could not have been operating as a generally countervailing influence. People who were working fewer than 30 hours per week were over-represented in the lower income groups, but there were no clear differences in the typical household incomes of respondents who were working 30–39, 40–48 hours, and even longer. Similarly, there was no linear relationship between the frequency with which the respondents worked at odd hours and their incomes: those who worked occasionally at odd hours had higher incomes than those who did so both regularly and never.

The income variable used in this analysis is the household's rather than the individual's. Household income is the better indicator of the

Table 11.5   Working at odd hours and leisure

	Regularly	*Occasionally*	*Never*
Last 12 months			
Types of leisure (no.)	2.9	2.6	3.1
Last 4 weeks			
No. of occasions	47	36	41
Total cost (£s)	318	339	456
Total time (hours)	85	76	92
N=	131	75	52

Source: National Leisure Survey pilot, 1999.

financial resources that are available for leisure, especially since so much out-of-home (and in-home) leisure is family leisure. Some respondents with low personal incomes could have lived in high-income households, but the reverse is far less likely, and there would inevitably have been a positive overall relationship between personal and household incomes. So the main reason why money was not generally countervailing against any negative leisure effects of long and unsocial hours of work can only be that, throughout the UK workforce as a whole, hours of work and income are not closely related. They may be related at an individual level. People who work shifts are likely to receive financial compensation, and those who work overtime are also most likely to receive extra pay or improved career prospects. But throughout the workforce as a whole, inequalities in earned incomes appear to depend more upon occupation than the number of hours that people work, or their scheduling.

There is no plausible interpretation of the evidence presented here other than that, while money makes a very clear difference, leisure is only weakly and unevenly responsive to hours worked.

Discussion

Negative findings can be just as significant theoretically, and just as policy-relevant, as the most positive research results. Whatever the findings, it is necessary to adjust theories to the facts. And the crucial facts here are that the slightly longer working hours in the UK compared with other EU countries, the marginal increase in hours worked by full-time employees since the 1970s, and the spread of employment at odd hours, cannot be seriously damaging to leisure because leisure is largely immune from the working-time effects that would be necessary to inflict the damage.

Why the griping?

Our evidence offers no justification or explanation for the griping that is standard among employees who work exceptionally long, or at odd, hours (see for example, Inkson and Coe, 1993; Oliver, 1998). Our findings are neither exceptional nor new in this respect (see Roberts and Chambers, 1985; Robinson and Godbey, 1999), though it is important to note that this applies only within the actual range of variation. People who currently work above-average hours do not generally work so long that they can do nothing except recover in the remainder of their time.

The griping does not reflect genuine injuries (to leisure at any rate), but appears to be basically a cultural norm. Not to complain would be culturally unacceptable: it would be to slight one's friends and family, or to indicate that one was unable to enjoy leisure time. Moreover, even if they can adjust and preserve normal levels of leisure activity, people who work abnormally long or unsocial hours may still feel entitled to complain at having to make the adjustments. In some cases the complaints will be part of a bargaining stance, indicating to employers that financial compensation or career rewards are expected.

Time buffers

Although disposable income grew more rapidly than free time throughout the twentieth century, the populations of even the most economically advanced countries do not appear to have joined the harried leisure class forecast by Linder (1970) whose main leisure problem was to be 'finding the time'. Most people, certainly those who work just normal full-time hours, still appear to possess plenty of literally spare time. Most leisure time is spent at home. Television alone accounts for roughly a half of all leisure time. This, plus listening to the radio, gardening and reading are the uses of leisure that expand when people retire or become unemployed (see Long and Wimbush, 1985; Marsden, 1982).

Television is rarely named as a particularly pleasurable leisure activity by any section of the population (see Robinson and Godbey, 1999). It is rarely a leisure priority. Rather it is how people occupy themselves when they have nothing better to do. Home-based leisure operates as a time buffer. It can be squeezed when hours of work lengthen, thus preserving people's priority uses of leisure. Home-based leisure was excluded from the calculations here in order to prevent this analysis doing no more than demonstrating a truism: that if people increase their working time they must spend less time doing something else.

Time deepening, sovereignty and elasticity

There are other ways in which people can protect their leisure from working-time effects. Time sovereignty refers to individuals' ability to decide exactly when something should be done. Some people have significant time sovereignty in their paid jobs: for example, they may be able to decide when during a particular evening, or which evening, they will work late. Koen Breedveld (1996a) has shown that in the Netherlands (and most likely everywhere else) sovereignty over paid working time tends to be a middle-class prerogative. However, all people will have substantial time sovereignty in respect of many of their leisure activities, especially in these days of 24-hour cities and the video-recorder.

Time elasticity refers to the ability to make time by doing things more speedily (housework is high on elasticity) or by paying someone else to do things that would otherwise have been done personally – meal preparation, car servicing and home decorating, for example. This latter way of achieving time elasticity will be another prerogative of the higher-income, generally middle-class, groups.

Time deepening refers to how people can do more than one thing at once. People may watch television and do housework simultaneously. In a similar way, it is possible to visit a historical city, enjoy a meal out, and visit a theatre, all within a single day trip.

Money and time

Within the existing range of variation, income effects are much more powerful than working-time effects on leisure; hence the rationality of those workers who have a choice deciding to maximize their incomes, even if this means working longer and/or at unsocial hours. Workers who behave in these ways are not usually debasing but enhancing their leisure.

Income accounts for much of the social class variation in uses of leisure. Class differences blur within the upper income groups when household income is controlled, though at the lower income levels clear class differences persist, presumably reflecting the middle class's greater ability, or inclination, to preserve otherwise normal patterns and levels of leisure activity, due to various combinations of culture, plus past and expected future earnings.

Income effects on leisure are especially powerful at the upper end of the income range. High incomes lead to people spending not only more money, but also more time, on out-of-home leisure, and experiencing more occasions in total. Getting into, then climbing up, these higher income levels, irrespective of the work schedules that this involves, is more likely to be a response to leisure values than workaholism.

Working-time policy

The data and arguments presented above are consistent with Koen Breedveld's (1996b) claim that the current furore about overworking is a storm in a teacup, largely whipped up by hype-books and media scares. The EU directive currently in force stipulates a 48-hour ceiling on working time, but this ceiling is easily breached. It can be ignored if employees consent to work longer. Of course, employees can be pressured into consent through fear of job loss or loss of promotion prospects, for example. Hence the argument for making the ceiling more rigid, and maybe introducing more 'protective' legislation restricting employment at odd hours.

All the hard evidence suggests that, on balance, such measures will not protect, but will jeopardize, the quality of leisure of those affected. There are no overall leisure disadvantages in working in excess of 48 hours per week, while the inconvenience to consumers would probably outweigh the benefits to the leisure of the workers affected if further restrictions were imposed on employment at 'odd hours'.

Exerting downward pressure on normal working time may still be justified on other grounds – in order to redistribute work in favour of the unemployed and older age groups, for instance. While they have been noted, no attempt has been made to intervene in these particular arguments. Downward pressure on working time may also benefit family life and relationships, but it is doubtful if there will be benefits for family leisure. Children's leisure is likely to be enriched or impoverished depending mainly on the routines of adult family members. According to the above evidence, women's own leisure does not benefit when they work for less than 30 hours per week. Rather, women's leisure benefits when they work for 40 hours per week or more. At present there is simply no leisure case for using either collective bargaining or state regulation to depress working hours, or to restrict work at what are conventionally defined as unsocial hours.

Acknowledgements

The research on which this chapter is based was funded by the Department for Culture, Media and Sport as a pilot study for a National Leisure Survey in which the sample will be considerably larger. The findings reported here should therefore be regarded as indicative rather than conclusive, and all the conclusions are strictly provisional. The author would like to acknowledge the contributions of the other collaborators on the project, namely, Fred Coalter, Mike Collins, Chris Gratton, John Haworth and Peter Taylor. Needless to say, all the views expressed in this chapter are solely the author's.

12
Routine Matters: Narratives of Everyday Life in Families

Elizabeth B. Silva

Introduction

In this chapter, I explore the everyday routines of people who live interdependently in family contexts. I consider everyday routines of women and men along two main axes. The first involves an exploration of routines as situated lived experiences. What do women and men see as constituting their routines? How do these routines matter to them? What matters in routines? The second involves the location of routines within these lived experiences. My key concern is with what routines reveal about 'gendered locations' and 'intersubjective negotiations' in contemporary British society. I see 'gendered locations' as those structures and circumstances in the lives of women and men where questions of differential power and privilege are central (Code, 1995). By 'intersubjective negotiations' I understand the constitution of subjectivity, as an interactive process, when lives are interconnected (Griffiths, 1995). I am also concerned to explore the links between routines and everyday life. How do routines shape, and how are they shaped by, everyday life? How does everyday life relate to broader contexts? Everyday life generally means the taken-for-granted continuum of the most mundane activities, and it has been strongly identified with women, because it has been linked with repetition and routine (Featherstone, 1992; Lefebvre, 1984). However, there is no singular or universal entity called everyday life, and I want to concentrate on a key aspect of the concept, which has linked the everyday to an implicit gendered location.

Routine is crucial to the organization of daily life. Yet a renewed concern with the everyday in cultural studies in the 1980s stressed the innovative dimensions of the everyday to the detriment of its repetitive character (Felski, 1999). Certeau (1984), for instance, stressed agency and resistance as an innovative practice of the everyday, yet in doing so his account lost sight of the mundane. However, feminist perspectives concerned with everyday life have stressed that the mundane is a major site of innovation in practices that challenge established patterns of living. A concern with the everyday has meant giving a place to the experiences of ordinary women, men and children. It emphasizes particular activities and spaces where bodies are ordinarily cared for and replenished. This suggests the need for the development of an innovative and challenging approach to the creation of knowledge, and to the understanding of the embeddedness of everyday life in wider social and economic contexts (Smith, 1987).

In the first section of this chapter I discuss recent theorizing in mainstream sociology about routine activities, and time changes in everyday life, particularly in relation to intimacy and risk. I then present my approach to an empirical study of home-life routines. The third section contains my core examination of the issues of gender and routine and households. I explore routines of work, housework, childcare and leisure in the home. In the conclusions I stress the centrality of interdependencies in the gendered negotiations about everyday routines and the limits that the care of children places upon adults' contingent choices.

Mainstream sociology and contemporary everyday routines

Recent mainstream sociological analyses have taken up feminist concerns with the organization and articulation of routine activities in social and economic processes extending beyond the scope of the everyday world. Giddens (1991, 1992), for example, has stressed that in late modernity the intimacies of the self are increasingly influenced by distant happenings. Day-to-day routines imply some social stability that helps contain anxieties of being vulnerable to the rapidly changing world. Because the overall framework of ontological security becomes fragile in modern social conditions, routines are of central importance: they hold at bay 'the threat of personal meaninglessness' (1991, p. 202) enabling the control of one's life circumstances. Beck (1992) has equally stressed the vulnerability of individuals in face of the fluidities and uncertainties of the 'risk society'. Beck and Beck-Gernsheim (1995) emphasized the acute significance of the connections of family life and women's work in and out of the home with wider socio-historical developments.

For Giddens (1992) the new form of intimacy characteristic of late modernity is identified by the concept of the 'pure relationship': a free choice of partners, contingent continuity of relationships, and the maintenance of individual boundaries. It is based on flexibly negotiated normative frameworks where people express their choices of how they want to live together, how they wish to communicate and collaborate. There is no imposed norm. Of course, this pure relationship model is an ideal type. Lesbian and gay relationships are closest to this model since they do not suffer from normative assumptions about gender inequalities. Heterosexual relationships are burdened by these changes, manifest in high divorce rates, growing cohabitation, more lone-parent households and rising numbers of women (particularly mothers) in employment. New narratives of family life have thus emerged. However, the newness of these narratives and the claims about their singularity have not been unchallenged (Silva and Smart, 1999).

As Jamieson (1998, 1999) and Smart and Neale (1999) remark, Giddens's analysis of family life is problematic. It does not focus on the significance of inequality and difference, nor does it give importance to having children for the contingency and fluidity of the pure relationship model. Giddens's model is of equal and financially independent childless individuals. This has consequences for his account of the importance of routines for ontological security. In Giddens's analysis routines are often conceived as social events that can be reflexively open to change, while 'caring routines' operate at an existential and psychological level. The analysis bears minimal sense of the practical activities so closely tied up with the everyday lives of women and men who care for children, and of the constraints that these pose for contingent actions.

Beck (1992; Beck and Beck-Gernsheim, 1995) has considered the growing significance of love in a social context of higher insecurity, risks and individualization. In this context children (and love for children) are regarded as important. For Beck-Gernsheim (1998) historical trends towards individualization have set up a process of 'staging of everyday life'. This is characterized by some key movements to coordinate and hold together biographies that tend to be pulled apart. People used to be able to rely on set rules and models but less and less can be taken for granted. The everyday is negotiated and planned, and resource distribution is discussed. 'Which burdens should be allocated to whom? Who should bear which costs? Which claims have priority? Whose wishes have to wait?' (p. 59). Tempos and abodes differ: family life is scattered between several locations, and there is no common temporal rhythm. It is difficult to tie together the threads of these different rhythms, responsibilities and priorities. The everyday lifeworld is increasingly mixed and many people living together come from different backgrounds. They choose to create a common world beyond the legacy of family and kin to construct an intercultural lifeworld. Many questions are a matter of negotiation and joint decision; some are individual: 'What do I want?' 'What is important to me?' For Beck-Gernsheim (1998), in place of traditional rules and rituals, contemporary family life is based on negotiations and decisions about everyday details of 'do-it-yourself' relationships.

These theories of late modernity stress the changing circumstances in which life is lived, away from the established routines of industrial societies and normative biographies. The post-industrial world has demolished certainties, brought about greater risks and made possible more creativity in the building of one's lifeworld and one's self. However, this picture is contested. Despite the high speed of change in the world, the current degree of fluidity and change in modern family living has been overstated. Fluidity has always been part of how families have lived their lives, but trends also point towards relative stability. There is both continuity and diversity in contemporary family life (Morgan, 1999; Silva and Smart, 1999). For instance, the continuing numerical dominance of two-parent families in current statistical trends cannot be taken to mean that this is the defining model of family life, even though this is the conventional model portrayed in public stories of 'happy families'. Attitudes, practices and meanings matter as much as statistics.

In her 'social analysis of time' Adam (1995) takes a similar view. She remarks that as certainties have been lost in the contemporary context, we have been left with a complexity that is untidy, awkward and unwieldy. A sensitivity to the complexity of social times requires among other things a dissolution of dualisms (such as male–female, material–immaterial) and a grasp of simultaneity and instantaneity. However, it is still important to measure, quantify and spatialize time. These are material expressions of how the personal, the embodied everyday life is implicated in (and implicates) wider phenomena. How do fluidity and change in contemporary living appear in the ways ordinary women and men, who are parents of (or live with, or care for) school-aged children, structure their everyday routines?

Narratives of routines: the study

The remainder of the chapter draws on an in-depth qualitative study of everyday routines involving participant observation and detailed semi-structured interviews. Fieldwork in 20 households, all containing school-aged children, was located in London (6 households), East Anglia (2), Lancashire (3), South Yorkshire (3) and North Yorkshire (6).[1] Eighty-two people were interviewed across the 20 families: 20 women, 17 men and 45 children (21 girls and 24 boys) between 5 and 16 years old. The overall study covers various aspects of life in contemporary homes besides the specific one with which this chapter is concerned. The study was originally designed as an ethnography of home life in Britain with the aim to investigate the relationship between people and technology in their domestic everyday life. The technology aspects are not explored in detail here (see Silva, 2000a and 2000b).

The sampling strategy aimed to cover a wide range of issues. Diversity in family life was taken into account through the inclusion of lone parents, lesbian households and a variety of ethnic backgrounds. None the less, although my sample reflects greater diversity than some other recent studies of UK family life, the majority of households in my sample still fit in with more conventional family models: in 16 families, the partners are all 'white' (four of these Jewish), heterosexual, married (one is previously divorced and has children from both previous and current marriages), British nationals (one is Canadian/British). Among the other families, two are heterosexual lone-parent families (one Afro-Caribbean, one white mother with mixed-race-parentage children), one is Asian (heterosexual and married), and the other is a lesbian household co-parenting with another lesbian household. The sample also reflects a range of income levels. Four families had incomes below £20,000 (two were very poor: lone parent on income support, or on student grant) and four above £40,000 (including one over £80,000). In this chapter I refer mainly to the everyday routines of the 37 adults in the sample, all of whom live with school-aged children.

In the process of data collection and analysis I have been sensitive to the fact that routines are not random, that they change according to circumstances and that they are located in culture, history and personal biography. The various circumstances of lives I studied contribute to sociological theorizing about everyday life, as they resonate with other lives, in other circumstances. They also give some indication of the limits of current theoretical adequacy.

I did not impose categories and structures of time on my interviewees' everyday lives. This is an *ex post* analytical construction. I was concerned with getting people to talk about what they do, about what happens as they do things. I wanted to get in-depth multiple narratives of their everyday lives. There were a number of sociologically relevant questions I wanted to pursue, which I explore in this chapter: how would accounts of routines relate to particular patterns of gender relationships in the home and in work-related matters? What kinds of ideas about 'the family' are expressed in everyday routines, and how are practices deployed in relation to these ideas?

Gender and family, as well as class, are routines, matters of daily accomplishment that are articulated in social, cultural and economic processes extending beyond the everyday world (Smith, 1987). These wider processes are currently characterized in the Western industrialized world by some important features: (i) we are increasingly moving away from the breadwinner and homemaker model of the family towards a two-earner model; (ii) we no longer have a clear split between workplace and home; and (iii), we no longer take for granted that pre-ordained models of family and work structure our everyday living. This implies that specific research questions need to be asked to account for these movements.

I generally asked people to tell me how a normal weekday would go by from the time they woke up until they went to bed. I asked them to think of a 'very common' day, 'an average day', when just their ordinary affairs took place. The specific manner in which I asked the question, and the context in which I asked it within the overall conversations varied. Reactions to my question also varied greatly. 'A normal *boring* day?' some would ask. 'There is no *normal* day.' Or, 'We never seem to have a routine. I think that's the trouble in our house!' 'Yeah, I mean sort of I suppose, depending on whether ... '.

The ways in which people kept track of their everyday narratives were also quite diverse. Some lost themselves in side-tracked accounts of events triggered by a recollection of some occurrence in the everyday. Normally men were either very brief or concentrated on workplace events. Because I was interested in home life I encouraged people (most often men) to tell me what happened in the home. 'What time do you get up? And then? What time do you get to work? How does the working day go? And then, ... the time after work? Is that how it went on today?' At times I would start by asking: 'What time do you normally get back home from work?' I also encouraged accounts of people's perceptions of their partners' and children's routines. Again, men had to be prompted more often than women. Women's routines appeared more generally imbricated with those of their children, in particular, but also with those of their partners.

Because some people's daily lives have different set patterns for different days of the week, we would normally talk about these differences. Time, space, activity and persons appeared as recurrent elements in the narratives of routines. Time routines were constructed around activities done in particular spaces, involving specific persons. The common ingredients of 'normal' routine included getting up, washing, having breakfast, giving children breakfast, taking children to school, doing childcare, setting off to work, commuting, doing housework (cleaning, cooking, washing, ironing), working, having personal time, engaging in relational time, and watching television. The activities most permeated with other concomitant activity (or activities) were childcare, housework, watching television, having personal time or engaging in relational time. Work was the most-preserved single activity done in isolation.

In graphic representations I made of the basic normal everyday routines of the 37 women and men, the portraits of time use, and the identification of the physical space where the activity (or activities) took place, demanded qualified interpretation. For instance, those people who appeared as spending their whole day at home also got out of the house to take children to school and pick them up, to do some shopping, errands of various sorts, and to engage in leisure activities. What mattered to me was that their perception of a 'normal', 'average', routine day meant spending all hours in the home. Other people who had similar patterns of activities remarked spontaneously on any specific times during the day when they were out of the home doing errands. After school hours there were clear times of unsettled spatial routine for most parents but in terms of routine patterns it was referred to as generally 'looking after the children'.

I shall discuss these patterns of everyday routines by reference to the role of gender in the theorizing of contemporary everyday family life. How is gender implicated in the location of routines and in the intersubjective negotiations between partners in concrete contexts of contemporary everyday life? I consider the debates on gendered time patterns in relation to the routines of the people I studied regarding work, housework, childcare and leisure.

Gender and routines

Feminists have challenged the idea of linear time, arguing that it is incompatible with women's everyday temporal experiences (Davies, 1990). These challenges have brought about an awareness of the gendered notion of time. However, epistemological dualistic frameworks are often employed in analyses of gendered time, creating a belief that it is possible to concretely oppose male and female times. The alleged boundary between masculine and feminine needs to be addressed. The definition of women's time as circular, repetitive and never ending draws attention to the embodied aspects of daily life. Male time is defined as linear, purposeful and achieving. Yet, when one acknowledges that gender identities are potentially multiple, unstable and contingent, the dualist opposition between a female time and a male time is dissolved (Odih, 1999).

However, the argument that women and men use time differently because of their distinct life situations is powerful and has real grounding. Gender is significant to variations of time in so far as women's subordinate economic and social positions result from practices of power that constrain their abilities to make decisions about their time and that of others. This opposition of largely undifferentiated categories of powerful men and powerless women, though, needs to be qualified. As with men, female experiences are not homogeneous, despite particular forms of masculinity and femininity prevailing at different historical periods. Gendered times are constructed in relations between women and men and they also change along the lifecourse. The construction of gendered routines is related to the gendered location.

In my study, how far do the everyday routines of women and men who live with school-age children differ? Is it possible to talk of a gendered routine pattern? How is this pattern constituted? The 37 personal narratives of routine show that time spent at home was very significant for most people. Only 16 individuals – 13 men and 3 women – spent equal or longer time away from home than in the home. Thus, women were more likely than men to spend longer hours in the home. This echoes a relatively traditional gender pattern, but variations within this trend were also interesting and not straightforwardly gendered. For instance, 4 men did not go out to work and 3 women had their everyday routines mostly away from home. The 37 accounts include 9 people who were at home all day long: 5 women and 4 men. This nearly equal gender split of the 'home-bound' group, however, contained different gendered home-life experiences. All of these men conducted paid work from home, while – with one exception – the routines of women who stayed at home all day were concentrated on childcare, personal time and housework. The one woman who worked from home had a routine pattern similar to the four men who worked from home, and all five had more fragmented routines than either their male counterparts who worked outside of the home, or the women who were full-time home-based.

These patterns show a combination of gender and routine not simply split along male and female lines but along lines of involvement with homely activities, mainly centred around the care of children. Activities for adults, male or female, were generally organized around the needs of children and normally only one adult was involved. Where the man cared for children he also did housework (but rarely the laundry), though no woman was present. Whenever a woman was present it was she who did the care of children, although a man may have helped, particularly in the evening routines (with homework, tea, play and bedtime rituals).

Mothering and caring for dependants are activities where the self gets the most subordinated to the needs of others. Women's ascribed domestic roles and subordinate position has meant that they generally have more experience of relational time. In the home, time is rarely demarcated between work, leisure and the personal (Adam, 1995; Sullivan, 1997). When men do 'mothering' their time becomes more 'relational' and the home tends to be gendered differently.

In my study there was plurality and difference among households. Looking at each individual and their household patterns, one had very little sense of a normative gendered pattern setting everyday routines overall. This is not to say that gender was unimportant. On the contrary, it is significant that only 4 men appeared to break out of the traditional mode of male routine in the home, and that 4 women remained in the traditional mode of female routine. It is, however, more important that 16 women did not operate within traditional female routine patterns of full-time housewifery, while 13 men did still model their everyday life according to the 'provider', 'sole-breadwinner' model of family. Out of these men, 5 had no involvement with the care of children or housework on a normal weekday, and 4 had some involvement in the evenings only.

These patterns were established in relation to concrete situations of the labour market and in interaction between partners. Although this interactive process does not indicate consensus about the outcomes, there was little sense of complaint or resentment about these routine patterns in the narrative accounts. However, current conflicts in the home between women and men are often conflicts over time (Silva, 1999). Some men use professional commitments as an argument against women's demands that they take on more work in the home (Hochschild, 1997). This may be a conscious strategy they are not ashamed to confess:

Elizabeth:	So you are at home by eight-ish?
Gabriel:	Yeah, usually home for eight or if I choose to, I'll ... just after seven.
Elizabeth:	Do you tend to see your kids before they go to bed or not?
Gabriel:	It goes through periods ... I tend, I tend to see them ... But – to be quite frank, I deliberately avoid getting back ... I tend to, to not rush back.
Elizabeth:	Is Tracy conscious of that?
Gabriel:	I think she probably is, yeah. I certainly am.
Elizabeth:	[Talking about Frances serving her husband.
Robert:	a meal at 9pm every day] Do you think you should do more?
Robert:	Eh?
Elizabeth:	Do you feel you should do more?
Robert:	I don't feel guilty, put it that way!
Elizabeth:	Why not?
Robert:	Don't see any reason why I should! No, I think it's just, I don't know really, I suppose it's just habit.

Frances worked part-time (job-share) in a bank. Robert's work time went from midday to 8pm. It is notable that in Frances's narrative of everyday routine serving Robert a meal at 9pm was a very matter-of-fact activity: uncontentious, taken-for-granted, very much as Robert saw it:

> Robert works every day, ... he finishes work at half past eight and gets home about nine o'clock at night so when he comes in at night, I then make a bite to eat for him, and I have a bite with him, and then we settle down to watch television at that point. (Frances)

For Tracy, who worked full-time from home, Gabriel's pattern also appeared uncontroversial:

> [The kids are in bed about 7.30pm.] When they're in bed – I usually have supper with Gabriel when he's back and – maybe about half past eight, quarter to nine, I will go and do another two or three hours' work if I need to.

Intersubjective negotiations appeared very relevant for the gendered locations of these individuals. These may have been related to more conventional patterns of gender relations, as seemed to be the case with Frances and Robert, or they may have resulted from modern reflexive choices to fit everyday life issues to life-stage circumstances, more in line with Beck-Gernsheim's (1998) argument:

> When they [the kids] were younger, things were quite different then because – I worked from home for two days a week, Tracy was lecturing at the college and I used the technology to move my hours around it. So I could take the kids to school and collect the kids from school, ... I'd work on a computer in the middle of the day and late in the evening and I'd still do a full day's work but I'd be looking after the kids as well. So – from that point of view, the technology enabled me to enable Tracy to – to – to do her teaching. I wouldn't have been able to do it any other way ... (Gabriel)

Doing housework *per se* did not figure strongly in the routine narratives of either women or men, although it was more present in the women's accounts. Childcare was a much more visible activity. Only two women did as much housework as childcare, whilst housework occupied *some* daily time for Wendy, Rena, Chris, Phil, Jane and Marc. Housework also took place mostly during childcare hours, with all those who had paid jobs, and also cared for children, doing their paid work mostly during school hours. Only two women did not have any paid work: Rosanne, a convinced housewife, and Lynn, a lone mother of four children with very low labour market skills.

The involvement of men in feeding children and themselves, and the not-a-big-issue approach to feeding husbands in the evening, illustrated by the earlier quotes, indicate that the effort in these activities was not remarkable. The easiness of tasks and the ability to combine managing home and children with working for pay was achieved by, on one hand, the availability of technological aids for everyday living, and, on the other, established patterns of daily routine. These set routine patterns of dealing with housework, and the technical artefacts in the home, usually involved a negotiated gender division of labour (in the less traditional homes), the help of older children, and also the help of other adults. Some of the better-off households bought some form of domestic time as they paid for cleaners, babysitters and childminders (all of whom were women). Some poorer and well-off families also enrolled the help of grandparents (more often grandmothers) in childcare, particularly with school runs and after school-care.

Marc and Diane had deeply egalitarian gender principles, which they applied to home management. Marc was an academic researcher and writer working from home, Diane a senior civil servant who worked long hours. Marc's everyday routines involved being up by 7.30am, getting breakfast for his children (two girls, aged 9 and 11, and one boy, 15), making his wife's sandwiches, taking the girls to school, tidying the house, doing his own work from home, being home for when the children got back from school, checking homework, having chats, cooking dinner. He cooked three evening meals a week, his son two. After meals the son tidied up and the daughters rotated various jobs: unloading the dishwasher, sorting out drawers. Marc and Diane had coffee in their private room, talked for about one hour, then returned to finish bits of their respective work before going to bed at about 11.30pm. Wednesdays also involved Marc doing the laundry and changing bedclothes (one of two men who did some laundry work).

In Brenda's household, very clear work rotas were set for the four children (a girl of 11, and three boys, aged 13, 10 and 11 months). Because of the baby, Brenda was working only three mornings per week. Her husband Colin, a self-employed builder, did nothing in the home. His routine involved getting up at 5.30/6.00am to be at work by 6.30am. At work he did 'what is to be done'. By 6.30pm he got back home, 'I have my tea, sit down and relax.' The only bit of housework he would involve himself with was 'sticking things in the dishwasher'. 'But no, I don't do the washing up. Brenda does that. It's her bit.' Brenda managed home with her children. Daniella, 11, said about washing-up:

> It is done in the dishwasher. The dishwasher does all apart from what doesn't fit in. On night times we have a day each: Charlie, myself, Eric, mum. We load, wash-up, wipe the worktops, empty bags in bin, the boys fight, they moan but get on.

About the laundry:

> It is mostly mum who does it. I do some to help her out, on Saturday. I get the washing and put it in the washer, then I change it over to the dryer, then put it on the basket. Mum does most of the ironing. I sometimes do some.

In another household, Chris worked as a 'lollipop lady', school playground supervisor, and as a hairdresser. Phil was an actor and a writer. Chris also gave the children certain jobs to do, mostly on Saturdays. 'It's a cleaning day ritual'. Greg, 13, did dusting and vacuuming. Georgia, 11, polished and sometimes 'hoovered'. Josh, 8, and Joseph, 6, did the windows, polished the pictures, tidied up their bedrooms and made their beds.

These people's lives appeared to conform to a pattern marked by their own working lives and by the school life of their children. How did leisure in the home conform to their choices of living? Only four partners mentioned the same getting up time. While the morning routines were quite separate for partners living together, with each one going to their own affairs, the evening saw the appearance of the television in the narratives, mostly after the children went to bed. Daytime television watching figured very little in the routine accounts of women and men, with two exceptions: Nancy, who switched it on first thing in the morning, when coming into the kitchen, and left it on until she went to bed, and Phil, who worked from home and timed his lunch break by the BBC One O'Clock News. Children in eight households watched television before going to school, with the television serving adults as a kind of 'electronic nanny'. However, the television was on for most of the day in a number of homes. During the research period televisions were found on at different times of the day in nine households, including the eight homes that used morning television as a 'nanny'. However, this did not necessarily mean that people were specifically watching a particular programme: for many, the television was on as 'background noise', 'for company', 'so I don't feel alone', or, as in Richard's account:

> I do bits and pieces of working or I'll watch some TV but – a lot of the times I just – I end up sitting in this state where I just literally drift over in my mind, so even if I'm watching TV a lot of the time I'm not really watching TV, it's just things drifting over in my mind.

Evening television watching fitted this mode for most people. Television was placed within a personal time of relaxation or of relating with one's partner. This was the everyday pattern for 24 individuals, with occasional evening viewing mentioned by 3 others. It was often a 'time of one's own'. However, 6 women and 4 men did not account for a role of the television in their everyday lives. This does not mean, though, that they never watched television. Four households were generally TV-free, although in only one of these households had a conscious decision been made not to have a television in the home:

> I experimented with a TV in my bedroom. It was not healthy for the relationship. Not having a TV makes us go out. We spend evenings

together, chatting. I talk on the phone to a friend. I don't want one. We don't, as a couple. (Diane)

There were particular characteristics about these four virtually TV-free households. Tracy, an architect, was the only woman in this study who worked from home. She looked after two sons out of school hours. Gabriel was also an architect, and they both caught up with work in the evenings. In the second household, Phil, an actor and writer, worked from home and was in charge of the daytime care of his four children. Chris's three jobs meant that she came in and out of the house at various times of the day and evening. In the evening they both shared the care of the children and had some time together. In the third household, Marc worked from home and looked after the two younger children out of their school hours, while Diane worked long hours and did not get directly involved in the home's daily affairs. Finally, in the fourth household Rebecca sometimes worked from home, and Eleanor out of the home. Evening routines changed depending on whether Rebecca's daughter was there (usually half of the week), but time was mostly spent replenishing oneself or the relationship.

In this study, then, home-based leisure did not have great significance and the main 'gadget for leisure', the television, appeared as a minor 'event' in the daily routine. Television was not central to the construction of everyday routines in these households. If some families tuned in to breakfast TV, after-school children's television and evening broadcasting programmes, television was by no means a relevant apparatus to the structuring of domestic time (cf. Silverstone, 1993). Perhaps this is a particularity of households with school-aged children.

Despite the flexible arrangements of working hours and some variation in the gender of the children's carer, the rigidity of school hours and the education system calendar appeared to structure most family arrangements. Family-time constructions appeared linked to dual-time schemes of workdays and holidays. For most people real family time happened at the weekend, mainly on Sundays. Interestingly this was the time that most of the women and men in my study spontaneously referred to as 'routine'. Sundays and other holidays were perceived as extraordinary because then time was in people's power. Personal needs and set routines were then less focused, and investment in the self and in relationships were at centre stage. The Sunday routine may have involved going to Mass, or going on family walks, engaging in particular forms of leisure, but more often it meant eating together. In a few cases this meant a proper Sunday dinner. Often the meal was just a time when people living together were available for each other.

Certainly children's affairs were prominent in the narratives of everyday routines. This is an empirical fact. But the analysis of time in home life, in particular the extent of 'choice' of routine patterns, is also a subject bound by complex explorations about the boundaries of the public and the private in people's lives, and in particular in family contexts.

Feminist writings on social time have identified a coexistence of public time, biological time, internal time, and so on, without a pre-established order. Sometimes these temporal orders are in conflict, and temporal priorities are also variable in the lifecourse. Temporal orders of reference in this study varied according to gender, labour market participation and the presence of small children. Even when women were not in paid employment, paid work gave a general meaning to time, because of its overall social dominance. This happens even when time is 'contaminated' by emotions and affections. Thus the distinction between what is public and private is ambiguous, and the boundaries are fluid and changeable. Clearly the choices of individuals and households showed fragmented and diverse patterns of everyday routines. The key setter of routine patterns for the women and men in my study was school hours. Second, it was paid-work hours, but these also varied. In the making up of the household routine the negotiations of gender locations were crucial. The care of children was central, but the gender of the carer (still mostly female), and the ways caring activities were organized, varied within each household's particular arrangements.

Conclusion

It became apparent in this study that patterns of everyday life, routines and habits must be firmly established for the effective conduct of everyday affairs. However, there are no set frameworks for this. My findings illustrate the trends pointed out in recent studies of the sociology of the family, and taken up in mainstream sociology, about family forms moving away from fixed or rigid notions of the 'proper' family. Even inside traditionally structured families, like some in this study, new normative guidelines are emerging. New types and qualities of relationships have appeared in practices of 'doing' family life. Routines matter great deal in this doing. They are diversely constituted and may change according to circumstances, but they do not change at random, or suddenly. Changes in everyday life routines go in pace with wider socio-economic transformations. The implicit identification between women and the everyday crumbles in the face of current trends. The fluidity of gender roles, even in family life, brings about considerations of personal choices about how to live, which have a strong impact on society and culture.

This study showed that the time problems in everyday life were usually different for women and men, but patterns of routine had a close relation with care activities in the home. Sometimes the gendered pattern was conventional; sometimes it was reflexively negotiated to conform to changing life circumstances. Men tended to do more when women were not present. Men's time tended to be less fragmented and more exclusively relational even when doing childcare. This indicates a complex process of change in gender location and intersubjective negotiations of women and men. Why do women usually acquire certain segments and styles of time? It is still assumed that women care for others and that their time is dependent time. This results from historical and sociocultural processes. Time is a resource, and being in charge of one's own time and of the time of others signifies having individual and social power. Women do have less power than men in heterosexual family life. Although power is also socially differentiated among women, and in this study some households drew on the paid or unpaid labour of women as domestic helpers, it is a common manifestation of male structural power that it has been taken for granted that women's time can be drawn upon (Jurczyk, 1998; Smith, 1987). This explains why in most heterosexual households women's routines were often more closely interlocked with those of their male partners and their children. The more closely children are interlocked with the adult's life, the more limited is contingency, and as contemporary practices stand, this is the case more with women than men. Inequality, however, may be less marked where both adults operate in a balanced way in their 'caring routines'.

Note

1. This project was partially funded within the ESRC 'Virtual Society' research programme, award number L132251048. Sixteen families are part of a broader study done with colleagues from the Institute of Communication Studies at the University of Leeds. The study of the other families was funded through research funds from the Department of Sociology and Social Policy, University of Leeds, and the National Everyday Cultures programme at The Open University. Data were collected from September 1998 until the end of 1999.

13
Roles, Rhythms and Routines: Towards a New Script of Daily Life in the Netherlands?

Andries van den Broek, Koen Breedveld and Wim Knulst

Introduction

Roles, rhythms and routines play an important part in daily life. Without some degree of fixed roles, rhythm and routinization, people would constantly be baffled by the numerous decisions they face. Roles, rhythms and routines make life predictable and allow us to concentrate on important matters. The fact that only certain events stand out as extraordinary underlines how unremarkably most daily pursuits go by. Familiar notions such as the evening and the weekend derive their meaning from the fact that those episodes possess a certain colour.

This analysis focuses on change and permanence in the usage and structuring of time. Men and women alike are facing an expanding set of tasks. This expansion has eroded formerly clear divisions of roles between housewife and male provider. Instead, both sexes now combine paid work and housekeeping chores. The casting in this new script has affected prevailing rhythms and pressurized familiar day-to-day routines. This chapter explores whether and how the roles, rhythms and routines of day-to-day life in the Netherlands have changed in the period 1975–1995 (cf. Van den Broek *et al.*, 1999).

Context

The postwar era in the Netherlands was one of reconstruction. In addition to the infrastructure, the social structure was also swiftly reconstructed, with institutions such as the Church, the nuclear family and labour relations perhaps giving greater structure and meaning to daily life in the 1950s than they had done in the interwar years. This also applied to the usage and structuring of time. The distinctive division of roles between the sexes and the clear distinction between work and leisure warranted an orderly usage and structuring of time. Gradually, Dutch society became less orderly. Informalization altered daily life, the personal rather than a person's role or class coming to the fore (Wouters, 1990). Institutional arrangements based on religious or socialist world-views lost ground, with the pluralization of values offering people greater freedom in the layout of daily life (Zijderveld, 1971). The diminished importance of formerly influential institutions enabled people to follow their own preferences. Both growing welfare and technological innovations (from kitchen utensils to contraceptives) were helpful in this respect. With the advent of the multiple choice biography, the entire walk of life became a 'Do-It Yourself' project.

Over time, the orderly usage and structuring of time became pressurized. The nuclear family, church rites and regulated working hours grew less dominant, exemplified in reduced limitations on leisure in general, and on Sunday leisure in particular. The gradual extension of individual agency now reaches beyond leisure, however. Fewer people leave the parental home to marry straight away; more people (at least temporarily) live alone or cohabit without raising a family. Fewer women regard housekeeping as a rewarding life; more women aspire to and achieve a professional career. In the 1950s, Dutch women were debarred from paid work and predestined to the role of housewife to a higher degree than their counterparts in surrounding countries. Over the past decades, this has changed rapidly, and the wedding ceremony no longer implies the end of a woman's professional life and her full legal capacities.

In 1996, the Dutch government further enhanced the liberalization of time. New legislation was passed that facilitated more liberal working hours and shop-opening hours, thereby sanctioning a process already well under way. Only school hours still hold their ground, though reduced working hours of staff may lead to shorter school hours in the future, a worrying prospect for dual-earning parents. The latter observation aptly illustrates that the newly emerging script of daily life may cause different rhythms to collide, also within the nuclear family. Rather than acting as a buffer, the schedule of the working mother adds to family scheduling problems.

The public and political debate on the structuring of time in the Netherlands focuses on two related issues: the pros and cons of a 24-hour economy and the temporal organization of a dual-earner society. The government justified the liberalization of working and shopping hours by presenting it, *inter alia*, as an attempt to balance the professional and private lives of dual earners. In practice, they are intertwined too. Many dual-earner households, for example, face a dispersion of working hours in the private household to weekday evenings and the weekend.

As a result of the dispersion of tasks between genders and over time, the distinctiveness of episodes like 'the evening' and 'the weekend' might fade. In addition, modern appliances like the microwave, the video and the Internet allow a greater temporal scattering of activities. Dinner can easily be reheated, movies can be watched whenever one wishes and information can be collected in the middle of the night. In short, an 'on-demand' use of time is emerging, with greater possibilities to do what one pleases at the time one prefers.

This chapter investigates whether roles, rhythms and routines regarding daily tasks have been subject to erosion. Hence, as advocated by Gershuny and Sullivan (1998), we attempt to move beyond more traditional applications of time-use studies that merely focus on duration of activities. In what follows, we will first analyse the *tasks* individuals fulfil and combine, and the extent to which tasks still constitute distinct roles. We will then consider *rhythms*, analysing the dispersion of tasks over the week and over a weekday, before finally addressing *routines*, investigating whether subsequent weekdays of individuals have become more alike over the years.

This chapter draws on Time Use Research data covering the 1975–95 period. The data were collected by two means. Time-budget information was collected by means of a diary in which respondents recorded their main activity in each quarter of an hour over the period of a full week in October, with the aid of a pre-coded list of activities. In the previous and subsequent week, additional information was gathered by means of questionnaires (Knulst and Van den Broek, 1998). As this chapter concentrates on paid work, housekeeping chores and the combination of both, the analyses refer to people aged 18 to 65, as it is during this part of the lifespan that people are most likely to face a combination of these tasks. For reasons of convenience, only the 1975, 1985 and 1995 measurements are used here (n = 950, 2,395 and 2,429 respectively).

Changing roles

The blueprint of the male-provider household features a clear division of roles. The advent of single-person and dual-earner households disrupts this casting. Instead, growing numbers of people combine paid work and housekeeping chores (Knulst and Van Beek, 1990), suggesting an entanglement of multiple roles within single individuals. It also suggests a blurring of roles: tasks no longer 'belong' to particular roles. In this section, individuals and tasks subsequently serve as the unit of observation. We will first analyse the tasks individuals fulfil and combine, then we will explore whether tasks still constitute roles. The dispersion of tasks over the population and the concentration of tasks in roles will subsequently serve as a means to assess whether roles have eroded.

This presupposes a standard measure that determines whether a person fulfils a given task. In our analysis, a person is regarded to fulfil a task if they take part in it for at least half of the amount of time on average spent on that task by 18–65-year-olds in the 1975–95 period. The average working time over the years, for instance, amounted to 19.6 hours per week. People working 9.8 hours or more here count as participants in paid work. As regards housekeeping chores, the average was 22.4 hours weekly, so the threshold value is 11.2 hours. The percentage of people facing multiple tasking refers to persons that exceed both threshold values (the other threshold values are shown in Table 13.3 below).

Judging by these criteria, participation in both paid work and in housekeeping increased over the 1975–95 period (Table 13.1). Beyond these average trends, diverging trends among women and men can be observed. While female labour participation more than doubled, male labour participation in 1995 had recovered to the 1975 level, following the lower levels of male employment in the 1980s recession. The growing female share in paid work narrowed the gap between the sexes. As regards housekeeping, a modest decrease in female participation was matched by a much more pronounced rise in male participation. Here, too, the difference in gender roles became smaller. Together, these developments point to a considerable blurring of formerly distinct roles.

Table 13.1 Participation in paid work, in housekeeping and multiple tasking, by gender, percentage among 18–65-year-olds, 1975-95

	Paid work			Housekeeping			Multiple tasking		
	1975	*1985*	*1995*	*1975*	*1985*	*1995*	*1975*	*1985*	*1995*
All	48	48	57	62	68	68	16	23	31
Women	17	26	39	96	96	90	15	23	32
Men	79	71	77	27	40	45	16	22	29

Source: SCP (Time Use Research 1975–95).

Although paid work was still a predominantly male activity in 1995, and housekeeping still a female one, both activities were less exclusively limited to either sex than was the case in earlier years (cf. Gershuny, 2000).

Housekeeping can be divided into a number of more specific chores. Here, six different chores are distinguished: preparing meals (including laying the table and washing up); cleaning the house; washing and ironing clothes; daily shopping; other shopping and childcare (Table 13.2). Although participation in childcare has remained largely unchanged, participation in the other tasks has changed over time, invariably rooted in a firm increase in male participation (particularly with respect to preparing meals and cleaning the house), often accompanied by a somewhat less marked drop in female participation. Although still predominantly a woman's burden, a considerable redistribution of housekeeping chores over the sexes can be observed.

Table 13.2   Participation in housekeeping chores, by gender, percentages among 18–65-year-olds, 1975–95

	Preparing meals (% > 3.7 hours)			Cleaning the house (% > 2.1 hours)		
	1975	1985	1995	1975	1985	1995
All	58	65	64	55	62	58
Women	97	94	87	93	90	82
Men	20	34	40	18	33	32

	Washing/ironing clothes (% > 0.9 hours)			Daily shopping (% > 0.7 hours)		
	1975	1985	1995	1975	1985	1995
All	48	52	53	65	70	71
Women	90	91	85	92	89	89
Men	7	11	18	38	51	52

	Other shopping (% > 0.7 hours)			Childcare[a] (% > 2.9 hours)		
	1975	1985	1995	1975	1985	1995
all	63	62	66	48	47	49
women	76	73	76	62	60	61
men	51	51	54	33	34	36

[a] refers only to parents with children that live at home.

Source: as for Table 13.1.

Combined (part-time) jobs in the formal economy and in the private household have increased the burden of the total package of tasks. Multiple tasking implies that people have a second shift next to their main task. Those involved in housekeeping more often also do paid work; those involved in paid work more often are engaged in house-keeping too. On average, the burden of the total package of tasks of 18–65-year-olds increased by 2.5 hours per week between 1975 and 1995 (cf. Peters, 2000).

We will now explore the question of whether tasks blur or still consti-tute distinct roles. One approach is to assess the extent to which a given task is combined with others. This has been calculated with respect to paid work and cooking (the left- and right-hand sections of Table 13.3 respectively). The extent to which paid work is combined with house-keeping chores expresses the extent to which housekeeping is per-formed by people for whom housekeeping is not the sole activity. This also reveals what particular chores are combined with paid work. People

Table 13.3   Participation in housekeeping chores among the working population, and participation in paid work and other housekeeping chores among the cooking population, percentage among 18–65-year-olds, 1975–95

	Working (> 9.8 hours) population			Cooking (>3.7 hours) population		
	1975	1985	1995	1975	1985	1995
Paid work (> 9.8 hours)	100	100	100	24	32	44
Preparing meals (> 3.7 hours)	29	42	49	100	100	100
Cleaning the house (> 2.1 hours)	24	39	41	87	82	76
Washing/ironing clothes (> 0.9 hours)	16	28	38	81	76	73
Daily shopping (> 0.7 hours)	43	55	60	89	84	84
Other shopping (> 0.7 hours)	52	53	58	75	69	72
Childcare[a] (> 2.9 hours)	37	36	41	62	58	57

[a] refers only to parents with children that live at home.

Source: as for Table 13.1.

with paid work became more involved over time in each of the six housekeeping chores distinguished here, some chores more than others.

The earlier observation that the role of the housewife is on the decline leads us to expect that fewer people participate in each house-keeping chore on a weekly basis (still using the threshold value to determine who is a participant). This implies that fewer people who participate in a given housekeeping chore also participate in the others. This was analysed by assessing what proportion of those partic-ipating in preparing meals also participated in the other housekeeping tasks (Table 13.3). The working time of those involved in preparing meals, which in the case of blurring roles should be on the increase, was also taken into account. Indeed, paid work rose among the cooking population, while their participation in the other housekeep-ing chores dropped, pointing to a blurring of roles.

That housekeeping as a specialized activity is on the decline implies the double expectation that fewer people perform each household chore on a weekly basis and that fewer people perform none at all. This expectation finds empirical support too (Table 13.4). A growing part of the population fulfils two or three of the housekeeping chores weekly, while fewer people perform all or none of these chores. Fewer people

Table 13.4   Number of housekeeping chores[a], by sex, percentage of the 18–65-year-olds[b], 1975–95.

	All			Women			Men		
	1975	1985	1995	1975	1985	1995	1975	1985	1995
No housekeeping chores	16	9	8	1	0	1	31	17	15
1 housekeeping chore	16	15	15	2	1	3	30	30	27
2 housekeeping chores	13	15	15	2	4	6	25	28	25
3 housekeeping chores	7	12	14	4	8	10	10	16	18
4 housekeeping chores	14	19	19	28	30	26	1	8	11
5 housekeeping chores	34	31	30	64	57	54	4	4	4

[a]as for Table 13.13, apart from childcare.
[b]apart from people living with their parents.

Source: as for Table 13.1.

are fully relieved of housekeeping chores and fewer are burdened by all those tasks. A breakdown of housekeeping chores by gender shows that the decrease in those without any part in housekeeping at all is due to increased male involvement, while the decrease in those involved weekly in each of the housekeeping chores is caused by a withdrawal of women from full-time housekeeping.

Although the gender difference in housekeeping became smaller, it is still considerable, the burden of housekeeping resting predominantly on female shoulders. Men spend more time per week than women on paid work (33 and 13 hours respectively in 1995), while women are more engaged in housekeeping and childcare (29 and 12 hours respectively). The former 'harmonious inequality' has only partly been erased. Daily tasks are less exclusively distributed along gender lines and cluster less clearly into well-defined roles.

Eroding rhythms

We will now assess whether the emergence of this new script of daily life also affects rhythms and routines, exploring first whether collective rhythms are losing ground because fewer people do the same activities at the same moment. First, the outlay of activities over seven days of a week is mapped out, followed by an analysis of the distribution of activities within a weekday.

In 1996, laws on working hours and shop-opening hours in the Netherlands were liberalized. In preceding years, those laws had already been supplemented by more and more exemptions. As a result, some degree of flexibilization had already been on its way in the 1975–95 period studied here. Flexibilization opens up the possibility that more paid work is done outside office hours. In reaction, concern has been voiced that evening and weekend paid work and the consequent de-synchronization of free time will interfere with collective (leisure) activities. In addition, worries have been expressed that the liberalization of shop opening hours prioritizes commercial rather than social and recreational objectives. The fear that family life will get crushed, church life will be hampered and social life will become scantier inspired churches to campaign publicly against the 24-hour society in 1998.

The discussion on working hours in the 24-hour society has focused solely on the timing of paid work, the timing of housekeeping chores apparently being regarded of minor importance. However, the timing of housekeeping chores appears to be of major importance too, as those who combine housekeeping with paid work might well choose or be forced to schedule their housekeeping chores for weekday evenings and/or over the weekend. This suggests that work outside office hours spreads into not only (or not primarily) the formal economy, but also (or rather) into the informal service economy of the private household.

The dispersion of tasks

In order to chart the dispersion of paid work and of housekeeping over the week, the proportion of 18–65-year-olds who are involved in either activity as the week unfolds was calculated. After dividing each day into six-hour episodes, the percentages involved in paid work and in housekeeping for at least two hours per episode were calculated (Table 13.5). Paid work was still concentrated in weekday mornings and afternoons in 1995. In each of those ten 'episodes' , around 40 per cent of the sample was at work (for two hours or more). In no other episode does the percentage exceed 10 per cent. Friday turns out to differ somewhat from other weekdays in this respect. The second most busy episodes are Saturday morning and afternoon, followed by weekday evenings.

The bulk of housekeeping is also performed on weekday mornings and afternoons, i.e. during 'office hours' , but is not as concentrated in the daytime weekday episodes as paid work. The percentages involved during those episodes are lower, while more housekeeping is being carried out in the evenings, on Sundays and, most of all, on Saturdays. Another difference with paid work is the differentiation between weekday mornings and weekday afternoons. The most striking difference, however, is the extent to which housekeeping extends beyond 'office hours' , especially on Saturdays; on Saturday afternoons in particular, the highest proportion of the population are involved in housekeeping (for at least two hours).

To map trends in the timing of paid work and housekeeping, the 28 weekly six-hour episodes were condensed into five types of episodes: weekday mornings and afternoons; evenings; nights; Saturday daytime; and Sunday daytime. For each type of episode, the average participation (for at least two hours) of 18–65-year-olds in paid work and housekeeping was calculated (Table 13.6). This revealed no major changes in the timing of paid work between 1975 and 1995. In daytime weekday episodes, about 40 per cent of 18–65-year-olds were

Table 13.5 Timing of paid work and housekeeping chores over the week, percentage of 18–65-year-olds involved in a given episode for at least two hours, 1995

	Paid work				Housekeeping chores			
	Night (00–06)	Morning (06–12)	Afternoon (12–18)	Evening (18–24)	Night (00–06)	Morning (06–12)	Afternoon (12–18)	Evening (18–24)
Sunday	1	2	4	2	0	10	24	7
Monday	1	42	43	6	0	26	40	8
Tuesday	1	43	43	7	0	25	35	8
Wednesday	1	43	41	6	0	25	35	8
Thursday	1	43	43	8	0	24	35	11
Friday	1	39	39	5	0	26	38	11
Saturday	1	9	9	3	0	30	52	5

Source: as for Table 13.1.

Table 13.6 Timing of paid work and housekeeping chores, percentage of
18–65-year-olds involved for at least two hours, 1975–95

	Paid work			Housekeeping chores		
	1975	*1985*	*1995*	*1975*	*1985*	*1995*
Mornings and afternoons of weekdays	39	37	42	37	36	31
Weekday evenings	4	5	5	6	7	8
Nights	1	1	1	0	0	0
Saturday morning and afternoon	7	7	9	41	42	41
Sunday morning and afternoon	2	3	3	14	15	17

Source: as for Table 13.1.

involved in paid work. A drop in 1985, when unemployment was relatively high, was followed by a rise to a somewhat higher level in 1995.
Changes 'outside office hours' were even smaller. The mass of paid
work remains concentrated in weekday mornings and afternoons (cf.
Harvey *et al.*, 2000). The timing of housekeeping reveals greater shifts.
Less housekeeping is being done in the daytime on weekdays, more is
dispersed to weekday evenings and to Sunday.

Focusing on proportions exceeding a two-hour threshold per
episode, shifts in the timing of paid work and housekeeping appear
modest. A somewhat different picture emerges when the focus is on
the numbers of hours that people are involved in paid work and in
housekeeping 'outside office hours' (Table 13.7). The volume of paid
work and housekeeping on weekday evenings (18:00–24:00 h.) and at
the weekend (06:00–24:00 h.) rose from 11.0 to 12.7 hours weekly, a

Table 13.7 Paid work and housekeeping chores on weekday evenings and at
the weekend, in hours per week, 18–65-year-olds, 1975–95

	Paid work			Housekeeping chores			Total		
	1975	*1985*	*1995*	*1975*	*1985*	*1995*	*1975*	*1985*	*1995*
On weekday evenings	1.1	1.3	1.4	3.1	3.5	3.6	4.2	4.8	5.0
At the weekend	0.9	1.0	1.3	5.9	6.2	6.4	6.8	7.2	7.7
Total	2.0	2.3	2.7	9.0	9.7	10.0	11.0	12.0	12.7

Source: as for Table 13.1.

dispersion shared evenly between weekday evenings (+0.8 hours) and the weekend (+0.9 hours). In both cases, half of that growth consists of paid work and the other half of housekeeping. So the initial situation, that obligations 'outside office hours' stem from housekeeping chores rather than from paid work, continues.

Weekly and daily rhythms

As mentioned earlier, commonplace indications like evening or weekend derive their meaning from the fact that such episodes possess a certain colour of their own. The above indicates that tasks are being dispersed between sexes and over time. This raises the question whether the colours of distinct episodes are fading. To assess whether this is the case, we will analyse the timing of activities over the days of the week and over the hours of a weekday.

The most marked differences in the distribution of activities over the week occur between weekdays and the weekend. But weekdays show differentiation too. As a result, the course of the week follows a recognizable pattern. The issue of whether this pattern is eroding relates to such issues as whether Monday is still laundry-day and whether certain activities are still not (to be) undertaken on Sundays. Despite some minor changes over the years, marked differences between the days of the week can still be observed (Table 13.8). Regardless of the dispersion of tasks to the weekend, Saturday and Sunday remain days at which relatively little paid work is carried out. As regards housekeeping, Saturday never stood out from weekdays and only Sunday differed, a

Table 13.8   Distribution of paid work, housekeeping chores and leisure time over the days of the week, in hours per day, 18–65-year-olds, 1975–95.

	Paid work			Housekeeping chores			Leisure time		
	1975	1985	1995	1975	1985	1995	1975	1985	1995
Sunday	3	4	5	21	21	23	95	96	91
Monday	37	36	42	34	34	32	56	56	53
Tuesday	37	36	43	32	32	30	57	57	55
Wednesday	36	35	41	32	33	30	59	60	57
Thursday	37	36	43	33	34	31	57	57	54
Friday	35	33	38	35	36	33	62	63	61
Saturday	8	7	11	34	35	35	86	87	84

pattern that did not change either. Both weekend days stand out as leisure days, though the general decline in leisure applies to the weekend as well.

At this level of abstraction, weekdays appear very similar. The one exception is that Friday gradually obtains a shade of its own, as the weekday on which relatively little paid work is done. The share of Friday in the workload on weekdays diminished from 19.3 per cent in 1975 to 18.4 per cent in 1995. It should be noted, however, that there is a decline in work on Fridays in a relative sense only. In absolute terms, more work is being done on Fridays nowadays, but the growth on other weekdays was more marked. Yet Friday is still firmly a weekday.

Several of the housekeeping chores have become more evenly distributed over the days of the week (Table 13.9). In 1975, cleaning the house was done more on Monday, and again at the approach of

Table 13.9 Distribution of housekeeping chores[a] over the days of the week, in hours per day, 18–65-year-olds, 1975–95

	Preparing meals			Cleaning the house			Washing/ironing clothes		
	1975	1985	1995	1975	1985	1995	1975	1985	1995
Sunday	0.9	1.0	0.8	0.2	0.3	0.3	0.0	0.1	0.2
Monday	1.0	1.1	0.9	0.7	0.7	0.6	0.4	0.4	0.3
Tuesday	1.0	1.1	0.9	0.5	0.5	0.4	0.3	0.2	0.2
Wednesday	1.0	1.0	0.9	0.6	0.6	0.5	0.2	0.2	0.2
Thursday	1.0	1.0	0.9	0.7	0.6	0.5	0.2	0.2	0.2
Friday	1.0	1.0	0.8	0.8	0.7	0.5	0.2	0.2	0.2
Saturday	0.9	0.9	0.8	0.5	0.6	0.5	0.1	0.2	0.2

	Daily shopping			Other shopping			Childcare		
	1975	1985	1995	1975	1985	1995	1975	1985	1995
Sunday	0.0	0.0	0.0	0.0	0.0	0.1	0.5	0.4	0.4
Monday	0.2	0.2	0.2	0.1	0.1	0.1	0.4	0.5	0.5
Tuesday	0.2	0.2	0.2	0.2	0.2	0.2	0.4	0.5	0.5
Wednesday	0.2	0.2	0.2	0.2	0.2	0.2	0.4	0.5	0.5
Thursday	0.2	0.2	0.2	0.2	0.3	0.3	0.4	0.4	0.5
Friday	0.3	0.3	0.3	0.2	0.3	0.3	0.4	0.4	0.5
Saturday	0.3	0.3	0.3	0.5	0.5	0.5	0.4	0.4	0.4

[a] without travelling time (because this cannot be specified per housekeeping chore).

Source: as fot Table 13.1.

the weekend, than on other weekdays. Monday also stood out as a peak day as regards washing and ironing clothes. Both patterns have been eroded over the years. The intensification of cleaning the house before the weekend disappeared, while Monday is still laundry-day, but less so than before. Having the house done at the break of weekend has become less desirable, or less realizable, while washing and ironing clothes was redistributed, not least to the weekend.

Saturday remained 'just another day' in terms of time spent on daily shopping and the most popular day for other shopping. By 1995, Sunday was still free from daily shopping, but other shopping had already entered the Sunday agenda. Given the liberalization of shop opening hours in 1996, daily and other shopping on Sunday may well have been on the rise since, causing further levelling out of former differentiation between the days. Preparing meals and childcare had already been spread out over the week at the outset, a situation that did not change. Apparently, the compelling character of daily care for food and children leaves little leeway for variation over the days. Although the distribution of tasks over the week shows a great deal of continuity, the specific days of the week lost some distinctiveness, as the pattern of tidying the house and clothes eroded.

It was observed above that tasks were dispersed not only to the weekend, but also to weekday evenings. On an average weekday like Tuesday, 26 per cent of housekeeping was performed 'outside office hours' in 1995, against 22 per cent in 1975. Again, this shift mainly involves tidying the house and clothes, and it may be expected that shopping has followed suit since 1996. As regards paid work, the shift from daytime to the evening was smaller (8 per cent in 1975, 10 per cent in 1995).

A sharper view at the daily weekday routines can be obtained by observing the timing of a set of concrete daily activities that, taken together, roughly constitute the layout of the weekday of the (working) population. For that purpose, peak times of nine daily activities were assessed, as well as the percentages of participants in those activities around peak time (Table 13.10). In terms of the location of peak times, the timing of daily activities on Tuesday was highly stable over the 1975–95 period. The peak time of three out of nine activities shifted by only 15 minutes, whilst the others remained unchanged. This image of stability is counterbalanced by the fact that the percentages involved at those peak times dropped markedly in some instances. Most change occurred with respect to eating, with fewer enjoying breakfast, lunch, or dinner during peak time. Whilst meals serve as a collective

Table 13.10 Timing of daily activities on Tuesday: peak time (the quarter of an hour following the time mentioned) and the percentage of 18–65-year-olds involved at peak time,[a] 1975–95

	Peak time			% involved at peak time		
	1975	1985	1995	1975	1985	1995
Getting up	07:00	07:00	07:00	37	35	36
Breakfast	07:45	07:45	07:30	37	28	29
Commuting from home to work[b]	07:45	07:45	07:45	44	41	42
Lunch	12:30	12:30	12:30	63	54	52
Commuting from work to home[b]	17:00	17:00	17:00	34	33	30
Dinner	18:00	18:00	18:15	59	55	46
Watching television[c]	20:00	20:00	20:00	45	43	42
Calling it a day	23:15	23:00	23:00	36	31	32

Notes:
[a] percentage involved in the peak quarter, in the preceding quarter and/or in the following quarter.
[b] percentage of those who worked during at least 15 minutes on Tuesday.
[c] peak time here is the hour following the time mentioned, the percentage involved referring to those who watched television for at least 15 minutes during that hour.

Source: as for Table 13.1.

anchorage in the sea of time to a lesser degree than before, lunch and dinner none the less remain the most important collectively shared markers of time, followed by the morning rush hour and watching television.

Patterns of commuting, watching television and going to bed also reveal a decreasing concentration during peak time, though less clearly so. The fuss the alarm clock causes in the morning did not change, neither in terms of timing nor in terms of the numbers affected. So, although the height of most peaks eroded, their temporal location was markedly stable: existing collective rhythms are not easily erased. The next section will address whether the watering down of the collective character of daily rhythms affected day-to-day routines at the individual level.

Fewer routines

In an era oriented towards ever-changing and eventful experiences, the word 'routine' has acquired a somewhat negative connotation. However, without daily repeated routines, we would continuously face a profusion of choices. This section will examine whether successive weekdays of individuals have grown less alike.

From observations about collective rhythms, no conclusions about individual routines can be derived. The fact that substantial numbers simultaneously have breakfast, rush to work, have lunch, watch television and go to bed does not imply that individuals undertake these activities at the same time on consecutive days. The presence of a collective peak does not mean that the same individuals take part in that peak on consecutive days. Stability of collective rhythms does not equal stability of individual routines. Moreover, collective regularities may erode while individual regularity remains constant. If, for instance, some of those commuting during rush hour decide to start travelling one hour earlier to avoid the traffic jams, their new routine would reveal the same level of individual regularity, while the collective peak at rush hour would be lower.

An assessment of stability of individual routines requires a comparison of individual time use on various days. Here, Monday and Tuesday will be compared for each individual in our database. Doing so for several years facilitates an account of the extent to which a person's Monday resembles that same person's Tuesday – or not. This was analysed with respect to the same weekday activities analysed previously (Table 13.11). For each activity, it was assessed what percentage of 18–65-year-olds began that activity at the same time on Monday and Tuesday, with a margin of 15 minutes earlier or later.

Two things catch the eye: the clear presence of individual day-to-day routines as well as a notable decrease in those routines. As regards the level of daily routines, lunch and dinner do not stand out as the most marked 'Zeitgebers' , as was the case with respect to collective rhythms (cf. Table 13.10). Comparing individual activity patterns on Mondays and Tuesdays, getting up, having breakfast and starting to work reveal the highest degrees of day-to-day routinization. After markedly pronounced routines in the morning, individual regularity drops as the day unfolds. The beginning of daily tasks appears more clearly defined and more commanding than the end of those tasks later in the day. The same holds for meals: from breakfast via lunch to dinner, the individual routine in timing declines. Second, individual day-to-day rou-

Table 13.11 Individual similarity in the timing of daily activities on two
consecutive weekdays (Monday and Tuesday),[a] percentage of
18–65-year-olds, 1975–95

	1975	1985	1995
Getting up	72	67	66
Breakfast	72	66	68
Starting to work[b]	78	74	70
Lunch	68	64	58
Finishing work[b]	65	58	52
Dinner	61	57	50
Starting watching television[c]	43	30	28
Finishing watching television[c]	41	36	36
Calling it a day	49	49	46

Notes:
[a] within a margin of one quarter earlier or later.
[b] percentage of those who worked at least 15 minutes on both Monday and Tuesday.
[c] percentage of those who watched television at least 15 minutes on both Monday and
Tuesday.

Source: as for Table 13.1.

tines eroded between 1975 and 1995, yet affecting activities in the
morning, as well as going to bed, relatively little. Apparently, daily
duties are most compelling in the morning, and are foreshadowed at
the end of the previous evening. The decline in individual routines
affected lunch, finishing work, dinner, and starting to watch television
most of all.

The above figures on the regularity in beginning and finishing paid
work relate only to people who worked on both days. The decline in
routines might be underestimated by these figures, since they do not
cover the possibility that more people work one day but not the other.
Indeed, the percentage of 18–65-year-olds working either Monday or
Tuesday increased from 10 per cent in 1975 to 12 per cent in 1995. The
more irregular labour schedule also eroded daily individual routines.
On the other hand, however, the percentage working on both consecutive weekdays increased from 42 per cent to 48 per cent. As work structures activity patterns, the effects of these two changes in the labour
market appear to compensate for one another.

The diminished compliance with collective weekday rhythms did
indeed, then, go together with diminished individual routines. As to
the latter, an analysis of the total individual use of time on Monday
and on Tuesday, by way of comparing all 96 15-minute episodes on

both days for each individual, points to the same. To allow such a comparison, the broad spectrum of all diverse activities was reduced to four types of activities: sleep and personal care, paid work, housekeeping and childcare, and leisure. For each of the 18–65-year-olds, we counted the number of 15-minute episodes during which a person was engaged in the same activity on Tuesday as on Monday. The number of episodes spent on the same activity dropped slightly, but statistically significantly, from 70.0 in 1975 to 68.4 in 1995. This is not a major shift. Yet one ought to keep in mind that the crude four-fold typology of activities and the great number of episodes with fixed activities did not make a major shift very likely to start with.

With an eye to regularities such as sleep at night, paid or domestic work during daytime and leisure in the evening, the use of most of the 96 15-minute episodes is more or less fixed. This makes the amount of change all the more telling. Within the margins of enduring stability of time use on weekdays, individual routines lost some ground. As regards the latter, it was observed earlier that Friday developed into a somewhat 'different' weekday. This does not apply to Monday or Tuesday, so our analysis of change in individual weekday routines focused on days on which change was least expected. This adds to the salience of the modest shift that was none the less observed.

Conclusion and discussion

Following reconstruction in the immediate postwar era, Dutch society went through a number of changes which pressurized the former structuring of time, such as the inflow of women in paid work, the advent of the dual-earner family, the flexibilization of working hours, and the secularization of society. In addition, the diffusion of technological devices like the washing machine, the microwave oven, the video recorder and the Internet enlarged the possibility to structure one's time in accordance with one's individual preferences.

This chapter has described change and permanence in the usage and structuring of time over the 1975–95 period with respect to paid and domestic work, focusing on roles, rhythms and routines in everyday life. The package of tasks of both men and women increased in numbers and diversity, eroding the clear former distinction between housewife and male provider. Members of both sexes more often combine paid and domestic work. On the one hand, this points to the entanglement of roles, as persons fulfil (parts of) various roles. On the other hand, this points to the blurring of roles, as tasks less clearly cluster into distinct roles. As more people combined part-time positions in the labour force and in the private household, time pressures grew.

The distribution of tasks over the sexes was accompanied by a distribution of tasks over time. Paid as well as domestic work is more often scheduled in the evening and at the weekend. Despite this distribution, week and day rhythms proved rather stable. Within the week rhythm, however, the pattern in the distribution of housekeeping chores over the week was weakened. And while the timing of the day rhythm hardly changed, it was complied with by fewer people. Yet, over the week and over a weekday, the collective timing of activities remained largely unaltered.

Individual routines, i.e. the repetitive character of an individual's activities, revealed more change over the years. The similarity in the timing of an individual's activities on Mondays and Tuesdays decreased, especially in the afternoon and the early evening. The main results are summarized in Figure 13.1.

It can be observed that, although roles, rhythms and routines were subject to change, time still does not elapse as a 'grey fog'. Furthermore, one should note that (gender) roles changed more than collective rhythms and individual routines. In light of the changing

---

Roles

- entanglement of roles: people combine various roles
- blurring of roles: tasks constitute roles less clearly (functional distribution of tasks)
- combined effect: multiple part-time positions and greater time pressure

Rhythms

- temporal distribution of tasks: tasks more often performed in the evening or at the weekend
- though largely stable, the week rhythmn faded somewhat
- timing of the weekday rhythmn was stable, but fewer numbers complied with it

Routines

- considerable level of individual routines in weekday timing of activities
- some fading of individual weekday routines

Figure 13.1 Change and permanence in roles, rhythms and routine

roles, the flexibilization of working-hour regulations, the decline in Christian rites, and the introduction of appliances that allow a more flexible use of time, it may appear to be rather surprising how well collective rhythms and individual routines have stood their ground.

Two things should be kept in mind. First, increased participation in paid work has brought greater numbers under the discipline of working hours, which enhances collective rhythms and individual routines. Second, our data report only on the realized use of time. The effort required to realize that use of time is beyond our range of vision. Indeed, the effort it takes to adhere to rhythms and routines in daily life may well have increased. In dual-earner families, women's time no longer functions as a buffer between the concurring school hours of children, shop hours for shopping, and the working hours of the male provider. Indeed, the working hours of women introduce an additional schedule into the family, making it more likely for the various rhythms to collide. Preventing this may therefore require more deliberate planning of time usage. On the other hand, the greater liberty to structure one's time as one prefers also brings greater responsibility for one's preferred use of time. New patterns of time usage do not occur automatically. The more the choice of and adherence to habits are a matter of personal deliberation, the more organizing talent is required.

Even if the actual use of time differs only marginally, people may experience more pressure from having to reflect upon and organize their own time. If and to what extent sticking to collective rhythms and individual routines indeed became more demanding over the years is beyond our range of vision. The call for more day care suggests that changing roles have made it more exacting to maintain rhythms and routines. In that case, the major change does not relate to those rhythms and routines themselves, but to the cost of complying with them.

14
Time for Life: Time for Being and Becoming

Davina Chaplin

Introduction

This chapter draws on an empirical research project focusing on the experiences and attitudes of a group of British owners of second homes in rural France: 29 unstructured interviews carried out between 1995 and 1997 were subsequently analysed using QSR NUDIST-4. The principles of grounded theory were adopted to evolve a thematic framework. One of the emerging themes was that of time, in relation both to escapes from working lives in Britain and to the routines and repetitions involved in the repeated visits to second homes. The ways in which the respondents conceptualize time in the context of their French homes reflect the rhythms of these lives in the broader framework of their year-round existences.

Time spent away from home, on vacation, is time out from daily life. Ryan (1997) argues that the expression associated with holidaying, 'the time of our lives', implies that time is not merely a chronological sequence but a social construct. Successful holidays, according to Ryan, involve a number of concepts of time, some of which are clearly applicable to second-home experiences: freedom from the normal regulatory constraints; the potential to experience natural time as a concept not associated with rhythms imposed by work; the opportunity to create memorable time which is an asset for the future; time which functions as a period of self-awareness (Ryan, 1997, p. 201). Inherent in some of these concepts are numerous paradoxes: for example, the fact that freedom from normal constraints of time is itself constrained by the period set aside for the holiday and by the need to return to normal life, leading, in turn, to self-imposed planning and scheduling of time to make the most of the holiday period.

The second-home owners interviewed in this study show a tendency to emphasize the other aspect of time in relation to holidays which Ryan identifies: not so much the time *of* our lives, but time *for* our lives. The importance of returning to the same place, rather than continually seeking out new places, reveals the difference between the mirage phenomenon, yearning for new paradises, in which to have *the time of one's life*, and the obverse of this, the creation of a context in which there is *time in which to live*, differently, more fully, at a different tempo.

Horizons

There is, however, another dimension to the time for living, which is about the shifts between the everyday perspective and a lifetime view. Alheit's (1994) account of the different horizons of time, everyday time and life time, and how individuals attempt to 'heal' the gap between the two, offers some useful pointers to understanding the shifting and linking process which is evident when people tell their stories. The telling of 'life stories' can be seen as attempts to synchronize the everyday time frame and the life time horizon which links past, present and future. The cyclical nature of everyday time, with its routines as well as its spontaneity, is mingled with the linearity and sequential character of the lifetime perspective (*ibid.*, p. 307). In the following extract, Louise oscillates between description of 'healing' time spent in the French home and a perspective on the career trajectory of her lawyer husband:

> The whole experience really, I love it there. I never feel as well, I feel relaxed, it's just a reflection on our own lifestyle, but when we first moved to London we had no ... we came here because of Peter's job and he had articles with a firm in the City and he's ended up staying there, he's a partner, he's just done ten years and it's incredibly hectic. But you don't have any idea of what it's going to be like, you don't realise how demanding ... He enjoys his job tremendously and he wouldn't change that at all, and I think he's incredibly lucky to have a job which really is for life and very few people have that. So of course we have to cope with that and all the demands that surround that. But when I say bolt hole that doesn't mean to say we don't enjoy our lives here, we do, they're very fulfilling in many ways, but they're also incredibly demanding. Almost to the point at times where it's too much, and if we didn't have France I don't know how well we'd cope. (Louise, 40s, teacher)

The horizons of everyday time and life time, of succession and intention, in the above narrative are suggestive of Aristotle's two time forms,
chronos (dating time), objective, discontinuous, atomistic, and *kairos*
(time which gives value), subjective, continuous, flowing, which are
brought together by Jaques (1982) into a two-dimensional conception
of time. Jaques holds that the two dimensions form alternating perspectives from which we view the world, and that for a balanced view
of time and life there must be a continual oscillation between the two
perspectives. The dimension of succession and the dimension of intention are both awarenesses of time in the individual.

The environment of the French home, it seems, allows its owners to
take a break from working lives, but, more importantly, the leaving
behind of their first-home environment signifies also a departure from
routine everyday situations. Alheit (1994) identifies this as a 'conjunc-
ture' which gives rise to 'the transgression of the everyday time frame',
which, he insists, is not a complete desertion of accustomed routine,
but, rather, 'appears to trigger off retrospective and prospective biographical analyses' (p. 309). As far as the French second-home owners
are concerned, there is an observable propensity to review their lives
from the perspective of the distance provided by the French environment and through the lens of a different temporality; there are
instances of narrative life histories which are sparked off by the story of
finding the French house but which then review experiences of previous houses, past holidays, careers and marriages, almost without any
prompting:

> I'm in a second marriage actually, so I had a maisonette in the first
> marriage and then a house with the first marriage, and then my
> husband now also had a house, you know, his own house, and
> hence the reason we bought the second home, was because we both
> had a house each, we were ready to live together and we had the
> money from one house to use. (Sarah, 30s, former catering manager)

Equally, interviewees often talk at length about their future plans and
projects in the context of the French property, but in a way which
then broadens out into a much wider frame of reference, for example
'downshifting' prospects, retirement plans, dreams of 'dropping out'
altogether and living permanently in France, and even a future which
continues in their children's lives:

> I think the whole project is going to be a two-generation thing,
> quite honestly. I think it's a long-term thing, but I mean that's

assuming that the kids will want to stay there and carry on, but for us, it's the fourth year now, isn't it? And I see at least another four or five years of work there doing places up, improving places, developing it, and keeping it going. There's plenty of work, it's non-stop, if it's not hedging it's planting crops, it's going harvesting later on ... (Bob, 30s, teacher)

I could tell I was like that and eventually I calmed right down, and then I sort of went so far down I was ... [laughs] lovely and relaxed and suddenly one day I was working down in the garden and I've never really liked gardening before, so that's been a change for me, and I thought I could really quite happily do this, I felt yes, I would miss things about England, I would miss friends, I would miss my job, but I did really really feel ready to do that. And that hasn't left me. That for me was a real sort of ... [watershed point] ... I think we've both said it's given us some kind of focus outside our life here in a way. But saying that it can be quite difficult having sort of two lives in a way ... (Fiona, 30s, teacher)

In the above extracts, Bob concentrates his thoughts on a prospective biography, whereas Fiona gives an insight into the moment when she suddenly felt she was 'ready' to live in France for good and started to think in terms of a change of focus, such that the retrospective narrative turns into a kind of mission statement for the future, while at the same time acknowledging the problems of the present, the conflicting elements of living 'two lives', as she puts it.

Tempo

For the majority of second-home owners, one of the chief attractions of living in France seems to be the different pace at which life is lived. It appears that there is a slowing down of the pace of life, at least for periods of the year, that is reflected in the experiences of 'being' in the context of the French home environment expressed by the respondents. The combination of their own familiar home environment and the feeling of *living*, not staying in a place, as holidaymakers do, is presented as something which is more effective than even the most restful of holidays. Even those who have retired from full-time work make comments about the pace of life and the pleasure of slowing down:

Here you can wander along, even at my advanced age! Just wander along quite gently, a nice little walk up to the *boulangerie* or the post office ... I think this is one of the advantages that we always say about this place is that you can just wander out, and reach quite a lot of places. (Edward, 70s, retired company director)

Everyone's laid back, the pace of life is so easy. (Alan, 60s, retired blacksmith)

However, for those who are still working, the contrast with the pace of their life in England is something which has a greater impact on them:

It really is the place where we unwind a bit and we have some family time and we get over the exhaustion and live at a more normal pace. (Louise, 40s, teacher)

Robinson and Godbey (1997), in their study of the way Americans use their time, refer to slowing down the pace of life as a major issue for the future. Taking issue with Schor's (1991) concept of the 'overworked American' in terms of the hours that Americans work, they nevertheless agree with her critique of the 'work and spend cycle' and the level of materialism reached. The pressure that Americans feel under, Robinson and Godbey maintain, is not because there is actually less free time, but because of the faster tempo to working lives, and the contribution this makes to people's perceptions of how hard (and long) they are working. According to their 1992 survey, a third of Americans always felt 'rushed'. This feeling also applied to many of the French second-home owners, particularly those employed in teaching:

Here, it's rushing about all the time, whereas there, the watch comes off and it doesn't matter what time we get up, go to bed or eat, whereas here there are so many time restrictions, everything goes by the clock ... over there it isn't. (Sandra, 40s, teacher)

Interestingly, in the American survey, a quarter of those surveyed blamed leisure activities as well as work obligations for the feeling of being rushed. As Robinson and Godbey observe, 'speed and brevity are more widely admired, whether in serving food, in the length of magazine articles, or in conversation' (1997, p. 48). 'Time-deepening' practices are adopted in order to cope with the 'time famine', which Linder (1970) identifies as a characteristic of contemporary consumption. These include doing more than one activity at once, speeding up a given activity or substituting a less time-intensive leisure activity for one that takes longer. All these forms of behaviour, which Robinson and Godbey observe most typically among upwardly mobile Americans, achieve a higher rate of doing but also cause great stress. They also mean that people 'take' from an activity, rather than 'give' themselves to it, in contrast to what the psychologist Csikszentmihalyi (1988) defines as refreshing 'flow' experiences, in which there is a letting go and a loss of all sense of time. One of the salient characteristics of 'flow' experiences is immersion in a task or activity, and some of the second homers expressed experiences of time in France in terms of being absorbed in pottering activities which induce a sense of timelessness:

> So there's always something, some sort of project ... I'm a lot busier than Richard. Part of my relaxation is, Richard calls it, Jane's off to tick round! I can actually go in the barn and appear four hours later and he says what are you doing? And I say, well, I just fiddled around with that and I've moved this ... (Jane, 40s, career consultant)

Others related this to a lack of awareness of clock time, especially as this affects meal times:

> *Pamela:* I mean we're not desperate about doing things, we do what we feel like on the day. If one of us doesn't feel like it we don't do it. Then sometimes we feel bad at the end of the holiday when we haven't achieved what we actually set out to do. So if we do a bit of work we generally have a late lunch, don't we?
>
> *Andrew:* Yea. Lose track of time, I suppose that's fairly typical ... come in and have lunch at about 4 o'clock! (Pamela and Andrew, 40s, civil servants)

The tempo aspect of time (rate or speed of activity) is constructed by many of the participants as an integral part of what they understand by 'the French way of life'.

> When we're with friends we tend to eat like the French do, just round a table and stay there and take a long, long time because it's just so easy and laid back, it's quite different to entertaining here which I don't enjoy very much. It's interesting, isn't it? But there *is* a difference, I think really it's geared up there for a very casual easy-going way of life and the dining room and the kitchen are ... you can chat to each other ... It's so much more relaxing than at home,

The dinner party thing which I've never been very good at! (Kath, 50s, self-employed transport manager)

Stress and de-stressing

Stress is something referred to by many of the home owners in the context of an escape syndrome. Physical labour, as opposed to mental, is constructed by some as the antidote to stress, as 'giving a part of yourself a break' as Bob puts it:

> We just relax, don't we? Yea, yea, I mean we've got such sort of types of stressful jobs, mentally stressful jobs, whereas if you then switch and you go over there, you know you're on a working holiday, but it's physical labour, so it's totally different and there-fore it's just the same as a rest really because you're not using your mind all the time, you give that part of yourself a bit of a break. (Bob, 30s, teacher)

The French rural lifestyle is perceived by the British second-home owners as not only slower in pace, but also existentially superior, because of the importance attached to allowing time for the savouring of experience, often gastronomic:

> I think we're different people. Partly because I think the French are laid back about everything, very philosophical ... certainly I think it has encouraged us to be similarly laid back and philosophical and to concentrate on things like wine and food ... (Ian, 50s, architect)

This is very much along the lines of what Robinson and Godbey (1997) argue is a critical variable in how satisfying future time use will be:

> We need to cultivate time-savoring skills, in order to appreciate the simpler delights of life as they are occurring: the taste of good food, the presence of good company, and the delights of good fun and silliness. (p. 316)

The inherent difficulty in changing to a 'more time to smell the roses' mentality is epitomized in a phrase, currently in use in Britain, to indi-cate proficiency and currency of knowledge and skill, 'up to speed'. More than anything else this phrase reflects the contemporary preoc-cupation with speed and pace of life, implying that slowness also means dullness or ignorance. However, for the second-home owners, slowness means something very different, albeit for only part of their lives, the time spent in France, as Jane emphasizes:

> Now we're slowing down, what we're going to do, if it's slowed down, before it used to be a major project, and often things we're doing ... that leads to a beer and a chat ... and it's just so *slow*, not just slow, laid back, you know, totally stress-free. (Jane, 40s, career consultant)

Resisting clock time

Many of the interviewees demonstrate the different pace of life through a lack of awareness of clock time, and the spontaneity this brings to their days. This reveals the symbolic nature of the clock as an oppressor and regulator: as Zerubavel remarks, that 'many people, when they are on vacation, often display a strong defiance of social constraints by deliberately refusing to wear a watch ought to be understood in this context' (1981, p. 49). The data from the project show how the respondents often make connections between the abandoning of clocks and watches and a free flow of being:

> The watch comes off, life is more spontaneous. (Sandra, 40s, teacher)

> You just go with the flow. (Richard, 40s, oceanographer)

> I think the only way I can describe it is the day can be totally fluid. (Jane, 40s, career consultant)

> I associate having the house there and our things ... our house there with also time enough to take life in and just to *be*. (Howard, 40s, GP)

One couple, both teachers, describe in detail the contrast between their stays in France and their lives in Britain, where not only clocks but also bells seem to rule their lives:

> The most wonderful thing was when none of us knew what day it was! We eventually worked out that it must be Wednesday, but I mean living the kind of life we do, your life is ruled by bells. I could tell you exactly all the time of the bells and when I realised that – never mind the date, I had no idea about that. I knew it was August,

but the fact that nobody could work out the day was just *brilliant!* (Fiona, 30s, teacher)

Spontaneity and synchronicity

Not knowing the day or date, or not knowing what the time is, are both related to not being controlled or regulated by mechanical devices or bureaucratic schedules. However, apart from the dizzy sense of freedom that this appears to generate, as it does for Fiona, there is another positive benefit: spontaneity. Zerubavel (1981) refers to the rigidification imposed by the scheduling and routines of modern life, of the duration of events or activities, their sequential order, the rate of recurrence of events or activities, all of which lead to a loss of spontaneity. Even purely biological activities are standardized: 'most of us get up, eat, and go to sleep not necessarily when we feel like it, but, rather, in accordance with a schedule' (p. 47). In contrast, many of the owners refer to unregulated eating and sleeping in France:

It's very, very peaceful and I sleep like the dead here ... you know, it's so quiet. I really, really unwind. I sometimes I have difficulty waking up all day ... just drowse, drowse, sleep, sleep, sleep ... (Diana, 50s, middle manager)

Spontaneity, according to Zerubavel, entails doing things at the rate one desires, in what order one prefers, and for as long as one likes, all of which is antithetical to routines and schedules. Some of the participants in the second-home project construct their typical days in France very much in terms of spontaneity. For example, this woman contrasts the hectic, time-constrained nature of family life in a northern city in Britain with the total lack of constraints during the stays in a hamlet near the Atlantic coast in France:

Here, it's rushing about all the time, whereas there, the watch comes off and it doesn't matter what time we get up, go to bed or eat, whereas here, there are so many time restrictions, everything goes by the clock ... Over there it doesn't ... I mean the children don't have a bedtime there, they go when they're tired, or when we go to bed, whereas here, you know, it's nine o'clock bedtime ... We have a clock in the kitchen but we don't look at the time at all. Just don't worry about that. We eat at all sorts of odd times, when we feel like it. (Sandra, 40s, teacher)

Spontaneity makes an irrelevance of aspects of time scheduling such as timing, synchronization and sequencing; it also brings with it an openness to serendipity, the delight of chance discovery, and even what Jung (1960) calls *synchronicity*: 'a meaningful coincidence of two or more events where something other than the probability of chance is involved' (p. 104). Satori (1999) redefines Jung's concept of synchronicity, emphasizing the relationship between an inner psychic state and an outward physical manifestation: 'Synchronicity is an event or series of events when the external and internal worlds affect each other, making meaningful experiences that change our lives' (p. 21). To be aware of synchronicity, it is necessary to be open to the moment, in a way that is made difficult, if not impossible, by adherence to rigid timetables and tempos. Satori relates this to the Greek *chronos* and *kairos* mentioned earlier in this chapter: synchronicity occurs at intersections in *kairos* and *chronos* time: 'We are in our busy chronos lives, going about our day, and suddenly something hits us ... Suddenly, we can find ourselves transformed by an event that puts us into the uncontrolled kairos time' (*ibid.*, p. 6).

Some of the accounts of finding the French house echo this sense of allowing *kairos* into one's life, as several women reveal. For example:

> We'd never seen it, it was part of a holiday, just the looking, as I think it is for most people ... so we had no real intention at all ... we happened on it by accident because we were supposed to go to St Jean les Églises but we hadn't got as far as that, night had fallen and thunderstorms had occurred ... so we checked in at Rochechouart. I get up very early ... so I stomped off, walked round the town and looked as one does at estate agents' windows and saw this, it looked fine, at a price we could justify ... with own little park and river! First category, aha I thought! I went in and said I wanted to go and see that, ... it was an incredible day, it was the day to buy places in France ... He said, it couldn't possibly be for us! So I knew I'd won ... [on seeing the house] I had a really welcome feeling, it was a very strange feeling, I felt happy and he [partner] said the same afterwards. (Valerie, 60s, accommodation agent)

References to 'strange' and 'welcome' feelings are quite common among the stories told, particularly by the women owners. The men, on the other hand, tend to represent synchronicity as strange and amusing coincidence. However, it is still the case that the men 'go along' with what the coincidences bring, surrendering to the intuitions and instincts which lead them to the purchase of a specific property in a specific place. In this way, the experience is an example of opening up to new opportunities, or, as the following owner expresses it, 'a new avenue':

I think it's opened up a new avenue in our life – it's given us a great interest. (Trevor, 60s, retired technician)

Routines and repetitions

The ways in which the unfamiliar and novel become routine and normal are also part of the story of working at consumption; just as the process of working on the house is consumed and enjoyed for its own sake, so too are the daily and weekly routines and habits. In contrast to the picture Giddens (1991) gives of rituals as 'coping mechanisms', the second-home owners often construct their routines as sources of pleasure and feelings of authenticity. In the following extract, a technician tells a story of slipping into habits of preparing, cooking and eating meals in France which he describes as feeling like the 'real life', unlike his life in suburban London, which feels like a 'sham'. He even uses the term domestic *'ritual'* to describe the change of rhythm and routine, which is a reflection of how he sees the difference between the habits of his urban British way of life and the simpler French one:

It's bizarre, it takes a day to get there, so we gradually get into it as it gets warmer. As we're passing Paris we're still worrying about work and who's looking after the cats, but by the time you get to Clermont Ferrand you've forgotten, you don't give a shit, and suddenly you realise this is the reason you come down because you slip into a different domestic ritual when you're there. You spend four hours cooking instead of just half an hour. And so everything's changed, you do things in a different way, it's a lifestyle. You do feel completely like a different person. *When you're there it feels like your life in England is not the real life, life in England is some sort of sham.* (Dave, 30s, technician – emphasis added)

Interestingly, Dave later referred to his life in France as 'just pretending to live there', revealing a paradoxical construction of the opposition between life in suburban London and rural France as sham versus real, but also reality versus pretence. For him escape is also an escapade, deriving from the switch of culture, something he describes as 'feeling like an adventure'. Simmel (1971) characterizes the adventure as 'a foreign body in our existence which is yet somehow connected with the centre'; Dave contrives his escape from everyday routine through the very routines or rituals he slips into in France, illustrating the structuring of freedom or the patterned nature of escapes from routines (Cohen and Taylor, 1992).

Yi-Fu Tuan (1998), in his book about culture as escape from nature, makes the point that escape, if it has the feel of clarity, is experienced as an encounter with the real, and that rituals can be defined in these terms: 'Participation in a ritual is participation in something serious and real; it is escape from banality and opaqueness of life into an event that clarifies life and yet preserves a sense of mystery' (p. 23). This sense of escaping from the banal everyday to encounters with different, and sometimes spiritually experienced, moments, almost akin to epiphanies, within chosen routine practices, is constructed by some of the owners as 'ritual' of the kind to which Tuan refers. Here another French home owner describes the early morning trips to buy bread as a 'ritual', or his daily 'fix':

> I go out every morning and nip down to C., which is about 7 kilometres ... it's my fix for the day ... it's *my* moment, it's my time ... I always have a piece of music for each holiday and I just play the same track over and over and over again, and on my journey and there was one, it was last year, but it was one aria, it was the Easter Hymn, from *Cavalleria Rusticana* and just as it got to the real crescendo, this buzzard took off and just flew straight up, and I thought this is life, this is the meaning of life, you know, this beautiful music, this great big bird flying over, and I sort of caught it as, I caught a view of it in the sun roof as I was driving along, and I was just crying as I got home, it was an odd thing! [laughs] (Richard, 40s, oceanographer)

If solitude is a feature of these ritualized experiences for men like Richard, the women more commonly link familiarity and routine with shared experiences. Here a woman with four children gives an account of the happiness she feels in her French home:

> You can't really put your finger on quite what it is, but it is a very nice, happy atmosphere ... I mean I think there is something about familiarity and everybody knowing ... and in some ways children are creatures of habit, they want the same sort of routine ... aren't we going to do this? (Annabel, 40s, property agent)

It seems that enjoying ordinary, simple things in a comfortable and comfortingly familiar ambience is achieved through a routine-making appropriation of the otherness of the environment, interacting with the French context in adapting elements of family life and adopting customs and practices which then become absorbed into the experience itself. Self-regulated routines are an important part of the process by and through which the consumers of the second home *make* and *do* their lives. In his account of the home as a material site for expression, Dant (1999, p. 72), citing the work of Michel de Certeau (1984), uses the term 'bricolage' to denote arts of 'making do' which are 'combined with ritual practices, habits and routines out of which the shape of everyday life emerges'. For Dant, rituals are neither a matter of conscious choice nor determined by social conditioning:

> Rituals may be followed knowingly because it suits the purposes at hand but these purposes might lead to a modification of the ritual, of material objects or of skills to meet varying situations or even to bring about variations in action, experience or environment. (Dant, 1999, p. 72)

The consuming and producing of dwelling in second-home contexts, perhaps more than in first homes (where there is less time and more social pressure to conform) amply demonstrates this kind of creative adaptation. The 'French' way of thinking or living is adopted, adapted and appropriated by the British owners and integrated into their patterns of consumption. The ceremonial and observance aspects of traditional forms of ritual are perhaps not apparent, but there is a sense in which routines and habits, lovingly repeated and carefully observed and savoured, are close to those traditions. The difference is that the actors have invented or adapted, adopted or chosen the habits for themselves, not because of any prescribed set of rules or codes. In this way, there could be said to be both a self-determined routinization of the exotic and a re-routinization of their lives, at least for part of the year. Changing contexts means changing gears, but also switching to appropriate forms of behaviour and practices, in a way which is constructed as profoundly different from conventional experiences of holiday places.

Time 'out' or ontological time

Returning to Jaques's (1982) two-dimensional conception of time, the experience of succession and the experience of intention, *chronos* and *kairos*, the second-home owners seem to be, to a greater or lesser extent, oscillating between the two aspects. The experiences of 'being' in the French home context expressed by the respondents are constructed as, on the one hand, time out from the confines of their lives and identities in Britain, and, on the other, as a recurring opportunity to pursue life goals, a more abstract, ontological time. Continuity and memory are important facets of these experiences, but so are future goals and expectations. Thus the two-dimensional conception of time, succession and intention, *chronos* and *kairos*, is mediated through the French lives of the participants. The active choosing to engage in routines embedded in these lives is a force for change for the owners, affecting the ways in which they construct their identities and anticipate their futures. The very fact of the long-term conversion and renovation process involved in the French project contributes to this change, and the repeated visits to the second home renew the past and refresh the future goals, both in terms of concrete achievement and personal growth. The temporal horizon is both nearer and further away: some owners talk about how the knowledge that the house is there, and that they will return to it, 'gets them through the winter in Britain'. In this sense the experience is of a cyclical time, but the other horizon is embedded in the long term, stretching back to the pre-purchase and purchase phases and forward to the distant future, of retirement or another way of life.

Robinson and Godbey (1997) conclude their book, *Time for Life*, on a reassuring note of optimism about the possibility of letting go, of 'accepting the gift of time' (p. 318). The shift from efficiency (wanting more) to appreciation (being aware of and valuing what one has, wanting less) is seen as the way to a sustainable society, but also the path to wellness, defined as '[a] balance among physical, emotional, spiritual, intellectual and social health.' (Alberta Centre for Well-Being, 1989, cited in Robinson and Godbey, 1997, p. 315).

In a number of ways the second-home owners demonstrate a change towards a conceptualization of time as natural as well as social time, a lived rhythm through which they are able to find a sense of well-being. In her treatise on natural and social time, Adam (1990) uses the term 'rhythmicity' to denote what she sees as a universal phenomenon, the ultimate source of life and form, fundamental to nature, including human nature, and preferable to the reversible time of Lévi-Strauss and Giddens: 'Rhythmicity, which entails cycles, structure, and processes with variation, would therefore be a more useful key concept for social theory than reversible time' (*ibid.*, p. 89).

This rhythmicity can be said to apply to what the second-home owners are doing in the consumption of their French lives: a process of learning to enjoy a more subjective 'temporal' time (Adam, 1990, p. 24). In part this relates to the control they claim to have over the part of the lives spent in their French homes, in contrast with the feelings of being subjected to the demands of daily life in urban Britain. It also derives from the active choices made about the time they spend in France, the simpler way of life into which they slip, the renewing of their acquaintance with place and community, and the building of a stock of memories which are enjoyed both in the present and in the future. It is time which is symbolized better by the wheel than by the line; it also resonates with a deeper feeling for life (de Grazia, 1974, cited in Hassard, 1990).

15
Collecting Time: the Social Organization of Collecting

Jackie Goode

Introduction: the collecting phenomenon

> Some people like to collect things, I like to collect experiences. This is the equivalent of buying the Mona Lisa (Millennium Eve reveller, New York's celebrations in Time Square).

> While Britain partied into the new millennium, a painting by Cézanne valued at three million pounds was stolen from the Ashmolean, the world's oldest public museum, and home to one of Britain's finest art collections.
>
> (Both extracts from *The Observer*. 2 January 2000)

These reports signal only a few of the social activities which constitute collecting. Definitions of collecting vary according to whether there is a focus on famous collectors (Elsner and Cardinal, 1994), on objects collected (Dant, 1999), or on practices followed (Belk, 1995), and on how closely one adheres to the model of the 'connoisseur', or takes a more inclusive position which encompasses lower-status activity. This study adopts a broad definition which seeks to examine collecting as a process which is made up of sets of everyday practices, socially organized around acquisition, and engaged in by large numbers of people from a variety of backgrounds. Collecting offers a window on a complex of individual, social, economic and cultural relations, and while the content of any one collection says a great deal about the person who created it, the 'collecting career' often encompasses several changes in choice of objects. Beyond the objects themselves, therefore, lie a number of common themes which illustrate the social and pro-cessual nature of collecting. Time is just such a theme.

Collecting is a prominent feature of social life. Between a quarter to a third of all adults are willing to identify themselves as collectors at any given moment (Pearce, 1998), and this may even be an underestimate since the figure was derived from a 'snap-shot' investigation; if all those who have had or will have collecting experience were included, the figure may be nearer to half the population.

The growth in collecting is evidenced by the huge number of antiques and collectors' fairs which take place all over the UK. Arrowsmith (1999) catalogues 315 large antiques and collectors' fairs and markets (those between 50 and 300 stalls) which take place regularly at indoor and outdoor sites across the country, drawing a mixture of serious collectors, professional dealers, bargain hunters or people just interested in antiques. Stall-holders surveyed displayed merchandise worth between £1,000 and £80,000. At a small number of prestigious 'datelined' fairs, the estimated stall value rose to many millions of pounds. To these sources may be added car boot sales, shops, mail order catalogues and the Internet.

Why now?

Popular writers and journalists, as well as academic historians, have attempted to explain what appears to be a sharp increase in all activities associated with collecting. To suggestions that there has always been a well-established and broadly based, but hitherto unrecognized, activity of collecting are added a number of themes: unsettled times (Burke, 1994), which enhance the value of nostalgia (Samuel, 1994); increasing affluence which allows the spread of what was once an exclusively high-status activity (Lacey, 1999; Platt, 1978); and a media agenda driven by commercial as well as artistic reasons (McRobbie, 1989) for wishing to increase interest in consumption.

Early psychological analyses consigned 'low-status' collecting exclusively to childhood (Olmsted, 1991), and this may account for negative conceptualizations of adult collectors as 'deviant'. Samuel (1994) refers to collectors as 'Clio's under-labourers' and 'memory-keepers' and locates 'mass' collecting within a broader historicist turn in national life. He identifies the media as active agents in promoting the twentieth-century phenomenon of 'heritage'. The impetus for this turn apparently lies in a heightened sense of disappearing worlds, exemplified by a whole series of separation anxieties: the deterioration of regional economies; threats to the living environment which put the taken-for-granted at risk; and the rise of cultural nationalism.

Corner and Harvey (1991) also observe that the media have inserted 'pastness' into popular narratives, but they prefer to align 'heritage' with 'enterprise', as two elements of an officially managed transition in national attitudes and culture during the 1980s.

Museums make a key contribution to this project. Traditionally focusing on the collection and the objects which comprise it, rather than with process and practice (Pearce, 1999), they now face a dilemma over objects collected without documentation and neutered of meanings derived from private ownership. How to recover something of the human experience behind the objects, without preserving only 'preferred memories' (Kavanagh, 1999)? Museums have recently begun to take an interest in 'everyday collecting', seeking to institutionalize the activities of small private collectors. The result is a debate within museum studies between those who suggest that private collectors form an important part of the community involved in preserving material culture, with the distinction between 'professional' and 'amateur' status becoming less and less salient (Martin, 1995), and those who wish to retain a distance from 'amateurs', as institutional collecting becomes more rigorous and intellectually focused (Knell, 1999).

All aspects of collecting have received increasing media attention. On television, the enduring popularity of *The Antiques Roadshow* has spawned a number of similar programmes; the interactive relationship between broadcast, print and electronic media is illustrated by the magazines and websites which now routinely accompany the TV programmes themselves; e-commerce caters for the global collector; at a local level, reports of collecting clubs appear in regional newspapers; and the 'money' pages of both broadsheets and tabloids regularly feature collecting as investment. Investment is certainly on the agenda for new groups of people with a heightened awareness of the need for financial self-provision; an interplay of demographics and economics may also be a factor in any increase in collecting.

Pricing in the collectables market is very fluid, however, and bargain-hunters can become disillusioned. The manufacture of 'new' collectables may be seen to act as a hedge against such risks, as well as alleviating the need to search charity shops and car boot sales. It remains to be investigated what the characteristics are of those who choose 'new' collectables, and whether they are distinct from collectors of 'old' goods. Collectors of merchandise produced in association with children's TV programmes and films, the epitome of the instantly created collectable, the 'Beanie Baby', and playground trading phenomena such as Pokemon and Digimon cards also invite further research.

Pearce's (1998) survey of contemporary collecting in Britain gives some insight into the dimensions of everyday collecting practices. Women are more likely than men to be collectors; most collectors live in families with partners and children; collecting is spread fairly uniformly across the age ranges; and 'socio-economic group is not a factor that greatly affects collecting practice' (*ibid.*, p. 29). The sizes of her respondents' collections were quite small (around twenty pieces each), and the typical cost of a single item was £5. This seems to represent a fairly modest scale of collecting given that goods to the value of £2.2 billions are bought and sold in antiques each year (*The Crime Squad*, BBC1, 21 February 2000). Of course, the price paid for an item is not necessarily the same as its value in the collectables markets. Furthermore, not all collectors actually know the size or monetary value of their collections, while those with very valuable collections may not wish to share the information.

Pearce's suggestion that gender rather than class or age is the most significant factor differentiating collecting practice echoes gender differences in relationships to personal possessions in general (Dittmar, 1991). Over and above collecting 'sex-appropriate' objects, Pearce suggests gender differences in collecting patterns, practices and motivations: men collect at special times and special places, and in order to organize their material, whilst women display their collections in the home, engaging in acts of remembering. How far such clear distinctions can be supported by more qualitative data remains to be seen.

Sociologists have paid very little attention thus far to contemporary collecting practices, despite the increasing emphasis on consumption (Campbell, 1995). What people do with objects after purchase, what 'possession and grooming rituals' (McCracken, 1985) they engage in, or what kinds of issues emerge around acts of disposal of goods acquired, all remain under-researched. My own study of collecting makes a contribution here, but also aims to go further. It conceptualizes collecting not only as a form of consumption, with purchasing taking place across a number of different sites, and with roles and rules which may resemble or contrast with more conventional consumption practices, but as an activity which is grounded in the familial, work and social lives of participants who are more than consumers. Collecting carries multiple meanings, as a set of social practices through which individuals are engaged in economic, social and cultural consumption and production. Both capital creation and identity creation have a place in the world of collecting, and the dynamics of their interaction change over time. In giving accounts of how their 'collecting careers' began and subsequently developed, and of what they are 'doing' in collecting, the interviewees in this qualitative study throw fresh light on this multi-faceted phenomenon.

Methodology

In applying sociology's increasing focus on material culture and issues of identity construction to an investigation of collecting, recent developments in the study of narrativity offer a way of tapping into how it is socially organized. Bal (1994) suggests that when what began as a series of haphazard purchases or gifts suddenly becomes a meaningful sequence, 'that is the moment when a self-conscious narrator begins to "tell" its story, bringing about a semiotics for a narrative of identity, history, and situation' (ibid., p. 101). But she does not go on to test this out empirically. Kaminsky and Myertoff's (1992) study of elderly Jews provides an illustration of narrativity as methodology. Respondents' recollections are conceptualized by the authors as part of a mourning process, acting as a unifying experience of the narrator's former self with the present self. In this 'remembering' of a life, time becomes accumulation rather than erosion. In contrast to the museum's narrative, an 'edited tale' is perfectly appropriate. Completeness is sacrificed for moral and aesthetic purposes, and 'preferred memories' are privileged.

The 'processual' approach to collecting adopted here seeks to capture both the story-telling capacity of objects themselves, and the organization of social relations (such as family, gender and class) across time which constitute what Finnegan (1997) calls the 'storying of the self'. Clio's memory-keepers may be connecting to the past as they mourn 'disappearing worlds', but collecting practices also reveal the ways in which the self being 'told' is socially connected within the present, and actively engaged with the future.

My work on collecting emerged from an academic interest in patterns of consumption, the operation of markets, and issues of identity. Although there had been qualitative studies of collecting in America (Belk, 1995; Olmsted, 1991), there have been no qualitative studies of everyday collecting, outside of clubs, in the UK. Setting out to rectify this brought some interesting early insights at the stage of recruiting interviewees. Although collecting is such a ubiquitous activity, not all of those who actually have a collection conceive of themselves as collectors (Soroka, 1990), and some who do identify themselves as such do so reluctantly because of their awareness of a putative negative image. Those who were sensitive to this worked hard to counteract any imputed application of it to themselves.

A focus on the social organization of collecting suggested the use of snowball sampling. This also offered the opportunity to investigate how far collecting cuts across such boundaries as age, gender and social class. Interviewees readily suggested other candidates, and almost every 'casual' conversation with colleagues and friends about the research currently being undertaken brought 'hidden' collectors out of the woodwork. But participants' own conceptualizations and presentations of their activities proved context-specific. For example, some people with collections engage in trading as part of their collecting, and they may be keen to claim an ascription of 'collector' in order to avoid inconvenient tax-related issues arising.

Another 'definitional' issue relates to *patterns* of acquisition. If a collection has been acquired 'by default' rather than in a systematic and uninterrupted way, the owner may disclaim 'collector identity'. The indications from the interviews, of gender differences in the time spent in collecting, and the way this time use is patterned, together with the implications of this for the ways in which their collecting practices have been conceptualized by themselves and others, are suggestive of explanations for why women's collecting has been 'hidden' in the past. But how far men and women are in fact 'doing' different things when they are 'doing collecting' proved less clear.

With an awareness of the need to negotiate these issues, and to avoid imposing implicit definitions, recruitment in fact posed few difficulties. A qualitative approach meant that the issues discussed could be pursued in more detail in the interviews themselves, and interviewees became highly reflexive respondents. As most qualitative researchers will recognize, being interviewed at length and in depth is an experience respondents frequently describe after the event in very positive terms, almost regardless of the subject. In addition to this familiar phenomenon, the definitional issues raised during recruitment may explain why the interviewees went on to give such full accounts: they had not only had a pleasurable but sometimes covert activity 'legitimated', and been asked to articulate practices which amongst other things constituted identity creation and expression, but they were being enabled to demonstrate the expertise that they had developed via these activities.

In the context of a negative public discourse, the researcher's task was not so much the traditional role of the sociologist of 'making the familiar strange' as making the 'strange' familiar. There was a 'de-pathologizing' dimension, confirmed by the occasional implicit invitation in interview to become co-conspirators against the inhibitory tendencies of disapproving others. On the other hand, it may not be overstating the case to see confronting the issue of disposal of a collection, in which so much of one's self is invested, as the breaking of a taboo, and here we are nearer to the traditional sociological task of trying to see what the respondents themselves may wish to avoid.

All interviews were recorded, fully transcribed, and analyzed both as individual case studies, and using Nud*ist, initially to trace common 'themes'. Early interviews were undertaken with 'mature' collectors (50 to 77 years) to enable a working model of a 'collecting career' to be developed. From a pragmatic point of view, the theme of 'time' was a useful analytical tool for selecting from a wealth of data, and the extracts presented are drawn from six interviews which illustrate certain themes associated with 'time' particularly well: personal, historical, future, 'real' and 'mythical' time. Extracts come from collectors of glass; teapots and dolls; textiles and historical documents; stamps and philatelic history; money boxes and ceramics; and music.

As with all qualitative analysis of 'rich' data, there is a temptation to become captured by the idiosyncrasies of the individual 'case,' and this is especially true of investigating activity which so clearly involves 'identity-work'. Using a 'time-lens' was also helpful in resisting this, as it supported a focus on the social organization of collecting as a set of social processes, and a view of the individual as a socially integrated interactive self, collecting time, spending it, taking 'time out'. Interviewees talked about their initial entry into what subsequently became a process of collecting; how their skills, knowledge and preferences changed over time; and the role of collecting in structuring time – collecting as a 'release' from other more onerous activities, as 'losing oneself', as 'escaping', as rising above life's mundanities.

Collecting is also engaging with material culture, being brought into an intimate relationship with 'things'. And the exact nature of this intersubjectivity is not coincidental for the collector. It is clear from these interviews that the particular objects a person collects, carries from other places and other times into the collector's present, enables the collector not only to spend time creating new sets of social relations – between themselves and objects, between themselves and historical eras, between themselves and actual others past and present – but also to engage in an imaginative act of *choosing time*. Some collections may indeed gesture to nostalgia for times past (Elsner and Cardinal, 1994), but it is the (re)creation of a particular period in their own biography, family history or cultural history which constituted the making of *mythical* time. In choosing which objects to collect, they were also choosing a mythical time to hold and keep. Telling their stories of 'collecting time' revealed the activity's multidirectional, imaginative and transcendental characteristics.

The following analysis is divided into three sections: revisiting the past; organizing the present; and maintaining a stake in the future.

Revisiting the past

Rites of passage and unfinished business

Collecting is a perfect vehicle for 'marking time'. For example, Barry's stamp-collecting began with those his father brought back for from his travels in the Navy. They were symbols of both parental love and the exotic places his father had visited. Early acquisitions often mark a rite of passage. For Lydia, moving house was a trigger to acquisition. Her first three teapots were part of a group of possessions which constituted 'home' as she was continually relocated as a medical student during the war. In what later became a larger collection of teapots, these three functioned as 'transitional objects' (Kenyon, 1999), maintaining continuities through times of change:

> There were three little teapots by then ... every time I moved, I had fourteen things that moved with me, including a gramophone, and a radio that had accumulators, and a microscope and a skeleton – they all went with me ... I was taking them as part of home, to make every place I stayed in home.

Such continuities may also be with an earlier historical period. Just as Herbert Read wanted to 'assert the role of the artist within the context of the machine age' (Dant, 1999 p. 135), some collectors seem to be re-installing the artist into the present by collecting small inexpensive objects on which the traces left by the craftsman are seen as purposeful displays of his skills. For Susan, her wine glasses hold the residue of the craftsman's labour and skill:

> It's seeing an object that I feel has had a lot put into it ... a lot of them are etched ... it's the fineness ... and design, and decoration, that perhaps is a *craftsman's* [original emphasis] decoration.

The etched glasses were also a vehicle for integrating different aspects of her own identity. She was influenced by her 'scientific' father to pursue chemistry as a career. Later she came to realize that her more 'creative' or 'artistic' side had become subdued. The glasses she collected symbolized *both* these aspects: she took pleasure in the scientific expertise which allowed her to 'read' the craftsmanship involved, but saw their delicacy and beauty as an expression of her more artistic self. Collecting enabled her to become a more 'all-round personality'.

For other collectors, the theme of loss and restoration was dealt with in ways which almost constituted a 'rewriting of history.' The loss of his mother's Dresden cup and saucer, bequeathed to another family member, seems to have acted as a spur to Dennis. Much of his numerous collection of china and ceramics were items he predicted would become collectable in the future. His collecting could be seen, in part at least, as a compensatory activity.

The same element appeared in Lydia's collection of porcelain dolls. Her mother, judging her to be grown-up enough to do without them, had thrown away the 'collection' of dolls she used to love dressing as a child. She was very sensible of this loss, as marking the time when you have to 'leave behind your childhood'. Not until retirement did she have time to make reparation, by learning how to make 'bespoke' dolls with porcelain heads, each magnificently dressed in period costume. After 50 or 60, she felt able to move on. 'Completion' in this context was the finishing of hitherto 'unfinished business.'

A classless society?

As June talked about her collections of fine linen, domestic textiles, and historical documents, she traced her current social position back to her family's more modest roots. Her prize item was a beautiful embroidered bedspread which had cost £200. She also collected domestic items which evidenced a different kind of skill – that of 'make do and mend' – which she saw as symbolizing her own family's skills. Her collections included items which appeared to act as a reminder not only of how far she had come in socio-economic terms, but of the domestic labour that went into the journey which produced her:

> I'm just attracted by the sheer sort of beauty of [the linen] and the workmanship in it ... I don't like to buy damaged linen but ... something like a baby gown or something children have worn and I can see little repairs, that doesn't put me off at all ... to me that's history. That's the girl who in whatever year was me.

Samuel (1994) posited only a unidirectional imaginary journey being made by consumers of heritage – from their own humdrum 'ordinary' world to a higher status 'romantic' one. He did not allow for the reverse journey, which was evident in some of these accounts: from middle-class status back to working-class roots. Not Lacey's (1999) 'bidding for class', or escaping from class, but returning to it in an act of memory, recognition and respect for others' labours, upon which one's personal progress has been built.

June also collected historical documents which provided insights into a higher-status way of life, one in which people from 'the Hall' did not expect their bills to be presented or paid immediately. In the contrast these documents provided of different sets of rules and values, according to class, there was an awareness that families like hers *were* 'a class', part of a different way of life. Collecting the documents was a process of making sense in class terms of where she is now.

Collecting and enjoying cultural capital

The interviews revealed 'staging posts' in collecting careers. Paul located the start of his 'collecting career' in adolescence, when, rather than aligning himself with his elders, he wanted to distance himself from all the music his parents liked: the BBC 'light' programme, the *Billy Cotton Band Show, Two-Way Family Favourites*. Hearing Humphrey Littelton's *Bad Penny Blues* in the 1950s was unlike anything else he'd ever experienced, and constituted for him 'a small act of rebellion' which was just what he was looking for. The fact that his older sister was alienated by the 'roughness' of this 'dirty music' made it an even more attractive vehicle to mediate 'growing up male'. His collecting of music placed his own history within that of a wider cultural history of Britain:

> I think it's all to do with growing up in the fifties when the only sort of music you heard from the media – didn't have TV then, but radio … was all controlled by other people … Teddy Boys … Mods and Rockers – these are people who for some reason won't accept being controlled by the adults – want to take a bit of control themselves – which I think I must've wanted to do at some early age.

It has also been a central constituent of identity construction. Paul disliked teachers, thought of himself as 'a flop at school' and had left as soon as he could. Later in life he realized that his collecting of music had made him quite an expert in his field:

> I hadn't completely rejected learning – I'd done loads of it, [but not] on their terms – 'them' being these grey people who stifle things.

As with the choice of objects themselves, selecting what to keep as 'cultural capital' is not coincidental for collectors: Barry, the philatelic historian was choosing a mythical time before the world had shrunk, in which the exotic can still give rise to wonder ('one wondered quite what was coming out of his kit bag next'); June, a time when groups in society may be clearly differentiated, but in which domestic labour really 'means something'; Lydia, a time in which one does not have to 'put away childish things'; and Paul, a time of independence, distinctiveness, and thrills.

Organizing the present

Finding the time

More mundanely, collecting is an activity which takes place in the social and cultural settings of the present, constituting friendships, family formations and maintenance. Sometimes these social relations are formalized, as with club membership. There the collector acts autonomously, the interactions constituting his or her identity as an individual. Nevertheless, accommodations may have to be made, 'pockets of time' to spend negotiated with others. At other times, collecting is simply part of the fabric of family life, highlighting family members' values, creating or uncovering conflict, providing mechanisms for exclusion or inclusion.

Susan's apparent 'materialism' had earned her the accusation from her sister of having 'a superficial life', while Paul had hidden the expenditure involved in his collecting from his first wife. He learned with relief from a dealer's magazine that this was a common practice:

> It was a story all about how to smuggle records into the house – [laughs] – which was something I'd done! Typically men – who don't want their wives to know how much they've spent – and they find ways of getting the price tags off or even smuggling the whole things into the house … that's what I used to do. And obviously not just me.

He also used listening to music his wife disliked as a conscious strategy to enable him to be separate from her, to retreat into another 'little world.' Using collecting activities as 'time out' also featured in Dennis and

Doreen's partnership. Undergoing an unpleasant divorce, Doreen spent hours every day for five months sorting out Dennis's collections (at the time of interview they filled a huge attic fitted with decks of shelving on three sides, as well as boxes stacked ceiling-high all around a large garage), and she found this 'therapeutic.' Often, then, collecting is inconspicuously fitted in with the everyday rhythms of family life, becoming dormant or 'active' according to the demands of family life-stage and competing priorities.

Spending time – alone or together?

How far an individual's collecting is undertaken separately from or together with a partner was in fact a common theme. Barry's visit to a collectors' fair was only possible because of other attractions York offered his wife. When the collector needs to spend time in 'possession and grooming rituals' (cataloguing stamps, preparing a display, laundering linen), this can provide their partner with a welcome opportunity to take time out themselves, perhaps legitimating a pub visit. Some interviewees resolved the dilemmas such decisions posed by encouraging their partner to begin a collection of their own. 'Hunting' became something they did separately but together. June used this strategy to prevent her husband constantly rejoining her at antiques and collectors' fairs to see if she had 'finished yet'. For Dennis, embarking afresh on a joint collecting career with Doreen meant that he was able to 'tutor' his new partner, and the 'master–pupil' relationship brought great satisfaction to both.

Stage posts in family formation

Paul also used his music collection as a way of furthering his 'courtship' of his current partner. When she moved in with him, he anticipated the pleasure of listening together to her selections. Unfortunately, she inhibited his habit of always having music on at home:

> She's a 'do-it' person ... I'm the passive consumer. For her, the ultimate is to do it. The next stage is to go and see it done and perhaps take part in it. Thirdly to passively see it done. Fourthly, if you have to, to buy a record of it. Fifthly, to have lots of records! [Laughter] 'Expensive wallpaper' – that's her phrase ... we've had some pretty difficult arguments.

The conflict had been partially resolved but in a way which affected on the way Paul was able to enjoy his collection: she bought him a

CD player for the car so that he could listen to his music there. But as he commented, 'You can't play vinyl in the car.'

Dennis's collecting career also acted as a tracer of his marriage career. By the time his third marriage ended, he had acquired so much that he had lost track of what he had. Doreen soon discovered what he himself had failed to notice: that her predecessor was giving away piecemeal his Tetley Tea merchandise and glassware before it could be removed. But Dennis needed to dispose of some of his collections, to create the space to start afresh with Doreen. This had brought its tensions. He professed to be happy to 'flog the lot' (apart from his prized collection of money-boxes) if he could get the right price. She was trying to decide what to keep and display, so that it could be properly appreciated. She described her predecessor's tastes as 'tacky'. Dennis simply acknowledged that 'we all like different things'. Besides, new tastes offer an opportunity for fresh collecting imperatives. Collecting was providing a means to incorporate Doreen's children, currently living with their father, into what he hoped would become their newly constituted resident family. He had discovered Doreen's daughter liked horses, and had started a new collection of things with horses on them. Collecting is a 'serial' activity in more ways than one.

Maintaining a stake in the future

Avoiding getting stuck in the past

For Paul, moving on was not due to exhausting the novelty of a particular genre, but to the fact that he no longer had the time to spend listening intensively to a single piece of music as he used to, until he knew it intimately. His sense of excitement was recaptured by venturing into new musical territory. This provided access once more to the thrill of searching out cheap issues of recordings, and to new learning. Importantly, it also enabled him to avoid getting 'stuck' in his youth. He looked back fondly, but saw himself and his collecting of music as located firmly in 'real time' as opposed to 'past times':

> For some people their musical interest is solely based on nostalgia. There are people of my age that are still desperate to hear Motown records from their prime youth time ... For most of us there's a period when – for me it was the groups I used to go and see. But I moved on. I've searched out other things. That time was very important to me, I don't put it down at all ... But I like to think that I'm not stuck there.

By no means 'stuck' in eras now gone, collectors reproduce the ingredients of their chosen 'mythical' time within the present. The vehicle of collecting allows them continuing access to these ingredients into the future. The need to recapture some of the essential elements of collecting – searching, discovery, the development of expertise, researching new genres – drive the collector's progress through a 'collecting career'.

Investing and preserving

Of course, what is often being collected and preserved at the same time is monetary value. This was frequently described as of secondary importance, and indeed it can be experienced as a burden, as Barry explained:

> It is another form of investment at one extreme, which is not the way I personally tend to look at it. I don't collect stamps the same way as one opens up a TESSA [savings account]. One does it because one has a pure love and interest in the whole art of philately. The value, although very nice, is secondary to the first love ... it's a kind of pleasure in one sense, 'wow, it's nice to know that's worth £500,' but there is the pain of thinking that some people might think you could be worth a visit of an unpleasant nature.

Financial investment was a much more prominent feature of Dennis's collecting. 'Buying up' what he hoped will become collectable in years to come was connected to his lack of access to an occupational pension:

> I was going to start flogging bits off when I get older, like my old age pension. It's better than putting money in the bank.

Over and above constituting continuing access to 'enchantment', and to financial investment, some collectors see themselves as custodians of more public treasures. In times of change, they are investing in a communal future. As June commented:

> I just think life is changing a lot ... unless somebody hangs on to those bits, in time they will be gone forever.

Trading occasionally at a *bric-a-brac* market as a way of upgrading her collections, she took great pleasure in explaining artefacts such as 'darning mushrooms' to the younger generation:

> Particularly the younger generation, they just say 'what do you mean? ... But you throw [worn socks] away!' ... I say 'yes, I know, *I* do *now*. But in fact, people couldn't afford to do that.'

What is being preserved here for future generations, who may become inured to constraints on consumption, is related to both a *domestic* identity, and a *national* identity:

> People don't do that work any more. Why do it if you can go into a shop and buy it? But it's also the skill as much as anything that's lost. It's only a domestic skill. It's nothing you'd write home over, but it is sad in a way ... I've never been mad on the *Beano* and *Dandy* ... [but] when you look back on those, it just epitomised a certain way of life in England really ... I think 'just look at that, it says this, it says that.' And it's telling us about a way of life that people had ... I don't feel like a miser hoarding ... just ... preserving a way of life ... so it still exists.

June's preoccupations highlight the fact that, for all the discourse of 'Englishness' in recent times, there has been very little which has recognized women's claims on a national identity, or explored its contours.

Bequeathing the self

All those interviewed had acquired collections of a considerable size and value. None of them knew precisely how many items they had nor the overall value of their collections, but it was not difficult to assess that they ranged in value from hundreds to many thousands of pounds. As a result of what had been invested in collecting the items, over and above money – time, expertise, ideological values, aesthetic appreciation, so much of one's self – disposing of them also demanded more time than some people had available. Disposal may require finding the right specialist journal in which to place an advertisement, or researching objects collected speculatively. Having tried to 'buy up' various categories of china to create 'collectability', Dennis suggested I could do the research necessary to realize their value.

As for the issue of the *final* disposal of their collections, these mature and 'experienced' collectors had already considered this. A variety of strategies were in use to address this problem, from giving away selected items to family members now; to seeking reassurance from the 'surviving' partner that the collection would be respected; to making (and modifying) a will which catered for the collection's disposal.

Leaving the collection to one's children was seen as the ideal solution, but it was far from clear that children would welcome such bequests. Barry wanted to avoid the burden created by idiosyncratic 'grand collections': 'Great grandfather made a collection of elephants' tusks and we've still got them all.' At the same time, he had no illusions that any members of his family would really continue to specialize as he had. He intended to make preparations by having his stamps valued at a particular auction house, enabling his children to realize their worth as 'a little extra nest egg'. June was also aware that her children might feel encumbered by complete collections of hers. Her will made them beneficiaries of selected bequests. Paul hadn't made a will as he was frightened to do so. He knew his collector friend would love to inherit, but he was not happy with this because he felt his friend was as much a dealer as a collector. Paul had given his partner's daughter one or two items as a present, creating pleasure for both. This 'testing out' had made him consider her as a beneficiary, but it was not a matter he had been able to resolve:

> There's a lot of other things that she'd quite like, but there'd be lots of other things that she'd have no interest in, so I don't know ... it's a difficult one.

It is a problem which he speculated many others of his generation of collectors will soon be facing. Auctioneers may be rubbing their hands in anticipation.

Conclusion

Although under-researched by sociologists, collecting is a further illustration of the processes of consumption, of buying and selling, of identity work, and of some of the post-purchase practices which constitute the intersubjectivity between consumers and the objects they acquire.

Qualitative research is rewarding because the respondents themselves are eager to share in the process of making sense of an activity which can be the focus of criticism from others. At the same time, the traditional skills of the sociologist are called upon when confronting those aspects of collecting which indicate the operation of a taboo. The theme of time is particularly useful in relation to collecting. It enables tracing links between the contemporary and the past, and between material and imaginary realms; it allows expression of the collecting *career* with its unrecognized beginnings, its rites of passage and its staging posts; and it gives access to multidirectional journeys, as a system of closure, of endings, as well as new beginnings.

A focus on the social organization of collecting provides unique material on social identity, as well as revealing how collecting mediates social relations. How far and in what ways these processes are gendered invites further analysis. Some gender differences in relation to objects collected were observable in these interviews, but a clear distinction between men collecting in a specialized and organized way and women engaging in acts of remembering could not be sustained. Differences in the patterning of time spent in the activities of collecting were embedded within men's and women's personal, cultural and family histories and their everyday lives, and these inevitably reflected gender relations, as well as changing class relations. In the enthusiasm and enjoyment, the 'thrills' expressed in creating and 'telling' their collections, these interviewees appeared to be engaged in broadly similar practices of acquiring objects which were beautiful and affirmatory to them, and which involved them, in various ways, in becoming themselves; in 'doing family'; and in cultural production.

The collecting career does not follow a linear trajectory. The heritage industry may have inserted 'pastness' into the everyday narrative representations of the present, but the evidence here suggests that in their everyday collecting, individuals are not getting stuck in the past, but are moving back and forth through time, using it creatively in the process. They are reinserting the present, in the form of the personal and the biographical, back into representations of the past. At the same time, they are incorporating their contemporary collecting practices into their current relationships. They are also confronting future relationships, by making plans to avoid burdening their own descendants, and by preserving what they perceive as important cultural values for future generations. The final disposal of a collection, which may be seen as the end of the story, poses a number of difficulties for collectors. But positive aspects of disposal are also shown to take place during the collecting career, as collectors complete unfinished business and move on; give as well as receive gifts; and create space and time for the continued pursuit of enchantment and re-enchantment. The development of the study of collectors and collecting has the potential to contribute to sociological understandings of consumption in both public and private domains, of experiences of involvement in the market, and of the cultural meanings which are attached to things in the twenty-first century.

Bibliography

Acker, S. (1997) 'Becoming a teacher educator: voices of women academics in Canadian faculties of education', *Teaching and Teacher Education*, 13, 1, pp. 65–74.

Acker, S. and Feuerverger, G. (1996) 'Doing good and feeling bad: the work of women university teachers', *Cambridge Journal of Education*, 26, 3, pp. 401–22.

Adam, B. (1990) *Time and Social Theory* (Cambridge: Polity).

Adam B. (1995) *Timewatch: A social analysis of time* (Cambridge: Polity Press).

Adam, B. (1998) *Timescapes of Modernity* (London: Routledge).

Agger, B. (1989) *Fast Capitalism* (Urbana: University of Illinois Press).

Alba, P., (1980) `Women's liberation or women's community?' *Bitches, Witches, and Dykes*, August, 4, 8.

Alheit, P. (1994) 'Everyday time and life time: on the problems of healing contradictory experiences of time', *Time and Society*, 3, 3, pp. 305–19.

Allen, J., Roth, J., Mulrennan, B., and Ronald, R. (1976) 'Reactions to Radical Feminist Caucus', *Broadsheet*, 41, pp. 10–15.

Anderson, B. (2000) *Doing the Dirty Work* (London: Zed Books).

Anonymous (1975) 'About the newsletter and the machine that prints it', *Woman*, 74, 4.

Anonymous (1983) 'Busy Lizzie' (Cartoon), *Broadsheet*, 108, 34.

Anxo, D. and O'Reilly, J. (2000) 'Working-time regimes and transitions in comparative perspective', in J. O'Reilly, I. Cebrian and M. Lallemont (eds) *Working-Time Changes* (Cheltenham: Edward Elgar).

Arber, S. (1999) 'Unequal partners: inequality in earnings and independent income within marriage', in L. McKie, S. Bowlby and S. Gregory (eds) *Gender, Power and the Household* (London: Macmillan).

Arkin, A. (1997) 'Hold the production line', *People Management*, 6 February.

Arrowsmith, W. (1999) *Antiques Fairs in England* (Bromsgrove: William Arrowsmith).

Austin Knight LTD (1997) *Call Centre, Practice Not Theory*, London: Austin Knight LTD.

Avineri, S. (1969) *Karl Marx on Colonialism and Modernization* (New York: Anchor Books).

Baker, P. (1993) 'Chaos, order, and sociological theory', *Sociological Inquiry*, 63, pp. 123–49.

Bal, M. (1994) 'Telling objects: a narrative perspective in collecting', in J. Elsner and R. Cardinal (eds) *The Cultures of Collecting* (Cambridge, Mass: Harvard University Press).

Baldry, C. (1998) 'Space: the final frontier', Paper presented at 16th Annual International Labour Process Conference, School of Management, University of Manchester Institute of Science and Technology, April.

Barber, B. (1996) *Jihad vs McWorld* (New York: Ballantine).

Bargh, C., Bocock, J., Scott, P. and Smith, D. (2000) *University Leadership* (Buckingham: Open University Press).

Bate, S. (1997)'Whatever happened to organisational ethnography?', *Human Relations*, 50, 9.

Beck, U. (1992) *Risk Society* (London: Sage).

Beck, U. and Beck-Gernsheim, E. (1995) *The Normal Chaos of Love* (Cambridge: Polity).

Becker, G. (1965) 'A theory of the allocation of time', *Economic Journal*, 75, pp. 493–517.

Beck-Gernsheim, E. (1998) 'On the way to a post-familial family: from a community of need to elective affinities', *Theory, Culture and Society*, 15, 3–4, pp. 53–70.

Beechey, V. and Perkins, T. (1987) *A Matter of Hours* (Cambridge: Polity Press).

Belk, R. (1995) *Collecting in a Consumer Society* (London: Routledge).

Belt, V. (1999) 'Are call centres the new sweatshops?', 'The Thursday Review', *The Independent*, 14 January, p. 4.

Bender, J. and Wellbery, D. (eds) (1991) *Chronotypes: The Construction of Time* (Stanford: Stanford University Press).

Bett Report (1999) *Independent Review of Higher Education, Pay and Conditions* (London: HMSO).

Bettio, F. and Prechal, S. (1998) *Care in Europe*, DGV Report no. CE-V/2-98-018-EN-C (Brussels: European Commission).

Bienefeld, M.A. (1972) *Working Hours in British Industry* (London: Weidenfeld and Nicolson).

Bitches, Witches and Dykes Collective (1980) 'How we started', *Bitches, Witches and Dykes*, August, pp. 2–3.

Blaxter, L., Hughes, C. *et al.* (1998) *The Academic Career Handbook* (Buckingham: Open University Press).

Blyton, P. and Trinczek, R. (1996) *The Reincarnation of Worksharing as a Response to Job Cuts: Assessing Recent Developments in Germany* (Düsseldorf: Hans Bruckler Foundation).

Bodanis, D. (2000) *E = mc²: A Biography of the World's Most Famous Equation* (Basingstoke: Macmillan – now Palgrave Macmillan).

Boden, D (2000) 'Worlds in action: information, instantaneity and global futures trading', in B. Adam, U. Beck and J. van Loon, J. (eds) *The Risk Society and Beyond* (London: Sage).

Borges, J.L. (1970) *Labyrinths* (Harmondsworth: Penguin).

Bosch, G., Dawkins, P. and Michon, F. (1994) *Times are Changing: Working Time in 14 Industrialised Countries* (Geneva: Institute for International Labour Studies).

Boulin, J.-Y. and Hoffman, R. (1999) *New Paths in Working Time Policy* (Brussels: European Trade Union Institute).

Bourdieu, P. (1984) *Distinction: A Social Critique of the Judgement of Taste* (London: Routledge and Kegan Paul).

Bowring, F. (1999) 'Job scarcity: The perverted form of a potential blessing', *Sociology*, 33, pp. 69–84.

Brannen, J., Meszaros, G., Moss, P. and Poland, G. (1994) *Employment and Family Life: A Review of Research in the UK (1980–1994)*, Employment Department Research Series No. 41.

Breedveld, K. (1996a) 'The double myth of flexibilisation: trends in scattered work hours and differences in time sovereignty', paper presented to conference on New Strategies for Everyday Life, Tilburg, the Netherlands.

Breedveld, K. (1996b) 'Working odd hours: revolution in time or storm in a teacup?', paper presented to World Leisure and Recreation Association Congress, Cardiff.

Broadsheet Collective (1978) 'Broadsheet supplement', with subscriber's copy of *Broadsheet*, 62, 5 pages.

Broadsheet Collective (1980) 'Broadsheet's collective', *Broadsheet*, 81, pp. 15–17.

Broadsheet Collective (1983) 'Collectively speaking', *Broadsheet*, 108, pp. 28–36.

Browne, J., Hargreaves, A., Kuiper, A., Livingstone, J., McKenzie, M., Novitz, R., Toberts, B. and Sewell, E. (1978) *Changes, Chances, Choices: A Report on the United Women's Convention 1977*, June, Christchurch.

Brownlie, C. (1970) 'Are you going to burn your bra?', Thursday, 1 October, 4–6, 26.

Burford, C. (2000) Re. Globalisation article, 5 August, 14:59 UTC. Comments on David Eisenhower's *Globalisation: Built on Lies*, 02/08/00, at: http://csf.colorado.edu/pen-1/2000III/msg01497.html

Burke, P. (1994) *Popular Culture in Early Modern Europe* (Aldershot: Scolar Press).

Burns, T. (1973) 'Leisure in industrial society', in M. Smith, S. Parker and C. Smith (eds) *Leisure in Industrial Society* (London: Allen Lane).

Busch, A. (1997) 'Globalisation: some evidence on approaches and data', *Globalization Workshop*, University of Birmingham Politics Dept, March.

Byrne, D. (1998) *Complexity Theory and the Social Sciences* (London: Routledge).

Calder, N. (1979) *Einstein's Universe* (Harmondsworth: Penguin).

Calvert, S. (1981) 'Theory, strategy and tactics in the Women's Movement', *Broadsheet*, 90, pp. 32–4..

Campbell, C. (1995) 'The sociology of consumption', in D. Miller, (ed.) *Acknowledging Consumption* (London: Routledge).

Capra, F. (1996) *The Web of Life* (London: HarperCollins).

Castells, M. (1996) *The Rise of the Network Society* (Oxford: Blackwell).

Casti, J. (1994) *Complexification* (London: Abacus).

CEC (1996) *Employment in Europe 1996* (Luxembourg: Official Publications of the European Communities).

Certeau, M. de (1984) *The Practice of Everyday Life* (Berkeley: University of California Press).

Chattoe, E. and Gilbert, N. (1999) 'Talking about Budgets: time and uncertainty in household decision making', *Sociology*, 33, 1, pp. 85–103.

Cilliers, P. (1998) *Complexity and Post-modernism* (London: Routledge).

Circle Collective (1978) 'Broadsheet bust-up', *Circle*, Winter, pp. 74–81.

Clark, P. (1985) 'A review of the theories of time and structure for organisation sociology', in S. Bacrach and S. Mitchell (eds) *Research in the Sociology of Organisations*, 4, pp. 35–79.

Clarke, J. and Newman, J. (1997) *The Managerial State* (London: Sage).

Clarke, W. (1973) *Einstein: The Life and Times* (London: Hodder and Stoughton).

Code, L. (1995) *Rhetorical Spaces* (London: Routledge).

Cohen, S. and Taylor, L. (1992) *Escape Attempts*, 2nd edn. (London: Routledge).

Colborn, T., Meyers, J. and Dumanoski, D. (1996) *Our Stolen Future* (Boston: Little, Brown and Company).

Cole, V. (1976) 'Editorial', *Broadsheet*, 44, pp. 12–13.

Collinson, D. and Collinson, M. (1997) 'Delayering managers: time-space surveillance and its gendered effects', *Organisation*, 4, 3, pp. 375–407.

Coney, S. (1973) *United Women's Convention, September 1973, Auckland* (Auckland: WEA).

Coney, S. and Cederman, S. (1975) 'How Broadsheet grew', *Broadsheet*, 31, pp. 31–2.

Cornell, D. (1995) 'Rethinking the time of feminism', in S. Benhabib, J. Butler, D, Cornell, and N. Fraser (eds) *Feminist Contentions* (London: Routledge).

Corner, J. and Harvey, S. (1991) 'Mediating tradition and modernity', in J. Corner and S. Harvey (eds) *Enterprise and Heritage* (London: Routledge).

Coser, L.A. (1974) *Greedy Institution* (New York: Free Press).

Coveney, P. and Highfield, R. (1990) *The Arrow of Time* (London: Flamingo).

Cowan, R (1983) *More Work for Mother* (New York: Basic Books).

Cowen, R. (1996) 'Performativity, post-modernity and the university', *Comparative Education*, 32, 2, pp. 245–58.

Crompton, R. and Harris, F. (1999) 'Attitudes, women's employment and the changing domestic division of labour: a cross-national analysis', in R. Crompton (ed.), *Restructuring Gender Relations and Employment* (Oxford: Oxford University Press).

Csikszentmihalyi, M. (1988) 'The flow experience and its significance for human psychology', in M. Csikszentmihalyi and I. Csikszentmihalyi (eds) *Optimal Experience* (Cambridge: Cambridge University Press).

Cuthbert, R. (ed.) (1996) *Working in Higher Education* (London: Open University Press).

Daly, K. (1996) *Families and Time* (London: Sage).

Dann, C. (1976) 'Behind the news: Maori women on the move', *Broadsheet*, 44.

Dant, T. (1999) *Material Culture in the Social World* (Buckingham: Open University Press).

Daphne (1974) 'The Trouble with Women's Workshop', *Wellington Women's Workshop Newsletter*, 26, pp. 2–7.

Datamonitor (2000) *Call Centres in Europe, 1996–2001* (London: Datamonitor).

Davies, K. (1990) *Women and Time: The weaving of the strands of everyday life*, (Aldershot: Avebury).

Davies, K. (1994) 'The tensions between process time and clock time in care work: the example of day nurseries', *Time and Society*, 3, 3, pp. 277–303.

Davis, S. and Meyer, C. (1998) *BLUR: The Speed of Change in the Connected Economy* (Oxford: Capstone Publishing Limited).

Deem, R. (1995) 'Time for a change: engendered work and leisure in the 1990s', in G. McFee, W. Murphy and G. Whannel (eds) *Leisured Cultures* (Eastbourne: Leisure Studies Association).

Deem, R. (1996a) 'No time for a rest? An exploration of women's work, engendered leisure and holidays', *Time and Society*, 5, 1, pp. 5–25.

Deem, R. (1996b) 'Border territories: a journey through sociology, education and women's studies', *British Journal of Sociology of Education*, 17, 1, pp. 5–19.

Deleuze, G. and Guattari, F. (1986) *Nomadology* (New York: Semiotext(e)).

Deleuze, G. and Guattari, F. (1988) *A Thousand Plateaus* (London: Athlone Press).

Dex, S. (1999) *Families and the Labour Market* (London: Family Policy Studies Centre/Joseph Rowntree Foundation).

Dex, S., Clark, A. and Taylor, M. (1995) *Household Labour Supply*, Employment Departmnent Research Paper No. 43 (London: Department for Education and Employment).

Dinerstein, A. (1997) 'Marxism and subjectivity: searching for the marvellous (prelude to a Marxist theory of action)', *Common Sense*, 22, 83–96.

Dittmar, H. (1991) 'Meanings of material possessions as reflections of identity: gender and socio-material position in society', in F. Rudmin (ed.) *To Have Possessions: A Handbook of Ownership and Property: Journal of Social Behaviour and Personality*, Special Issue, 6, 6.

Doudeijns, M. (1998) 'Are benefits a disincentive to work part-time?', in J. O'Reilly and C. Fagan (eds) *Part-Time Perspectives: An international Comparison of Part-Time Work* (London: Routledge).

Durkheim, E. (1984) *The Division of Labour in Society* (Basingstoke: Macmillan – now Palgrave Macmillan).

Duncan, S. (1995) 'Theorising European gender systems', *Journal of European Social Policy*, 5, 4, pp. 263–84.

Eagle, A. and Argent, (1978) 'Herstory: lesbian feminism in action', *Circle*, summer, pp. 8–11.

Elsner, J. and Cardinal, R. (1994) *The Cultures of Collecting* (Cambridge, Mass: Harvard University Press).

Englestadt, F. and Kalleberg, R. (eds) (1999) *Social Time and Social Change* (Oslo: Scandinavian University Press).

Equal Opportunities Commission (1999) *Facts about Men and Women in Great Britain 1999* (Manchester: Equal Opportunities Commission).

Eriksen, T. (2001) *Tyranny of the Moment* (London: Pluto Press).

Ermath, E. (1992) *Sequel to History* (Princeton: Princeton University).

Esping-Andersen, G. (1990) *The Three Worlds of Welfare Capitalism* (Cambridge: Polity Press).

European Commission (1998) *Job Opportunities in the Information Society* (Luxemburg: European Commission).

European Commission (1999) *Directorate-General for Employment, Industrial Relations and Social Affairs: Employment in Europe 1998* (Luxemburg: Office for Publications of the European Comunities).

European Foundation (1997) *Working Conditions in the European Union: The Second Survey* (Luxembourg: Office for Official Publications of the European Communities).

Eve, R., Horsfall, S. and Lee, M. (eds) (1997) *Chaos, Complexity, and Sociology* (California: Sage).

Evetts, J. (1990) *Women in Primary Teaching* (London: Unwin Hyman).

Evetts, J. (1994) *Becoming a Secondary Headteacher* (London: Cassell).

Exworthy, M. and Halford, S. (eds) (1999) *Professionals and the New Managerialism in the Public Sector* (Buckingham: Open University Press).

Ezzy, D. (1997) 'Subjectivity and the labour process: conceptualising "good work"' *Sociology*, 31, 3, pp. 427–44.

Fagan, C. (1996) 'Gendered time schedules: paid work in Great Britain', *Social Politics: International Studies in Gender, State and Society*, 3, 1, pp. 72–106.

Fagan, C. (2001) 'Time, money and the gender order: work orientations and working time preferences in Britain', *Gender, Work and Organisations*. 8, 3, pp. 239–66.

Fagan, C., Warren, T. and McAllister, I. (2001) *Gender, Employment and Working-Time Preferences in Europe* (Luxembourg: Office for Official Publications of the European Communities).

Fajertag, G. (1996) 'Working time policies in Europe: recent trends', paper presented to conference on New Strategies for Everyday Life, Tilburg, the Netherlands.

Farnham, D. and Jones, J. (1998) 'Who are the vice-chancellors? An analysis of their professional and social backgrounds 1990–1997', *Higher Education Review*, 30, 3, pp. 42–58.

Featherstone, M. (1992) 'The heroic life and everyday life', *Theory, Culture and Society*, 9, 1, pp. 159–82.

Featherstone, M. (2000) 'Archiving cultures', *British Journal of Sociology*, 51, pp. 161–84.

Felski, R. (1999) 'The invention of everyday life', *New Formations*, 39, winter 1999–2000, pp. 15–31.

Ferlie, E., Ashburner, L. *et al.* (1996) *The New Public Management in Action* (Oxford: Oxford University Press).

Fernie, S. and Metcalf, D. (1997) '(Not hanging on the telephone): payment systems in the new sweat shops', *Centre for Economic Performance* (London: LSE).

Ferri, E. and Smith, K. (1996) *Parenting in the 1990s* (London: Family Policy Studies Centre).

Finnegan, R. (1997) '"Storying the self": personal narratives and identity', in H. Mackay (ed.) *Consumption and Everyday Life* (London: Sage).

Ford, P., Goodyear, P. *et al.* (1996) *Managing Change in Higher Education* (Buckingham: Open University Press).

Forman, F. (1989) 'Feminizing time: an introduction' in F. Forman and C. Sowton (eds) *Taking our Time: Feminist Perspective on Temporality* (Oxford: Pergamon Press).

Forman, F. and Sowton, C. (1989) *Taking our Time: Feminist Perspective on Temporality* (Oxford: Pergamon Press).

Forth, J., Lissenburgh, S., Callender, C. and Millward, N. (1997) 'Family friendly working arrangements in Britain', *Labour Market Trends*, October.

Foucault, M. (1979) *Discipline and Punish: The Birth of the Prison* (Penguin: Harmondsworth).

Foucault, M. (1980) *Power* (London: Tavistock).

Foucault, M. (1982) 'The subject and power', in H.L. Dreyfus and P. Rabinow (eds) *Beyond Structuralism and Hermeneutics* (Brighton: Harvester Press).

Foucault, M. (1992) *The Order of Things: An Archaeology of the Human Sciences* (London: Routledge).

Freeman, J. (1972) 'The tyranny of structurelessness', *Berkeley Journal of Sociology*, 17, pp. 151–64.

Frenkel, S., Tam, M., Korczynski, M. and Shire, K. (1998) 'Beyond bureaucracy? Work organisation in call centres', *The International Journal of Human Resource Management*, 9, 6, pp. 957–79.

Fulton, O. (1996) 'Which academic profession are you in?', in R. Cuthbert (ed.) *Working in Higher Education* (Buckingham: Society for Research into Higher Education/Open University Press).

Fulton, O. (1997) 'Mass access and the end of diversity? The academic profession in England on the eve of structural reform', in P. Altbach (ed.) *The*

International Academic Profession: Portraits from Fourteen Countries (Princeton: Carnegie Foundation for the Advancement of Teaching).

Game, A. (1991) *Undoing the Social* (Buckingham: Open University Press).

Game, A. (1998) 'Travel', *International Sociology*, 13, pp. 41–58.

Game, A. and Pringle, R. (1984) *Gender at Work* (London: Pluto Press).

Garhammer, M. (1998) 'Time pressure in modern Germany', *Society and Leisure*, 21, pp. 327–52.

George, D. (2000) 'Driven to spend: longer hours as a by-product of market forces', in L. Golden and D. Figart (eds) *Working Time* (London: Routledge).

Gershuny, J. (1992) 'Change in the domestic division of labour in the UK, 1975–87: dependent labour versus adaptive partnership', in N. Abercrombie and A. Warde (eds) *Social Change in Contemporary Britain* (Cambridge: Polity).

Gershuny, J. (2000) *Changing Times* (Oxford: Oxford University Press).

Gershuny, J., Goodwin, M. and Jones, S. (1994) 'The domestic labour revolution: a process of lagged adaptation', in M. Anderson, F. Bechhofer and J. Gershuny (eds) *The Social and Political Economy of the Household* (Oxford: Oxford University Press).

Gershuny, J. and Sullivan, O. (1998) 'The sociological use of time-diary analysis', *European Sociological Review*, 14, 1, pp. 69–85.

Giddens, A. (1984) *The Constitution of Society* (Cambridge: Polity).

Giddens, A. (1987) *Social Theory and Modern Sociology* (Cambridge: Polity Press).

Giddens, A. (1990) *The Consequences of Modernity* (Stanford: Stanford University Press).

Giddens, A. (1991) *Modernity and Self-Identity* (Cambridge: Polity).

Giddens, A. (1992) *The Transformation of Intimacy* (Cambridge: Polity).

Giddens, A. (1996) *In Defence of Sociology* (Cambridge: Polity Press).

Giddens, A. (1999) *Runaway World* (London: Profile Books).

Gleick, J. (1999) *Faster: The Acceleration of Just About Everything* (London: Little, Brown and Company).

Glucksmann, M.A. (1998) 'What a difference a day makes: a theoretical and historical exploration of temporality and gender', *Sociology*, 32, 2, pp. 239–58.

Golden, L. and Figart, D. (2000) *Working Time* (London: Routledge).

Goodnow, J.J and Bowes, J. (1994) *Men, Women and Household Work* (Oxford: Oxford University Press).

Grazia, S. de (1974) 'Time and work', in H. Yaker (ed.) *The Future of Time* (New York: Anchor Books).

Gregson, N. and Lowe, M. (1994) *Servicing the Middle Classes* (London: Routledge).

Griffiths, M. (1995) *Feminisms and the Self* (London: Routledge).

Gurvitch, G. (1990) 'Varieties of time', in J. Hassard (ed.), *The Sociology of Time* (Basingstoke: Macmillan – now Palgrave Macmillan).

Hakim, C (1991) 'Grateful slaves and self-made women: fact and fantasy in women's work orientations', *European Sociological Review*, 7, 2, pp. 101–21.

Hakim, C. (1996) *Key Issues in Women's Work* (London: Athlone Press).

Halford, S., Savage, M. *et al.* (1997) *Gender, Careers and Organisation* (Basingstoke: Macmillan – now Palgrave Macmillan).

Halsey, A.H. (1992) *Decline of Donnish Dominion* (Oxford: Clarendon).

Halsey, A.H. and Trow, M. (1971) *The British Academics* (London: Faber and Faber).

Hardill, I., Dudleston, A.C., Green, A.E. and Owen, D.W. (1999) 'Decision making in dual career households', in L. McKie, S. Bowlby, and S. Gregory (eds), *Gender, Power and the Household* (London: Macmillan – now Palgrave Macmillan).

Hareven, T. (1982) *Family Time and Industrial Time* (Cambridge: Cambridge University Press).

Harris, P., Thiele, B. and Currie, J. (1998) 'Success, gender and academic voices: Consuming passion or selling the soul?, *Gender and Education*, 10, 2, pp. 133–62.

Harvey, A., Gershuny, J., Fisher, K. and Akabari, A. (2000) *Statistics on Working Time Arrangements Based on Time Use Survey Data* (Halifax/Colchester: Saint Mary's University/University of Essex).

Harvey, D. (1989) *The Condition of Postmodernity* (Oxford: Basil Blackwell).

Harvey, D. (1996) *Justice, Nature and the Geography of Difference* (Oxford: Blackwell).

Hassard, J. (1990) 'Introduction: The Sociological Study of Time', p. 118 in J. Hassard (ed.) *The Sociology of Time* (Basingstoke: Macmillan – now Palgrave Macmillan).

Hawking, S. (1988) *A Brief History of Time* (London: Bantam).

Hawking, S. (1993) *Black Holes and Baby Universes and Other Essays* (New York: Bantam).

Haworth, J.T. (1997) *Work, Leisure and Well-Being* (London: Routledge).

Hayles, N.K. (1999) *How We Became Posthuman* (Chicago: University of Chicago Press).

Heaphy, B., Donovan, C. and Weeks, J. (1999) 'Sex, money and the kitchen sink: power in same-sex couple relationships', in J. Seymour and P. Bagguley (eds) *Relating Intimacies* (Basingstoke: Macmillan – now Palgrave Macmillan).

Hedgland, D. (1974) 'Submissions: a personal protest on behalf of the house-bound woman', *Wellington Women's Workshop Newsletter*, 17, pp. 3–4.

Held, D., McGrew, A., Goldblatt, D. and Perraton, J. (1999) *Global Transformations* (Cambridge: Polity).

Henkel, M. (2000) *Academic Identities and Policy Change in Higher Education* (London: Jessica Kingsley).

Henley Centre (1996) *Teleculture Futures* (London: The Henley Centre).

Hey, T. and Walters, P. (1997) *Einstein's Mirror* (Cambridge: Cambridge University Press).

Hill, S. (1991) 'Why quality circles failed but Total Quality Management might succeed', *British Journal of Industrial Relations*, 29, pp. 541–68.

Hinrichs, K., Roche, W. and Sirianni, C. (1991) *Working Time in Transition* (Philadelphia: Temple University Press).

Hochschild, A. (1983) *The Managed Heart* (Berkeley: University of California Press).

Hochschild, A. (1990) *The Second Shift* (London: Piatkus).

Hochschild, A. (1996) 'The emotional geography of work and family life', in L. Morris and E.S. Lyons (eds) *Gender Relations in Public and Private* (Basingstoke: Macmillan – now Palgrave Macmillan).

Hochschild, A. (1997) *The Time Bind* (New York: Metropolitan Books).

Hoeg, P. (1995) *Borderliners* (London: Harvill Press).

Hoffman, B. and Dukas, H. (1986) *Einstein* (London: Paladin).

Holliday, S. (1996) 'Trends in British work, leisure and the quality of life', paper presented to conference on New Strategies for Everyday Life, Tilburg, the Netherlands.

Hörning, K., Gerhard, A. and Michailow, M. (1995) *Time Pioneers* (Cambridge: Polity Press).

Horrell, S. (1994) 'Household time allocation and women's labour force participation', in M. Anderson, F. Bechhofer and J. Gershuny (eds) *The Social and Political Economy of the Household* (Oxford: Oxford University Press).

Horrell, S. and Rubery, J. (1991) *Employers' Hours of Work Survey* (London: HMSO).

Imken, O. (1999) 'The convergence of virtual and actual in the Global Matrix', in M. Crang, P. Crang and J. May (eds) *Virtual Geographies* (London: Routledge).

Inglis, D. and Holmes, M. (2000) 'Toiletry Time: Defecation, temporal strategies and the dilemmas of modernity', *Time & Society* 9, 2, 223–45).

Inkson, K. and Coe, T. (1993) *Are Career Ladders Disappearing?* (London: Institute of Management).

Intratest Burke Sozialforschung (1998) *Employment Options for the Future: Field Report* (Prepared for the European Foundation for Living and Working Conditions).

Irigaray, I.. (1980) 'When our lips speak together', *Signs*, 6, 1, pp. 69–79.

Jackson, P.R. and Taylor, P.E. (1994) 'Factors associated with employment status in later life', *Work, Employment and Society*, 8, pp. 553–67.

Jackson, S. and Scott, S. (1996) 'Sexual Skirmishes and Feminist Factions: Twenty-Five Years of Debate on Women and Sexuality', pp. 1–31 in J. Jackson, and S. Scott, (eds) *Feminism and Sexuality: A Reader* (Edinburgh: Edinburgh University Press).

Jamieson, L. (1998) *Intimacy* (Cambridge: Polity).

Jamieson, L (1999) 'Intimacy transformed? A critical look at the "pure relationship"', *Sociology*, 33, 3, pp. 477–94.

Jaques, E. (1982) *The Form of Time* (London: Heinemann).

Johnson, M. (1979) 'United women's convention: A herstory', *Circle*, 32, pp. 3–9.

Joshi, H. and Davies, H. (1992) 'Day care in Europe and mothers' foregone earnings', *International Labour Review*, 132, 6, pp. 561–79.

Jung, C.G. (1960) *Synchronicity* (Princeton: Princeton University Press).

Juno Collective (1977a) A Juno Special: Special Supplementary Issue of *Broadsheet*, January.

Juno Collective (1977b) 'Lesbian feminist lifestyles in Palmerston North', *Juno*, 2, pp. 5–7.

Juno Collective (1977c) 'Is Lesbian Feminism Pro WLM?', *Juno*, 3, p. 34.

Jurczyk, K. (1998) 'Time in women's everyday lives: between self-determination and conflicting demands', *Time and Society*, 7, 2, pp. 283–308.

Kaminsky, M., and Myertoff, B. (1992) 'Life history among the elderly: performance, visibility, and re-membering', in M. Kaminsky and B. Myertoff (eds) *Remembered Lives* (Ann Arbor: University of Michigan Press).

Kavanagh, G. (1999) 'Collecting from the era of memory, myth and delusion', In Simon J. Knell (ed.) *Museums and the Future of Collecting* (Aldershot: Ashgate).

Kay, G. and Mott, J. (1982) *Political Order and the Law of Labour* (London: Macmillan – now Palgrave Macmillan).

Kedglery, S. (1972) 'Women in Politics', *Listener*, 71, 1719, p. 19.

Kelly, K. (1995) *Out of Control* (Menlo Park, Calif.: Addison-Wesley).

Kenyon, L. (1999) 'A Home from home: students' transitional experience of home', in T. Chapman and J. Hockey (eds) *Ideal Homes?* (London: Routledge).

Kerfoot, D. and Knights, D. (1994) '"Into the realm of the fearful": power, identity and the gender problematic', in H. Radtke and H. Stam (eds) *Power/Gender: Social Relations in Theory and Practice* (Thousand Oaks: Sage).

Kiernan, K. (1991) 'The roles of men and women in tomorrow's Europe', *Employment Gazette*, 99, 10, pp. 491–9.

Knell, S.J. (1999) 'What future collecting?', in S.J. Knell (ed.) *Museums and the Future of Collecting* (Aldershot: Ashgate).

Knights, D., Calvey, D. and Odih, P. (1998) Report Stages 1–5, *Unpublished Reports*, University of Keele.

Knights, D., Calvey, D. and Odih, P. (1999) 'Social managerialism and the time-disciplined subject: quality–quantity conflicts in a call centre', 17th Annual International Labour Process Conference, School of Management, Royal Holloway University of London, March.

Knights, D. and Kerfoot, D. (1994) '"The best is yet to come": searching for embodiment in managerial work', in D. Collinson and J. Hearn (eds) *Men as Managers, Managers as Men* (London: Sage).

Knights, D. and McCabe, D. (1998a) '"Ain't misbehavin"? Opportunities for resistance within bureaucratic and quality management innovations', *Sociology*, 34, 3, pp. 421–37.

Knights, D. and McCabe, D. (1998b) '"Another one bites the dust": engendering the problems of masculinity in the management of innovation', *Zeitschrift für Personalforschung*, 12, 2.

Knights, D. and Odih, P. (1995) 'It's about time! The significance of gendered time for financial service consumption', *Time and Society*, 4, 2, pp. 205–33.

Knulst, W. and van Beek, P. (1990) *Tijd Komt Met de Jaren* (Den Haag: Sociaal en Cultureel Planbureau).

Knulst, W. and van den Broek, A. (1998) 'Do time-use surveys succeed in measuring "business"?' Some observations on the Dutch case, *Loisir et Société*, 22, pp. 563–72.

Kreitzman, L. (1999) *The 24 Hour Society* (London: Profile Books).

Kristeva, J. (1981) `Women's Time', *Signs* 7, 11, pp. 13–35.

Lacey, R. (1999) *Sothebys, Bidding for Class* (London: Warner Books).

Landes, D. (2000) *Revolution in Time* (London: Viking).

Lash, S., Quick, A. and Roberts, R. (eds) (1998) *Time and Value* (Oxford: Blackwell).

Law, J. (1994) *Organizing Modernity* (Oxford: Basil Blackwell).

Lazzarato, M. (1996) 'Immaterial labour', in P. Virno and M. Hardt (eds) *Radical Thought in Italy* (Minneapolis: University of Minnesota Press).

Leccardi, C. (1996) 'Rethinking social time: feminist perspectives', *Time and Society*, 2, 3, pp. 353–81.

Lefebvre, H. (1984) *Everyday Life in the Modern World* (New York: Transaction).

Lehndorff, S. (2000) 'Working time reduction in the European Union: a diversity of trends and approaches', in L. Golden and D. Figart (eds) *Working Time* (London: Routledge).

Lemert, C. (1997) *Postmodernism is Not What You Think* (Oxford: Blackwell).

Leonard, P. and Malina, D. (1994) 'Caught between two worlds: mothers as academics', in S. Davies, C. Lubelska and J. Quinn (eds) *Changing the Subject* (London: Taylor and Francis).

Lewis, J. (1992) 'Gender and the development of welfare regimes', *Journal of European Social Policy*, 2, 3, pp. 159–73.

Lewis, J. (1993) *Women and Social Policies in Europe* (Cheltenham: Edward Elgar).

Lewis, S. (1997) '"Family friendly" employment policies: a route to changing organisation culture or playing about at the margins?', *Gender, Work and Organisation*, 4, 1, pp. 13–23.

Linder, S. (1970) *The Harried Leisure Class* (New York: Colombia University Press).

Livestre, J. H. (1979) 'Dear Woman', *Woman*, 117, pp. 6–7.

Lockwood, D. (1992) *Solidarity and Schism* (Oxford: Clarendon Press).

Long, J. and Wimbush, E. (1985) *Continuity and Change* (London: Economic and Social Research Council/Sports Council).

Lorentz, H., Minkowski, H. and Weyl, H. (1923) *The Principles of Relativity* (London: Methuen).

Luke, T. (1998) '"Moving at the speed of life?" A cultural kinematics of telematic times and corporate values', in S. Lash, A. Quicke and R. Roberts (eds) *Time and Value* (Oxford: Blackwell Publishers).

Luttwak, E. (1999) *Turbo-Capitalism* (London: Harper Perennial).

Marsden, D. (1982) *Workless* (London: Croom Helm).

Marsh, C. (1988) *Exploring Data* (Cambridge: Polity Press).

Martin, P. (1995) '"I've got one just like that!": collectors, museums and community', *Museological Review*, 1, 2, pp. 77–86.

Martin, W.H. and Mason, S. (1998) *Transforming the Future* (Sudbury: Leisure Consultants).

Marx, K. (1858: 1973) *Grundrisse* (Harmondsworth: Penguin Books).

Marx, K. (1867: 1976) *Capital* (Harmondsworth: Penguin Books).

Marx, K. and Engels, F. (1976) *Collected Works. Vol. 6* (London: Lawrence and Wishart).

Massey, D. (1993) 'Politics and space/time', pp. 141–61 in M. Keith, and S. Pile, (eds) *Place and the politics of identity* (Routledge: London).

Matthews, R. (1999) 'Do we all have a nasty dose of hurry sickness?', *The Express*, 14 October, pp. 44–5.

Matthews, R., Feinstein, C. and Odling-Smee, J. (1982) *British Economic Growth 1856–1973* (Oxford: Oxford University Press).

McCracken, G. (1985) *Culture and Consumption: New Approaches to the Symbolic Character of Consumer Goods and Activities* (Bloomington, Ind.: Indiana University Press).

McCurdy, C. (1979) 'Women's Studies Assoc. (sic) Conference', *Broadsheet*, 73, pp. 6–7.

McGoldrick, A.E. (1983) 'Company early retirement schemes and private pension schemes: scope for leisure and new lifestyles', *Leisure Studies*, 2, pp. 187–202.

McNeill, W. (1995) *Keeping Together in Time* (Cambridge, Mass.: Harvard University Press).

McRae, S. (1986) *Cross-Class Families* (Oxford: Clarendon).

McRae, S. (1989) *Flexible Working Time and Family Life*, PSI Research Report 701 (London: Policy Studies Institute).

McRobbie, A. (ed.) (1989) *Zoot-suits and Second-hand Dresses* (London: Macmillan – now Palgrave Macmillan).

Meikle, P. (1976) (ed), *United Women's Convention 1975* (Wellington).

Melucci, A (1989) *Nomads of the Present: Social Movements and Individual Needs in Contemporary Society* (London: Hutchinson Radius).

Merz, J. and Ehling, M (eds) (1999) *Time Use – Research, Data and Policy* (Baden-Baden: Nomos).

Mol, A. and Law, J. (1994) 'Regions, networks and fluids: anaemia and social topology', *Social Studies of Science*, 24, pp. 641–71.

Morgan, D. (1996) *Family Connections* (Cambridge: Polity).

Morgan, D (1999) 'Risk and family practices: accounting for change and fluidity in family life', in E. Silva and C. Smart (eds) *The 'New' Family?* (London: Sage).

Morrison, M. (1992) *Managing Time for Education* (Coventry: Centre for Educational Development, Appraisal and Review, University of Warwick).

Morrison, M. (1995) 'Teaching to Time: Supply Teachers' Lives and their Work', unpublished PhD thesis, University of Warwick.

Mouffe, C. (1992) 'Feminism and radical politics', in J. Butler and J. Scott (eds) *Feminists Theorise the Political* (New York: Routledge).

Mulgan, G. and Wilkinson, H. (1997) 'Well-being and time', in G. Mulgan (ed) *Life After Politics* (London: Fontana).

Munro, R. (1998) 'Identity, culture and organisation', Course outline, *Undergraduate Handbook*, Department of Management, Keele University.

Murdoch, J. (1995) 'Actor-networks and the evolution of economic forms: combining description and explanation in theories of regulation, flexible specialisation, and networks', *Environment and Planning A*, 27, pp. 731–57.

National Committee of Inquiry into Higher Education (1997) *Higher Education in the Learning Society* (London: HMSO).

Neary, M. (2000) 'Labour Moves: A Critique of Social Movement Unionism', unpublished paper, Department of Socioloigy, University of Warwick.

Neary, M. and Taylor, G. (1998) *Money and the Human Condition* (London: Macmillan – now Palgrave Macmillan).

Nippert-Eng, C. (1996) *Home and Work* (Chicago: University of Chicago Press).

Noon, M. and Blyton, P. (1997) *The Realities of Work* (Basingstoke: Macmillan – now Palgrave Macmillan).

Novitz, R. (later Rosemary Du Plessis) (1978) 'Marital and Familial Roles in New Zealand: The Challenge of the Women's Liberation Movement', in P.G. Koopman-Boyden, (ed), *Families in New Zealand Society* (Wellington: Methuen).

Nowotny, H. (1994) *Time: The Modern and Postmodern Experience* (Cambridge: Polity).

Nyland, C. (1986) 'Capitalism and the history of worktime thought', *British Journal of Sociology*, 37, 4, pp. 513–34.

Odih, P. (1998) 'Gendered Time in the Age of Deconstruction', unpublished PhD thesis, University of Manchester Institute of Science and Technology.

Odih, P. (1999) 'Gendered time in the age of deconstruction', *Time and Society*, 8, 1, pp. 9–38.

Office for National Statistics/Equal Opportunities Commission (1998) *Social Focus on Women and Men* (London: The Stationery Office).

Oliver, J. (1998) 'Losing ground', *Management Today*, June, pp. 32–8.

Olmsted, A.D. (1991) 'Collecting: leisure, investment or obsession?' *Journal of Social Behaviour and Personality*, 6, 6, pp. 287–306.

Orloff, A. (1993) 'Gender and the social rights of citizenship: the comparative analysis of gender relations and welfare states', *American Sociological Review*, 58, 3, pp. 303–8.

Pateman, C. (1989) 'Feminist Critiques of the Public/Private Dichotomy', pp. 118–40 in *The Disorder of Women: Democracy, Feminism and Political Theory* (Cambridge: Polity Press).

Pearce, S.M. (1998) *Collecting in Contemporary Practice* (London: Sage).

Pearce, S.M. (1999) 'Collections and collecting', in S.J. Knell (ed.) *Museums and the Future of Collecting* (Aldershot: Ashgate).

Peters, P. (2000) *The Vulnerable Hours of Leisure* (Amsterdam: Thela).

Pfau-Effinger, B. (1998) 'Gender cultures and the gender arrangement – a theoretical framework for cross-national gender research', *Innovation*, 11, 2, pp. 147–66.

Phillips, A. (1991) *Engendering Democracy* (Pennsylvania: Pennsylvania State University Press).

Plant, S. (1997) *Zeros and Ones* (London: Fourth Estate).

Platt, J. (1978) 'Economic Values and Cultural Meanings: the market for antiques', paper presented to the BSA Annual Conference, University of Sussex.

Postone, M. (1993) *Time, Labour and Social Domination* (Cambridge: Cambridge University Press).

Poulter, L. (1977) 'Movement Demands and Issues', *Juno* Special Issue, January pp. 10–11.

Price, R. and Bain, G. (1988) 'The labour force', in A.H. Halsey (ed.) *British Social Trends since 1900* (London: Macmillan – now Palgrave Macmillan).

Prigogine, I. (1997) *The End of Certainty* (New York: The Free Press).

Prigogine, I. and Stengers, I. (1984) *Order Out of Chaos* (London: Heinemann).

Rabinow, P. (1995) *Making PCR* (Chicago: University of Chicago Press).

Ray, P. (1982), 'Feminism's New Frontier', *Listener*, 102, 2224, 1719.

Ray, P. and Lloyd, A. (1979) 'Ten Tough Years', *Listener*, 91, 2049, 1820.

Reed, M. and Harvey, D. (1992) 'The new science and the old: complexity and realism in the social sciences', *Journal for the Theory of Social Behaviour*, 22, pp. 353–80.

Reeves, R. (1999) 'The mad rush to save time', *The Observer*, 3 October, p. 17.

Rikowski, G. (1999) 'Education, capital and the transhuman', in D. Hill, P. McLaren, M. Cole and G. Rikowski (eds) *Postmodernism in Educational Theory* (London: The Tufnell Press).

Rikowski, G. (2000a) 'Messing with the explosive commodity: school improvement, educational research and labour-power in the era of global capitalism', paper presented at the British Educational Research Association Conference 2000, Cardiff University, September.

Rikowski, G. (2000b) 'Marx and the future of the human', paper presented at the seminar on Marx, Individuals and Society, Birkbeck College, University of London, October.

Ritzer, G. (1992) *The McDonaldization of Society* (London: Pine Forge).

Ritzer, G. (1997) '"McDisneyization"' and "post-tourism": complementary perspectives on contemporary tourism', in C. Rojek and J. Urry (eds) *Touring Cultures* (London: Routledge).

Roberts, K. (1998) 'Work and leisure: the recent history of a changing relationship', *Vrijetijd Studies*, 16, pp. 21–34.

Roberts, K. (1999) *Leisure in Contemporary Society* (Wallingford: CAB International).

Roberts, K. and Chambers, D. (1985) 'Changing times: hours of work/patterns of leisure', *World Leisure and Recreation*, 27, 1, pp. 17–23.

Robertson, R. (1992) *Globalization* (London: Sage).

Robinson, J.P. and Godbey, G. (1999) *Time for Life* (University Park, Penn.: Pennsylvania University Press).

Rose, M. (1994) 'Skill and Samuel Smiles: Changing the British Work Ethic', in R. Penn, M. Rose and J. Rubery (eds) *Skill and Occupational Change* (Oxford: Oxford University Press).

Rose, N. (1999) *Power of Freedom* (Cambridge: Cambridge University Press).

Roseneil, S. (2000) *Common Women, Uncommon Practices: The Queer Feminisms of GreenHam* (London and New York: Cassell).

Roy, D. (1990) 'Time and Job Satisfaction', pp. 155–67 in J. Hassard (ed), *The Sociology of Time* (Basingstoke: Macmillan – now Palgrave Macmillan).

Rubery, J. (1997) 'Working time in the UK', *Transfer*, December.

Rubery, J. (1998) 'Working time in the UK', *Transfer*, Brussels, December.

Rubery, J. Fagan, C. and Maier, F. (1996) 'Occupational segregation, discrimination and equal opportunity', in G. Schmidt, J. O'Reilly and K. Schomann (eds) *International Handbook of Labour Market Policy and Evaluation* (Cheltenham: Edward Elgar).

Rubery, J., Smith, M. and Fagan, C. (1997) 'Explaining working-time patterns by gender, societal and sectoral effects', in G. Bosch, D. Meulders and F. Michon (1997) *Working Time: New Issues, New Norms, New Measures* (Brussels: DELBEA).

Rubery, J., Smith, M. and Fagan, C. (1998) 'Gender, societal effects and working-time regimes', *Feminist Economics*, 4, 1, pp. 71–102.

Rubery, J., Smith, M. and Fagan, C. (1999) *Women's Employment in Europe* (London: Routledge).

Russell, Marcia, (1979) 'United Women's Convention: No Bed of Bread and Roses', *Listener*, 91, 2048, 2021.

Ryan, C. (1997) 'The time of our lives or time for our lives: an examination of time in holidaying', in C. Ryan (ed.) *The Tourist Experience* (London: Cassell).

Sainsbury, D. (1994) *Gendering Welfare States* (London: Sage)

Samuel, R. (1994) *Theatres of Memory, Vol 1* (London: Verso).

Satori, J. (1999) *Synchronicity* (Boston: Butterworth Heinemann).

Sayer, D. (ed.) (1989) *Readings from Karl Marx* (London: Routledge).

Schor, J. B. (1991) *The Overworked American* (New York: Basic Books).

Schor, J. (1998) 'Beyond work and spend', *Vrijetijd Studies*, 18, pp. 7–20.

Schutz, A. (1967) *Phenomenology of the Social World* (London: Heinemann Educational Books).

Scott, J. and Tilly, L. (1980) 'Women's work and the family in nineteenth century Europe', in A. Amsden (ed.) *The Economics of Women and Work* (London: Penguin).

Sewell, G. and Wilkinson, B. (1992) 'Someone to watch over me: surveillance, discipline and the just-in-time labour process', *Sociology*, 26, 2, pp. 271–91.

Seidler, V. (1989) *Rediscovering Masculinity* (London: Routledge).

Seule, J. (1978) 'A Space of One's Own', *Broadsheet*, 64, pp. 6–7.

Seymour, J. (1988) 'The Division of Domestic Labour: a Review', *Working Papers in Applied Social Research No. 13*, Faculty of Economic and Social Studies, University of Manchester.

Shaw, J. (1998) ''Feeling a list coming on'': Gender and the pace of life', *Time and Society*, 7, 2, 383–96.

Sheller, M. and Urry, J. (2000) 'The city and the car', *International Journal of Urban and Regional Research*, 24, December.

Shields, R. (1997) 'Flow as a new paradigm', *Space and Culture*, 1, pp. 1–4.

Silva, E.B. (1999) 'Transforming housewifery: dispositions, practices and technologies', in E. Silva and C. Smart (eds) *The 'New' Family?* (London: Sage).

Silva, E.B. (2000a) 'The material and the moral in everyday life', paper presented at the Inaugural Symposium of the National Everyday Cultures Programme, Open University, May.

Silva, E.B. (2000b) 'The politics of consumption @ home', *Pavis Papers*, 1, Open University.

Silva, E.B. and Smart, C. (1999) 'The "new" practices and politics of family life', in E. Silva and C. Smart (eds) *The 'New' Family?* (London: Sage).

Silverstone, R. (1993) 'Time, information and communication technologies and the household', *Time and Society*, 2, pp. 283–311.

Simmel, G. (1971) *On Individuality and Social Forms* (Chicago: Chicago University Press).

Simmel, G. (1980) *Essays on Interpretation in Social Science* (Manchester: Manchester University Press).

Slaughter, S. and Leslie, G. (1997) *Academic Capitalism* (Baltimore: Johns Hopkins).

Smart, C. and Neale, B. (1999) *Family Fragments* (Cambridge: Polity).

Smith, D. (1987) *The Everyday World as Problematic* (Milton Keynes: Open University Press).

Soroka, M.P. (1990) 'Collecting collectors: A cautionary note', paper presented at the Popular Culture Association National Meeting, Toronto.

Sorokin, P. and Merton, R. (1990) 'Social-time: A functional and Methodological Analysis', pp. 56–76 in J. Hassard, (ed) *The Sociology of Time* (Basingstoke: Macmillan – now Palgrave Macmillan).

Spain, D., and Bianchi, S. (1996) *Balancing Act* (New York: Russell Sage Foundation).

Speakman, S. and Marchington, M. (1999) 'Ambivalent patriarchs: shift workers, breadwinners and housework', *Work, Employment and Society*, 13, 1, pp. 85–105.

Steward, B. (2000) 'Changing times: the meaning, measurement and use of time in teleworking', *Time and Society*, 9, 1, pp. 57–74.

Strange, S. (1986) *Casino Capitalism* (Oxford: Blackwell).

Strathern, P. (1997) *Einstein and Relativity: The Big Idea* (London: Arrow).

Sullivan, O. (1997) 'Time waits for no (wo)man: an investigation of the gendered experience of domestic time', *Sociology*, 31, 2, pp. 221–39.

Sullivan, O. (2000) 'The divisions of domestic labour: twenty years of change?' *Sociology*, 34, 3, pp. 437–56.

Taylor, M. (ed.) (1999) *British Household Panel Survey User Manual* (Colchester: University of Essex).

Taylor, P. and Bain, P. (1998) 'An assembly line in the head: the call centre labour process', paper presented to the 16th Annual International Labour

Process Conference, University of Manchester Institute of Science and Technology, March.

Thompson, A. (1979) 'A Women's Culture as a Separate Culture', *WSA Conference Papers*, pp. 51–54.

Thompson, E.P. (1967) 'Time, work-discipline and industrial capitalism', *Past and Present: A Journal of Scientific History*, 38, pp. 56–176.

Thompson, E.P. (1991) 'Time, work discipline and industrial capitalism', in E.P. Thompson (ed.) *Customs in Common* (Harmondsworth: Penguin).

Thompson, J. (1975) 'Editorial', *Broadsheet*, 26, 9.

Thrift, N. (1996) *Spatial Formations* (London: Sage).

Thrift, N. (1999) 'The place of complexity', *Theory, Culture and Society*, 16, pp. 31–70.

Trowler, P. (1998) *Academics, Work and Change* (Buckingham: Open University Press).

Tuan, Y-F. (1998) *Escapism* (Baltimore: Johns Hopkins).

Turetzky, P. (1998) *Time* (London: Routledge).

Tyrell, B. (1995) 'Time in our lives: facts and analysis in the 1990s', *Demos Quarterly*, 5, pp. 23–5.

United Women's Convention Commitee (1979), *United Women's Convention: Easter 1979* (Hamilton: University of Waikato).

Urry, J. (1996) 'Sociology of time and space', in B. Turner (ed.), *The Blackwell Companion to Social Theory* (Oxford: Blackwell).

Urry, J. (2000) *Sociology Beyond Societies* (London: Routledge).

van den Broek, A., Knulst, W. and Breedveld, K. (1999) *Naar Andere Tijden? Tijdbesteding en Tijdsordening in Nederland, 1975–1995* (The Hague: Sociaal en Cultureel Planbureau).

Victoria University Wellington (VUW) Feminists (1978), 'Group Restructure', *VUW Newsletter*, 8, pp. 1–2.

Wainwright, D. (1997) 'Can sociological research be qualitative, critical and valid?', *The Qualitative Report*, 3, 2.

Wajcman, J (1998) *Managing Like a Man* (Cambridge: Polity).

Waldrop, M. (1994) *Complexity* (London: Penguin).

Wallerstein, I. (1991) *Unthinking Social Science* (Cambridge: Polity Press).

Warr, P. (1983) 'Work, jobs and unemployment', *Bulletin of the British Psychological Society*, 36, pp. 305–11.

Warren, T. (2000) 'Diverse breadwinner models: a couple based analysis of gendered working time in Britain and Denmark', *Journal of European Social Policy*, 10, 4, pp. 349–71.

Watkins, P. (1993) 'Finding time: temporal considerations in the operation of school committees', *British Journal of Sociology of Education*, 14, 2, pp. 131–46.

Watson, G. (1994) 'The flexible workforce and patterns of working hours in the UK', *Employment Gazette*, July.

Weber, M. (1930) *The Protestant Ethic and the Spirit of Capitalism* (London: Unwin University Books).

Westwood, S. (1984) *All Day, Every Day* (London: Pluto Press).

Whipp, R. (1994) 'A Time to be Concerned: A Positional Paper on Time and Management', *Time and Society*, 3, pp. 99–116.

Woman '74 (1975) *Proceedings of the University Extension Seminar*, 1415, September 1974 (Hamilton: University of Waikato).

Woman Collective (1977) 'Five Years of "Woman"', *Woman*, 98, pp. 1–4

Wouters, C. (1990) *Van Minnen en Sterven: Informalisering van Omgangsvormen rond Seks en Dood* (Amsterdam: Bert Bakker).

Young, M. (1988) *The Metronomic Society* (London: Thames and Hudson).

Young, M. and Schuller, T. (1988) 'Introduction: towards chronosociology', in M. Young and T. Schuller (eds) *The Rhythms of Society* (London: Routledge).

Zerubavel, E. (1981) *Hidden Rhythms* (Berkeley: University of California Press).

Zerubavel, E. (1990) 'Public-time and Private-time', pp. 168–77 in J. Hassad (ed) *The Sociology of Time* (Basingstoke: Macmillan – now Palgrave Macmillan).

Zijderveld, A. (1971) *The Abstract Society* (New York: Anchor Books).

Zohar, D. and Marshall, I. (1994) *The Quantum Society* (New York: William Morrow).

Zuzanek, J., Beckers, T. and Peters, P. (1998) 'The harried leisure class revisited: Dutch and Canadian trends in time use from the 1970s to the 1990s', *Leisure Studies*, 17, pp. 1–19.

Zuzanck, J. and Mannell, R. (1998) 'Life cycle squeeze, time pressure, daily stress, and leisure participation: a Canadian perspective', *Society and Leisure*, 21, pp. 513–44.

Index